Jump Cut!

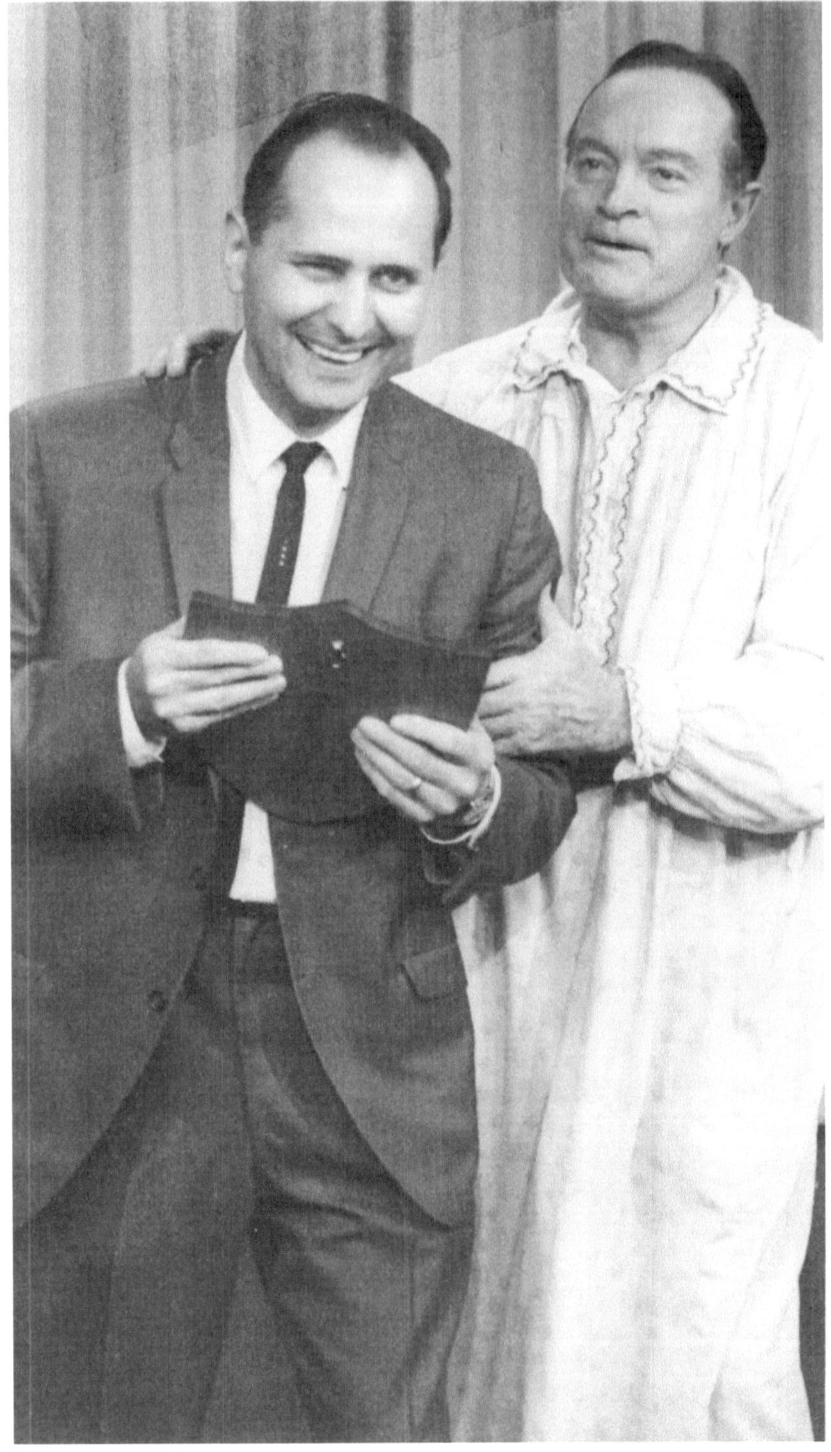

JUMP CUT!

Memoirs of a
Pioneer Television Editor

by

ARTHUR SCHNEIDER, A.C.E.

with a foreword by
GEORGE SCHLATTER

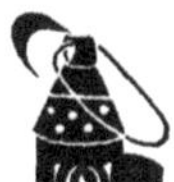

McFarland & Company, Inc., Publishers
Jefferson, North Carolina, and London

Front cover: hands holding 2″ spliced videotape

Frontispiece: Author and Bob Hope with "jump cut" award

British Library Cataloguing-in-Publication data are available

Library of Congress Cataloguing-in-Publication Data

Schneider, Arthur, 1926–
    Jump cut! : memoirs of a pioneer television editor / by Arthur
Schneider ; with a foreword by George Schlatter.
       p.   cm.
    Includes index.

    ISBN-13: 978-0-7864-0345-5
    softcover : 50# alkaline paper ∞

    1. Schneider, Arthur, 1926–   . 2. Motion picture editors—United
States—Biography. 3. Motion pictures—Editing. 4. Video tapes—
Editing. 5. Television—Production and direction. I. Title.
TR849.S35A3   1997
778.59'3'092—dc21
[B]   97-2505

Manufactured in the United States of America

McFarland & Company, Inc., Publishers
Box 611, Jefferson, North Carolina 28640
www.mcfarlandpub.com

Acknowledgments

Few people get a chance to write their biography. Without the help of the many friends I've made over the years in the television and motion picture industries as well as my family, I, too, would have found it impossible. After dedicating almost four decades of my life to editing film and videotape, working very long hours most of the time, I made my decision to retire in 1988.

My wife, Dee, and I have been married for more than four decades, which is an indication of her love, devotion and strength—qualities that enabled her to bring up our children and handle the everyday chores I was not around to take care of. For that I am ever grateful. She continues to be always helpful and by my side in retirement.

I am also thankful that our children, Robert and Lori, have found their niche in the television industry and have become prominent in their own right. Maybe Bob Hope was right when he told me, "Next the grandchildren."

Contents

Foreword

by George Schlatter
(Producer, *Rowan and Martin's Laugh-In*)

Bob Hope gave Art Schneider the nickname "Jump Cut" in 1965, but it wasn't until we delivered the pilot for *Laugh-In* that the name "jump cuts" took on its real meaning and its present importance. Up until then, jump cuts were to be avoided at any cost. By design, the *Laugh-In* pilot had hundreds of jump cuts which were deliberate and artfully executed by Art Schneider. That was the idea—no fat, no air, no waits, just *jokes*. Sometimes we didn't even do set-ups, just the punch lines. That editing technique has now been used, abused and misused in what is currently referred to as the "MTV" style of editing. Some people call this "mindless eye candy." Others are not so kind. Personally, I think some of it is wonderful, and I think it is a shame when people malign Art's art of "jump cuts"—an art form he created through infinite patience, understanding, endurance, eagerness to learn, and willingness to get rid of the "old" and accept the "new."

Until *Laugh-In*, television was radio with pictures. You could just listen to television and not miss too much. The *Laugh-In* editing forced you to *watch the screen*. We did a verbal joke at the same time as a sight gag while funny words appeared across the bottom of the screen. Go try to explain that to an editor who had not seen someone do it before. Sometimes jokes lasted two or three seconds. We had some visual bits that were only on screen for two or three frames, but it all had to fit together into a coherent mosaic of humor.

Much of *Laugh-In* was in the script, but a lot of it happened in the editing room through the effort of our co-producer, Carolyn Raskin, and Art Schneider. People today just would not understand the amount of hours this took, and the amount of devotion and adventure that went into those early days of *Laugh-In*. To my way of thinking, no one has ever duplicated the wit and creativity that Art Schneider and the people who worked with him put into *Laugh-In*.

I first met Art when he was a young editor at NBC. At that point, videotape had just come into existence. Until then, radio shows were broadcast live to New York and then performed again for the West Coast three hours later. When television came in, shows were broadcast live to New York. A process was developed involving something called "kines." These were kinescopes, films shot off a monitor. They looked like they had been shot through a blanket. They were in black and white and really not very good.

When color television arrived on the scene, it brought with it the necessity for videotaping shows so they could be broadcast and later rebroadcast coast-to-coast in color. In 1964, the techniques involved were still very primitive. The colors were over-saturated and there was no way to edit. Art Schneider and a few other pioneers began to develop a process for editing two inch videotape using microscopes and razor blades and sticking it together with glue and metallic tape. This was a tedious and painfully precise procedure. Art and I worked together on numerous specials using the new technology. However, nothing really could have prepared us for *Laugh-In*.

It is difficult now to imagine, but in the *Laugh-In* pilot we had all of the countless cuts made in the booth when we shot the show. In addition, we had over 500 of these physical slices made on two inch videotape. We also had hundreds of tiny film splices. And the procedure that Art and Carolyn followed to edit, dub and sweeten the soundtrack was even more complicated than the video edits. No one today could duplicate once what Artful Art did each and every week on *Laugh-In*. Art will go into all of this in much more detail later in this book. After reading his story, you may understand the legacy he gave to our industry. When you do, I would suggest kneeling facing East with your hands tightly clasped in front of your chest to acknowledge the contribution these people made. While you're there, you may want to do a pratfall...it always worked for us. Don't you remember the tricycle rider?

Until recently, we were creatively ahead of what could be done technically. We had ideas, but it was impossible to execute them with the technology that was available back then. Now the technology is way ahead of creativity. Electronic editing on Avid makes it possible to produce concepts and visual effects that are as yet unthought of. Today, television and motion pictures desperately need more geniuses like Art "Jump Cut" Schneider who will push producers, directors and writers to make use of the technology developed by Art and others who followed. Video editing is now a viable "Art" form, jump cuts and all.

Read the book and appreciate some of our video heritage. I know I do. I just hope Art has some jokes in here someplace—succinctly edited, that is.

Introduction

My professional career covers nearly 40 years as a film and videotape editor. In the early days, I was something of a pioneer because television was in its infancy and nobody really had any idea of the impact this medium would have. I marvel at the advances we've made in the industry since I began my training as a film editor at the University of Southern California in 1949. Motion pictures and television gradually merged over the years—something the film industry thought would never happen—and editing tools today are astonishingly versatile and efficient. Still, it takes the skill and creativity of a human being to give continuity to the story since, after all, an editor is a story teller. I should also point out that motion picture film is still used extensively as the recording medium in television even though the end product may be released on videotape.

This book is an insight into how television post-production, particularly editing, evolved over the past five decades. It is also a detailed account of my activities as an editor as well as an innovator in the development of equipment and techniques that allowed us to be far more creative than earlier methods. The book also relates my favorite stories about the motion picture and television personalities and directors I've met and worked with over the years, as well as humorous anecdotes.

I started my editing career with NBC in 1951, and the Bob Hope comedy specials were my first major assignment. I've devoted an entire chapter to the stories and people involved. I also was very much a part of the original *Laugh-In* series and have devoted another chapter to its history.

During my tenure as a film and videotape television editor, I accumulated more than 700 screen credits; many videotape editing awards including seven Emmy nominations and four Emmy Awards; and many other accolades from within the academic community and the television industry. This book covers my professional career up to my retirement and is based on the notes I've kept through the years. It begins with a brief history of my late high school days and college years, the period that helped me eventually find the direction I wanted to take in life. I hope this book will inform and entertain you and bring to the surface some of the forgotten personal history about the mesmerizing medium of television.

CHAPTER ONE

Growing Up

Someone once said that three of the key people involved in film or television productions are the writer, the director and the editor. Of course we also know that it takes many more talented people in all areas, but I feel that these three are vital in order for a production to get off the ground successfully. Without a good script, there is no story. Without a good director, the story may be poorly interpreted. Without a good editor, the well-written and -directed script can be ruined.

The television industry started more than 45 years ago. I was fortunate to get in on the ground floor in 1951. I was really blazing new trails since in those early days, there were no "rule books" and we had to be inventive as well as creative. They were the really fun days because, in a sense, most production people walked around with blank stares on their faces since the technology at the time was new to everyone and they had no idea how to take advantage of it. Engineers designed this new hardware but they were not the ones who had to use it. So we often devised ways to get around technical problems without making it obvious to the client. You really couldn't do any wrong because no one really knew enough about the technical end to know themselves. We were, in effect, pioneers in this fledgling industry.

However, before I get into my career in the television industry, I'd like to briefly tell you what got me started and eventually steered my career into film and videotape editing. One thing that most likely triggered my interest in motion pictures and television was a trip my father and I took from New York to California in 1942.

My father had a friend who worked for 20th Century–Fox studios as a set decorator at the Western Avenue lot in Hollywood. Although visiting the studio was not originally part of our trip, we thought we might get a tour of a real movie set and maybe even see some stars. As it turned out, my father's friend was able to get us onto the set of a picture called *My Gal Sal* starring Rita Hayworth. We arrived on the set which was part of an old theater and I saw Rita Hayworth sitting on a half moon type of swing, singing a song. The humongous Technicolor camera was mounted on rails fastened to the top of several dozen rows of theater seats. These rails, called dolly tracks, allowed the camera to move forward and backward. The camera was enclosed in a huge soundproof box called a "blimp" so that the noise of the camera would not be picked up by the microphone. I would guess that the box covering the camera was about two feet wide by three feet high by about four feet long.

I was awestruck by all the people scurrying about the set and the director sometimes barking commands to the extras (but not, I noted, to the star, Rita Hayworth, who was always treated with great respect). She was singing a song that was prerecorded, and the soundtrack came from a large speaker on one side of the stage. During my brief visit that day, Hayworth must have sung that same song six times. One reason was that the camera had to change angles and that meant she had to repeat certain sections of the song in order for the camera to film different angles or views of her. Each time a camera repositioning was required, about a dozen men came out from nowhere to lift the camera off the dolly tracks and put it on a tripod. Meanwhile, Hayworth was taken to her dressing room while the changes to the camera position were being made. This hurry-up-and-wait approach was quite typical of the way motion pictures were made in those days. That brief glance into "Tinsel Town" and moviemaking generated a strong desire in me to someday become a part of this business. Little did I know that after I graduated high school and after several false starts and nine years later, I would become heavily involved in ways I had not even dreamed of. My father and I returned from that trip and I went back to school and reality.

When I was a freshman in high school in Brighton, New York, a suburb of Rochester, I was more interested in flying and building model airplanes than studying. My grades suffered as a result. I was a "C-" average at best. I had a couple of girl friends but with no car and little money, it was tough to date. I had a paper route but my take-home pay was $4.50 a week, hardly enough to do much of anything with. When I was 13, I got an after-school job working for my uncle at his pharmacy. He also had a soda fountain where I would make sodas, and other drinks. Every Thursday, he offered ten cent chocolate sodas and when my friends would come in, I would add extra chocolate or ice cream. Even with this second job in my young career, I still wasn't making enough to have a steady girl friend. I was also somewhat shy and wasn't really aggressive towards girls. My first love was still building and flying model airplanes, so most of the money I earned went towards buying model supplies.

My father ran a radio parts business. In 1948, he bought one of the first black and white television sets made by a company called Hallicrafters. It was in a metal box about two feet square, had a seven-inch picture tube and weighed about 40 pounds. We used to watch the stock car races from Buffalo, some 90 miles away, and could only get good reception when the atmospheric conditions were right—that is, when clouds acted as a reflector so that the signal could be bounced off them. (This is also called a "skip" signal.) When this happened, we could see a somewhat snowy-looking signal. But even though the pictures were mediocre at best, I was intrigued with television. My mother helped run the radio business and took care of the books. She died when I was 12 years old after our trip to California and left some money for my brother Ed's and my education. My father couldn't operate his radio parts supply business, run the household and take care of two sons who were not the easiest to get along with.

As teenagers, my brother and I used to get into mischief and were constantly being disciplined but managed to stay out of any real trouble. Ed is 16 months younger than I am and we used to fight sometimes until we were bloody. I really don't know why we fought or how we survived without killing each other. We were just a couple of typical teenagers. My father remarried more than a year after my mother's death, partly in hopes his new wife would be able to handle us. That did not work out very well since we both resented someone taking our mother's place, especially a stranger. She insisted we call her Ruth. Although Ruth tried very hard to be part of the family, it was many years before my brother and I would finally accept her. My father and his second wife had two children, Eugene and Judy. They are both very close to me and I have never considered them anything but my real siblings.

I had three hobbies as a teenager: chemistry, photography and model airplanes. We used to make Molotov cocktails and other chemical experiments mostly with things that went boom. Our "lab" was in the basement of our home. It had eight swing-away windows for ventilation around the foundation. One day when my parents were not home, I decided to generate some hydrogen gas for one of my experiments. I put zinc in some acid and went upstairs to answer the telephone. When I came back down, I struck a match to light the Bunsen burner. In an instant, there was a dull roar and the sound of breaking glass. There was so much hydrogen gas built up in the confined basement area that when the gas was ignited, the force blew out all eight windows. When my parents returned, I was grounded for a month, and I used the next eight paychecks to pay my father back for the window repair.

My chemistry experiments ended for good the day Ed and I decided to make skyrockets. We had made several rockets and were trying to ignite one of them. Ed put a lighted match to the fuse he had made, and it began to burn slowly. When the fuse burned inside the rocket, it seemed to go out. Then he poked a small stick in the end, and instantly the rocket started to burn and shot off into space. However, Ed did not get his hand out of the way fast enough and was severely burned across the knuckles. When my father returned from shopping that day, he asked Ed how his hand was burned. Ed and I tried unsuccessfully to come up with an explanation. That did it. My father took all our chemicals and hardware and dumped them in the trash. It was the best thing he could have done because we might have done even more damage to ourselves and maybe our home if we had continued. Luckily he never found out about our attempts to make nitroglycerin, which fortunately never worked anyway.

My second hobby, photography, included a darkroom in our basement where I even experimented with color printing. Amazing as it might seem, I was actually able to get pretty decent results from this process using some very primitive equipment. Years before Polaroid was invented, I used to impress my friends with the speed with which I could take a picture, develop it and make a print (generally under ten minutes). I would take a picture in black and white, run to my darkroom, develop it, and while the negative was still wet, make a print from it, also wet, to show my friends. Even these soggy prints amazed them.

My next job was as a clerk in a supermarket in Rochester, near our home. I was making pretty good money and even began to save some of it. This was a time in my life when I was trying new things as most teenagers do. I was anxious to learn to fly. One day, one of my friends dared me to smoke a cigar, the biggest mistake I ever made. After only about ten puffs, I got violently ill and threw up. Forget that idea. I never really liked the smell of cigarettes so I secretly tried to smoke corn silk in an old corn cob pipe. That was nothing, but my dad caught me. He wisely offered me a choice: I could smoke, or I could learn to fly, but I could not do both.

I thought for a while and told him I didn't like smoking and that I really did want to fly. I promised him I would never smoke again, something I'm glad I agreed to when I was young. I soloed in Rochester soon after I turned 16. What I couldn't understand was that at 16, I was old enough to fly an airplane but I would have to wait until I was 18 in order to get a driver's license. For two years, I had to hitchhike to the airport.

As teenagers, Ed and I were being quite difficult, and our insensitivity was taking its toll on both parents. My mother had left some life insurance money which my father used to send my brother and me to military school. He needed a respite from child-rearing for a time. We were sent some 2,000 miles away to the highly-rated Wentworth Military Academy in Lexington, Missouri. We went by train and were on our own to enroll and handle all the other things generally done by parents. The first six weeks were hell, partly because my brother and I were "new boys" or "plebes" and had to take all the crap thrown at us by older students. Since this was a military school, we had to salute officers, take military training including target practice, and go on "bivouacs" or camping trips as well as march in parades every weekend. We learned etiquette, table manners, and had to eat a "square meal" which is moving your utensil at right angles from the plate to your mouth. Every Sunday, to our disgust, we would have brains and scrambled eggs for breakfast.

The other problem was that we were really homesick and depressed. I resented being away from home and friends and having to study from 7 to 9 P.M. six nights a week. Every 30 minutes or so, the hall monitor would come into our room to see if we were really studying. At first, I would hide comic books inside my textbooks and read them instead of studying. However, I quickly noticed that only those cadets who were on the honor roll were allowed off campus on weekends. I was stuck in my room and very depressed. After about four or five weeks I ran out of both self-pity and comic books. I decided to buckle down and really began to study. Actually, I found it rather easy because part of our class work was learning how to study, something I never learned in public school because of too many distractions.

When the next grade report came out, I was amazed to find that I had made the honor roll. I stayed on it for the rest of the two years I attended Wentworth. When I finally got the hang of it, studying was easy. I attribute my scholastic success to dedicated teachers without whom I would not have made it. I was now allowed to go into town every weekend and even made the MP (military police) unit. I carried an empty pistol

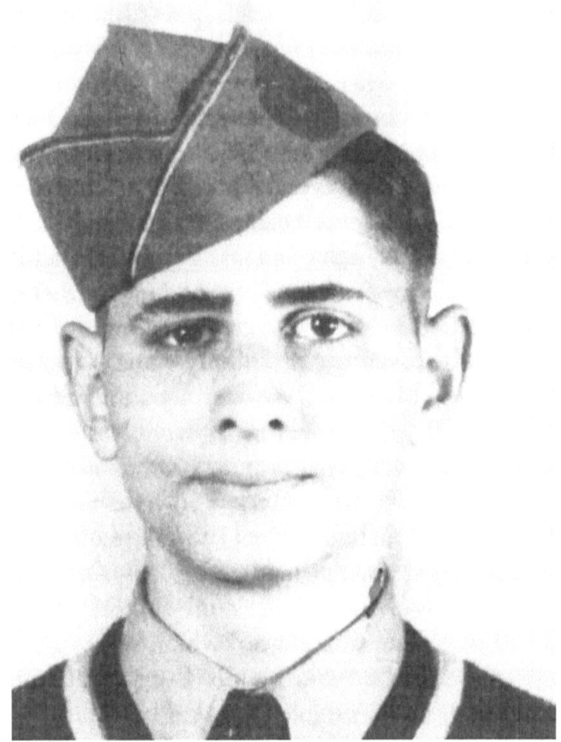

Author as 17-year-old in military school, 1947 (Wentworth Military Academy, Lexington, Missouri).

holster and looking real sharp in my military uniform even though I was only 16.

Because Wentworth was so expensive, my brother and I were only able to stay for two years; I left at the end of my junior year. My senior year was spent back at Brighton High School in Rochester, where I graduated with a B+ average which allowed me to get into the University of Southern California in Los Angeles. It's hard to believe that when I enrolled in USC in 1948, a semester unit cost just $15. Today it exceeds $250 a unit.

I was always interested in airplanes and wanted to design them. After graduating high school, I was admitted to USC as an aeronautical engineering student in the fall of 1948. However, this division was located in Santa Maria, California, at the Alan Hancock airport, several hundred miles north of Los Angeles. After a few months of mental pain attempting to learn the required math classes, I decided to switch to mechanical engineering. I soon found out that any kind of engineering required more advanced math than I cared to learn.

My next attempt was to become an airplane and engine mechanic, a profession I felt would require very little math. I loved to tinker with engines, and I thought it would be fun to take them apart and rebuild them. I learned welding, hydraulics, and a multitude of other skills that I even enjoy in retirement today. I rebuilt a nine cylinder, 450 horsepower radial aircraft engine from the bottom up. It was a thrill to hit the ignition switch on the engine test mount and hear it roar to life. But after thinking about it, I decided I didn't want to be a "grease monkey" all my life.

Just after the Christmas of 1948, I decided to move to Los Angeles to see what was available on the main campus. I was somewhat discouraged because I continued to discover that the math and other courses were far more difficult than I imagined and I didn't want to end up stumbling through any more engineering courses. The evening before I was to leave for L.A., we had a big Christmas party. My roommate, an ex-fighter pilot, got drunk and so did I. I was so drunk, several fellows strapped me in my bunk along with dozens of ice cubes so that I couldn't move. I spent the night shivering and barfing.

The next day I had the worst hangover. I was absolutely miserable. I went to the school cafeteria and asked the cook what to do for a severe hangover. He told me to drink a quart of tomato juice with several teaspoons of Tabasco sauce, black pepper and God knows what else. He fixed the drink for me and I guzzled it down even though the taste was horrible and it burned my throat. I went back to the dorm and took a nap. When I awoke, my hangover was gone! I was flabbergasted. I didn't feel that great but at least I was able to get on the bus and make it to L.A. without heaving my guts.

A friend of mine told me to check out the Department of Cinema, located at the main campus in Los Angeles. The cinema building used to be an old livery stable and the sound stage used to be a barn. I was fascinated with all the motion picture cameras, cranes, dollies, and lights. This was it. I changed my major once again and began my cinema training in 1949. I was looking forward to learning and playing with all the neat motion picture stuff. I learned most every phase of production and post-production including camera, sound, writing and directing. I soon felt I wanted to specialize in film editing. I was quite active in extracurricular activities, including becoming the secretary of the student chapter of the Society of Motion Picture Engineers (SMPE). I wanted in the worst way to become a member of Delta Kappa Alpha, an honorary cinema fraternity, but needed an "A" average for one semester to become eligible. I chose my elective courses very carefully, managed to get that "A" average and was soon taken into that organization.

In 1949, one of my fellow USC cinema students talked me into joining the naval reserve for a four-year tour of duty to be part of the photographic team of the Armed Forces Radio Service (AFRS), a naval subsidiary. I would go to meetings once a month and shoot lots of 4 × 5 black and white still photos with the navy supplying all the film and flashbulbs. In July of 1950, we went on a two-week cruise to the Panama Canal and Equador aboard a destroyer, the USS *Ulhman* (identified as DD 687). We were also shooting a Navy recruitment film in 16mm color. Not only was I shooting still photos every day, but I had to carry a 16mm professional Mitchell movie camera weighing about 45 pounds on a tripod up and down ladders and tight stairways on board the destroyer. Many times I felt like chucking the camera overboard even if it did cost $25,000.

Every evening, I was one of two sailors assigned to develop and print several hundred still photos shot by all the photographers aboard ship. I resented it because everyone else was at the back of the ship watching movies while I was in the ship's infirmary sweating and developing and printing pictures. Since we were approaching the Equator, the heat and humidity were playing havoc with our film stock. The ship's infirmary was used as a darkroom because it was the only place we had cold, fresh water to wash the negatives and prints.

When we crossed the Equator in July of 1950, we all had to go through an initiation called the "Solemn Mysteries of the Ancient Order of the Deep." This meant everyone, including officers and, in this case, the captain. Those who were to be initiated were called "Pollywogs" and those who had already been through this ordeal were called "Shellbacks." Once initiated, you were given a permanent identification card. If you lost the card, you had no proof of initiation and had to go through this horrible mess again.

Part of the initiation included going through a canvas tube just large enough so that you could only slide, not crawl through on your belly. Into this canvas tube they dumped all the ship's garbage of the day. We were forced to slide through this 30-foot-long tube while Shellbacks stood outside beating us with soft canvas bats called "shilleaghs." At the end of the tube, you were grabbed, your mouth was forced open and quinine was squirted into your mouth. Quinine is used to cure malaria and is very bitter. At this point, they smeared lard mixed with gravel in your hair. Then you were thrown into a large tank of water saturated with fluorescent dye marker, a greenish-yellow substance that stains your skin.

While floundering around in this tank, you were hit with water from a high pressure fire hose which forced you under the surface. Just before you drowned, they hauled you out and the initiation was over. However, your skin had a warm yellow-green glow from the dye which lasted almost a week even with daily showers. When I tried to remove the lard and sand from my hair, the crew had turned off all the fresh water and only salt water was available to wash with. Believe me, you cannot wash with salt water. I had to comb the stuff out of my hair and wait for the fresh water to be turned on again.

I was one of the first to go through the initiation since I then had to start taking pictures of all the other Pollywogs going through the process, including the captain. I was lucky to go through first, because as soon as you completed the initiation, you were considered a Shellback, identifiable by the yellow-green color of your skin. The last person to go through the line felt the brunt of everyone else who had been initiated. There were some 150 sailors behind me. I felt sorry for the last guy through the line. I think it was the captain.

Although we did not go through the Panama Canal, we did tour the city and tried to go across the Gatun Lake locks, one of several in the canal. The navy bus we were on was just a tad too wide for the lock gate itself and the wheels got stuck on the guard rails, jamming the bus so tightly that we had no choice but to climb out the windows and edge our way back. We were there in July of 1950 and the rain came like clockwork, just about two P.M. every day. It came down in buckets but only lasted for a few minutes. We were in Panama for three days, then left for Guayaquil, Equador, to work with their navy in demonstrating how to set off depth charges.

The Ecuadorian sailors were ushered aboard and the order came to fire the first charge from the fantail of the destroyer. But someone forgot to set the depth deep enough so that it would not affect our ship. When the charge exploded underwater at a very shallow depth, I would guess about 50 feet or so, it lifted the back of the destroyer several feet in the air, knocking several of us to the deck. The geyser of water that hit us

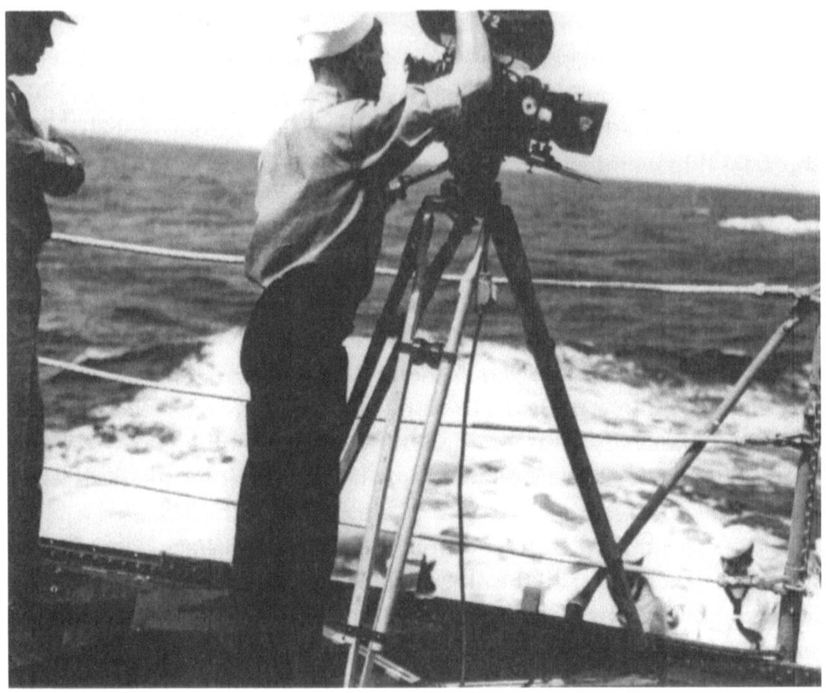

The author as Navy photographer, 1950.

drenched everyone on deck, including the officers of both navies, all in their "Sunday best." There was hell to pay but I managed to avoid the wrath of the captain since I was shooting still photos at the time.

Our shore leave was limited and we were bored essentially doing nothing but getting a tan from the equatorial sun that heated that metal deck so effectively. Since most of the officers and crew had already left to visit the town, several of us decided to sneak off the ship and go sightseeing. We managed to get off the ship without being noticed and started down the main street of town, more of a wide dirt path than a street. Since we were all hungry, several of us went into a restaurant and bought some fried chicken. A few hours later, most of us came down with dysentery. I was sick as a dog, but the ship's doctor had no sympathy for us since we were told to avoid eating in town where sanitation was nonexistent. (Of course, we hadn't listened, thinking we were invincible and that nothing could harm us.) Just before returning to the ship, one of the guys bought a baby alligator and took it on board. He didn't realize that even though this alligator was a baby, it had a vicious snapping bite. This sailor dumped the gator into one of the ship water ballast tanks and for all I know it's probably still in there today.

To top it off, when we returned to the ship, the officer of the day discovered we were AWOL and provided punishment I hope I never have again. Four of us were sent to the boiler room and had to stand guard duty four hours on and four hours off for 48 hours. The humidity and heat were so intense, I lost about 12 pounds and my uniform nearly fell off my skinny body. After that wild but interesting summer cruise, I was anxious to get back to class.

I really looked forward to going to class each day because it was easy for me to learn all the technical things about filmmaking and the creative aspect of editing. The USC Cinema Department made a short comedy in 1950 called *The Filmmaker*. I was not only part of the crew but also did a little acting. I set up lights, recorded sound and generally had fun. But when it came time to get in front of the camera, I felt a little awkward. It was fun, but I decided that I would limit my on-camera appearances.

Early in my first year at USC, I was asked to join a social fraternity called Pi Lambda Phi. The house was more than a mile from the main campus, off center of fraternity row. I moved in and thought this would be great fun and a chance to meet girls. There was quite a variety of personalities in the house including the Vukavich brothers, famous USC football heroes. I soon found out that the only thing most of the fraternity members wanted to do was party. It seemed there was a party every night and two on weekends! I remember an incident where several frat brothers got drunk and bodily lifted a VW Bug onto the porch of the house, turning it sideways in the process. The next day, the owner of the car was horrified to find his car on the porch, so blocked in that it took most of the day to get it off again. Needless to say, that student missed all his classes that day.

The fraternity house was not exactly what I had envisioned. It was quite old and in desperate need of repair. As I later found out, many times it came close to being shut down by the health department. Since many of the fraternity brothers were intent on partying most every night, I wasn't able to study much. This began to bother me since I wasn't getting some of my assignments in on time. I made up my mind I was going to get an education. My father paid for most of the tuition and expenses and I helped out by working in the film processing lab, running the film projector for various classes and doing odd jobs for people to earn extra income. However, after a particularly noisy and drunken party, I finally quit the fraternity and moved out.

In 1950, I hitched a ride back to my home town of Rochester, New York, with three friends in their convertible. They were going back to New York City and were to drop me off. We left Los Angeles at the beginning of Christmas vacation and drove the shortest route across country, stopping only for pit stops and meals. It took us three days and 18 hours. After the first day with no showers, we all began to smell ripe. Each time we'd stop in a restaurant or diner, we would sit on alternate stools because we couldn't stand to be that close to each other. It was even worse when we climbed back into the car. We often would drive with the windows all the way down, even when the outside temperature was below freezing, to keep the B. O. from suffocating us. What an experience.

During that vacation, I asked my dad to loan me money for a used car (it was nearly impossible to get around L. A. without one). He finally agreed and loaned me the money to buy a used 1950 Oldsmobile 88 two-door coupe with low mileage. It was actually a very nice car. When I drove it back to L. A., I spent only $47 in gas cross-country. Try that today! Somewhere in Texas where there are miles and miles of nothing but miles and miles, I decided to see how fast the car would go. I floored it and watched the speedometer needle hit 120 MPH. Looking far ahead, I saw what looked like a mirage in the desert. As I approached it, the mirage didn't seem to change much. Suddenly, I realized that it was not a mirage at all but real water running across the road. I slammed on the brakes and hit the water, a small spring (about 50 feet wide) which spun the car around 180 degrees in the opposite direction going about 70 MPH. I pulled over and listened to my heart pounding in my chest as I realized what a close call I had. Believe me, after I turned the car around and started up again, I drove that car about 35 MPH all the rest of the way to California.

I rented an apartment closer to school and moved in with another Cinema student, Don Stern. We split the rent on a guest house behind the home of a family named Wynn. The owner was a mailman, a fine gentleman, and his family treated us very well. This sort-of "bungalow" behind their home was really a very small one-bedroom and bath with a parking space for two cars next to it. It was clean and well-maintained but had almost no storage space. I got a good deal on a new spare tire and had nowhere to store it so I stuffed it between our two beds, the only place I could keep it without tripping over it.

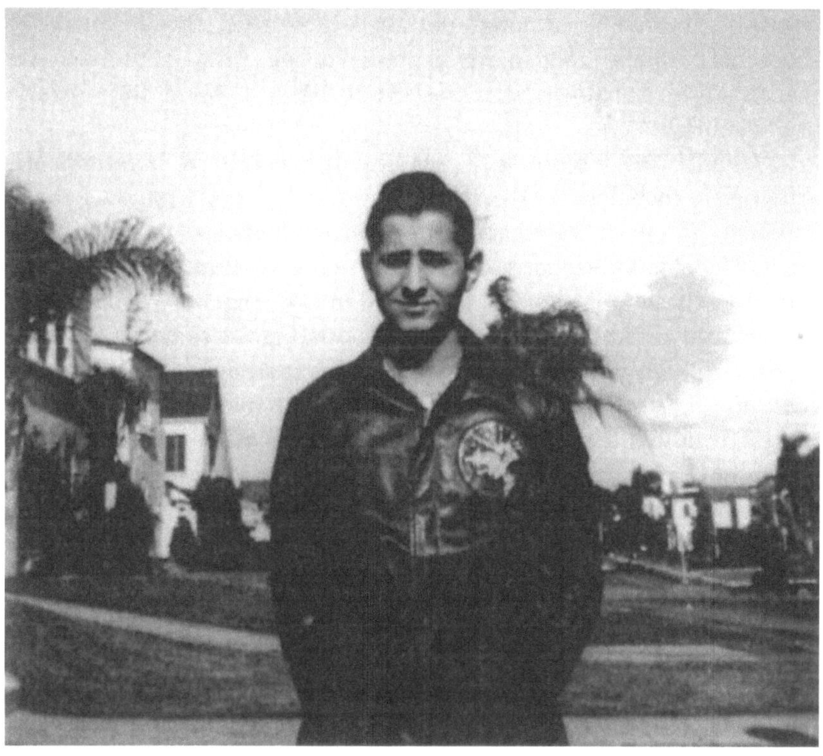

The author as a young pilot and college student (USC).

There was a time when Don and I got involved in a "pyramid club" so that we could get a free 21-inch black and white television set. All we had to do was to get 21 of our friends to buy their own TV set through this club. Ha! We ended up making payments on the set for two years and never got anyone interested in buying even one set.

In my senior year, I was asked by one of my professors, Sid Solow, then president of Consolidated Film Industries (CFI) in Los Angeles, if I would be interested in taking over the USC 16mm film processing lab since the student manager was graduating. I would be teaching some 22 other students the 16mm film processing operation. I jumped at the chance since I would not only be paid but I could get all my film raw stock and processing for free. I also was making the magnificent sum of $60 a week working six days a week. Heck, that was a good deal for me. I owned a 16mm film camera and I needed a way to get free film. I also discovered that by using ordinary film print stock, I could shoot it as a camera negative. The results, although not great, were good enough for me to shoot lots of footage to gain experience in editing. The only problem was that this print stock was so insensitive to light, it would only work in bright sunlight.

When I wasn't working, I was heavily involved in extracurricular activities in the Cinema Department. I worked on every project I could. I used to go out on weekends with other students just to shoot background footage for school projects. One night we needed to get a long, smooth dolly shot of Figueroa Boulevard in Los Angeles. We decided to use one student's car as a camera car by mounting the camera and wedging the tripod in the front bumper. To guide it straight, we thought we could use the streetcar tracks that ran down the middle of the street as makeshift dolly tracks. But after a couple of tries, we found out that the wheels of the car would slip in and out of grooves in the tracks, giving a very bumpy picture. So we let half of the air out of all four tires and drove the car down the tracks. This time it worked great.

Another activity I enjoyed was shooting film of basketball games for the coaches at USC. Every Friday night, about 2,000 feet of 16mm movie film was shot by several cameramen, including me. As soon as the game was over, I would develop and print all the film. I stayed up all night until I had assembled those 20 rolls onto one large 2,000 foot film reel ready for the coaches to view by eight A.M. Saturday morning. The experience I gained with these projects convinced me more than ever that I wanted to be a film editor.

CHAPTER TWO

Working in Early Television

Late in my senior year at USC, I went to a technical meeting spon sored by the Society of Motion Picture Engineers (SMPE) and was introduced to a man from NBC in Hollywood who said he was looking for a part-time film editor to work on syndicated television programs. In 1951, the only method of archiving television programs was on 16mm film, which was recorded and printed for a two-week delay across the country. This was many years before the transcontinental television cable, microwave towers or satellites. Programs in those days were either live or recorded on film and generally seen two weeks later across the country. There were no other choices.

The next day, I drove to NBC in Hollywood (located at Sunset Boulevard and Vine Street) and went in for an interview. This fellow grilled me for about four hours. About the only thing he didn't use was a rubber hose. At the end of the interview, he actually said, "Don't call me, I'll call you." I thought that was the end of my chance to work at NBC. However, that Friday, this fellow called me back and asked if I could come to work on Monday. I said yes and the job lasted more than 17 years.

I came to work at the NBC Studios in Hollywood on September 16, 1951. It now seems that most jobs I've had in my career end up with me working in the basement. This was no exception. The NBC Studios were built in 1937 for their West Coast radio network. In 1948, modifications were made to replace some of the radio studios with television equipment. I remember Studio "G," a former radio studio, was modified especially for Groucho Marx's *You Bet Your Life* television program. Since quality was of prime importance, the program was photographed on 35mm black and white motion picture film with four cameras. In addition, Studio "D" was converted to television to be used for the daily Dinah

Shore 15-minute television series sponsored by Chevrolet. Do you remember their slogan "See the USA in Your Chevrolet"? All television broadcasting was in black and white until 1954, when a few live color broadcasts were aired.

I endeavored to complete my senior year in college and work but my hours were very irregular. One day I would be in at 9 A.M. and the next day at 2 P.M. For a while, I tried to finish the semester but the erratic hours were taking their toll. At this time, I felt that it was more important to keep this job than to get a degree. It turned out to be the right decision for me. I lacked only 12 units to get my bachelor of fine arts degree and I felt that at some later date when I had regular hours, I would do that. As it turned out, I never got regular hours and was not able to complete those few units. Many years later, I wrote to USC asking if there was any way I could get my degree without completing those missed units. They sent me a very polite letter stating that many other former students had asked the same question. They were all given the same answer: No one gets a degree from USC without earning it by completing all the required courses. Even famous and successful alumni who had not completed all their credits but tried to get their diplomas were turned down flat.

In 1951, NBC television was only a few years old. Black and white cameras were everywhere. At the Sunset and Vine street facility, Studios E and F were assembled from field equipment normally used for remote productions and were meant to be temporary, but they stayed that way until all the NBC Hollywood studio facilities moved out to Burbank in 1954. I remember a cooking show with Chef Milani in Studio E directly above my editing room. I could smell the food cooking as it wafted through the ventilation system. When the show was over, we would run up the stairs to eat the food prepared that day. (The food was always given away to the cast and crew since it was not practical to store it.) It was mostly Italian but sometimes the chef made salads as well. If I was one of the first in the studio, I would get the biggest helping.

Often, when commercials were being shot, the props and other items would be given to the crew after the shoot since the commercial agencies didn't want to lug these items back to their office. I still have some Halloween napkins, plates and other props from a Hallmark commercial—items which today are more than 50 years old! We would also get cleansers, soap, hair spray and a multitude of other things that were generally quite useful. The only props they would not let us have after they finished shooting were the automobiles.

In order to record television programs for later distribution, a specially designed motion picture camera was pointed at a high-intensity five-inch television picture tube known as a kinescope. This special kinescope tube had a blue phosphor face since the film used to photograph the TV image was most sensitive to blue light. The television recording made by this method was called (for obvious reasons) a kinescope recording, or "kine" for short. This equipment was used to make delayed broadcast films of programs to be shipped across the country about two weeks after the live broadcast. I'm sure many of you have seen black and white kinescope films on programs using material from television programs made before the advent of videotape. These old black and white kinescopes sometimes had a telltale horizontal flickering bar (or "shutter bar") in the middle of the picture.

When I started work at NBC, I was called a Group 2 TV engineer, an all-encompassing name that covered anyone involved in technical operations including production (cameras, sound, lighting, etc.) or post-production (film processing, kinescope recording or editing). Some 15 years later I was upgraded to a Group 5 supervisor. At first, my primary job was to run the kinescope cameras and record television programs based on the needs of the network. In order for the rest of the country to view West Coast-originated prime time or local programs, we would record some programs on orders from the NBC syndication division. These programs would be recorded on 16mm black and white kinescope film as a negative image, developed in our own lab and sent to a commercial film laboratory for multiple release printing at times, often on the order of 30 copies. Along with the negative picture image, we recorded an optical sound track that would later be used to print the program sound onto the final release prints.

My secondary job was to synchronize the picture image with the optical sound track, put identifying leaders on the film and send it to the lab for printing. From time to time I would have to edit out some objectionable language or fix a technical problem so that the print, when viewed by audiences around the country some two weeks later, would not contain these irregularities. When the first print (known as an "answer print" or a "first trial print") came back from the lab, it was my job to evaluate it for picture and sound quality, scratches or dirt. If any of these problems

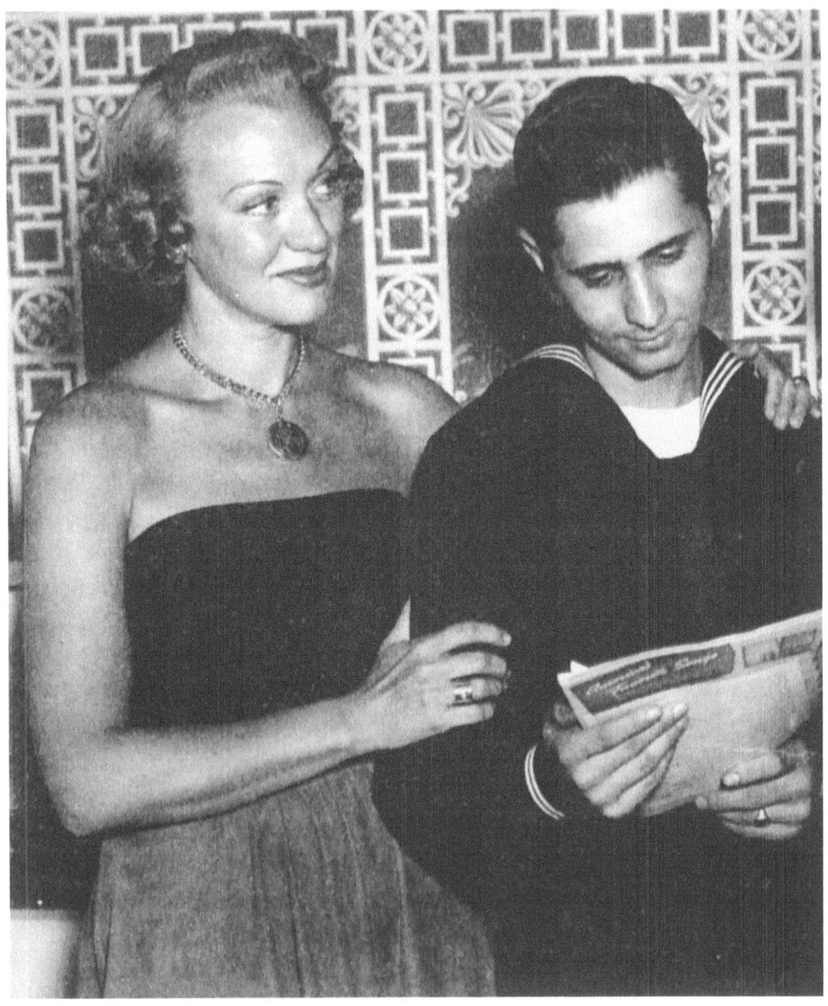

Author with actress Eve Arden, 1950.

occurred, I would send the print back to the lab for corrective action. Scratches were rarely a problem but dirt specks and density problems had to be monitored carefully. If the sound track wasn't printed at the right density, it would exhibit spitty "S's" or other types of audio distortion.

Early in 1952, the transcontinental cable was installed from the East to the West Coast, allowing us to record programs live from New York. This new and innovative technique allowed West Coast audiences to see

New York-originated programs at the same clock time as the audience in New York. Later, the cable was replaced by microwave towers that increased picture quality somewhat. However, there were sometimes signal breakups due to one technical problem or another or even atmospheric conditions. Today, television programs are sent around the world by satellite.

It is impractical for West Coast audiences to watch live programs originating at 8 P.M. Eastern Standard Time from the East Coast since many West Coast families would just be sitting down to their 5 P.M. P.S.T. dinners. Because the 16mm kinescope film is not really very good in terms of sharpness and picture quality, NBC invested in several new 35mm cameras specially designed to make high quality kinescope recordings. These new cameras would be used to record live programs from the East Coast as part of a new time zone delay process, enabling West Coast audiences to see the same program three hours later at the same clock time as East Coast audiences did when the program was live.

Basically, the process worked this way. Let's take as an example Milton Berle's *Texaco Star Theater*, which was broadcast live at 8 P.M. from New York every Tuesday night. Because of three different time zones in the US, 8 P.M. on the East Coast is 5 P.M. on the West Coast. Milton Berle's program would be sent to the West Coast by microwave transmission and recorded at 5 P.M. West Coast time. Two cameras (one 35mm and the other a 16mm backup) would start recording one minute before 5 P.M. to be sure they were up to speed. The primary 35mm camera was used to record the first half of the one-hour program. It recorded a negative picture and a separate 16mm magnetic soundtrack which ran in synchronization with the film.

The 35mm primary copy was then sent to a local Hollywood film processing lab a short distance away where a crew was standing by just for this purpose. The backup or protection copy was a 16mm kinescope film with a positive picture image that had its soundtrack on the same piece of film and was processed locally in NBC's own small processing plant. This was so as not to "put all our eggs in one basket." If the 35mm master film was damaged or didn't get back to NBC in time, we could actually run the 16mm backup film and not lose the program. In all the years of doing this, we only were forced to use the backup film once or twice.

When projected over the television system, the 35mm negative image would be electronically reversed for broadcast to a positive "print"-like image. When recording a program that was more than a half-hour in length, an appropriate amount of overlap between half-hours was necessary in order to be able to switch over to the next half-hour in a continuous manner. Two minutes before the first half-hour ended, a second pair of cameras (one 16mm and one 35mm) were started to provide a program content overlap so that during broadcast, the director would be able to seamlessly switch over to the second half hour of the program.

During the recording of the program, I would carefully watch the program during that two-minute overlap to find an appropriate point at approximately the half-hour point so as to know where to punch tiny changeover cue marks into the film in the upper right hand corner of the frame. These marks were used to cue the studio director to start the second projector and when to make the actual switch from part one to part two. These cue marks were actually punched into the film itself with a triangular hand punch. My first choice of where to make a reel changeover was in a fade to black since any missed frames would not be seen on the air. This could be at the beginning or end of a commercial break or within the program content itself. The first set of four consecutive punch marks was made exactly eight seconds from the switch-over point. A second set of four were punched exactly one second from the switch-over point where the director would switch to the second half hour.

Thirty-five mm film runs at 90 feet per minute so a 30-minute program is 2700 feet in length. It should be noted that a 30-minute roll of film was actually closer to 34 minutes in length (about 3100 feet), allowing for startup footage and overlap time on longer programs. When the first half-hour roll of 35mm film was stopped, the film magazine was removed from the camera and sent to the darkroom. There the film was put in a light-proof black paper bag, then into a metal film can, wrapped with tape, and given to a messenger to deliver to the lab some 15 minutes away. I should mention that I was a young lad of 21 and slight of build. The film magazine and the roll of film inside the magazine together weighed 52 pounds. Lifting that magazine over my head, approximately six feet off the ground, to mount it on top of the camera was no easy task. After some four years of hoisting those heavy magazines over my head, I didn't exactly look like Charles Atlas, but I did gain many new muscles in my arms.

A point of interest. When the NBC Studios later moved to Burbank, one of the people they hired as a film messenger was a fellow by the name of Jim Nabors. Jim was jovial, hummed tunes and always had a good word for everyone. He loved to sing and we sometimes found him singing opera while strolling down the halls of NBC. We used to kid around with him and found him to be a conscientious person. He would pick up the film, hop into his car and drive the 15 minutes to Hollywood, then return to Burbank, pick up the second half-hour roll of film and again drive to Hollywood. On the second trip, he would pick up the developed film of the first half-hour and return it to me in the editing department. Jim would do this all evening long. During this period, Steve Allen had his own variety show on NBC. One day Jim Nabors got his big break on *The Steve Allen Show*. The rest is history. Even after Jim Nabors became a star, any time he would see me in the hallway, he would stop to chat.

When the film was returned from the lab, it was in a large blue cardboard box almost two feet in diameter. I would then carefully, and I mean *carefully*, remove it from the box by first putting an aluminum flange on one side through the plastic core in the middle of the roll. Then, with great agility, I'd turn the box and the film with the flange on it over on the table so that I could put another flange on the other side of the film in a sandwich fashion. The reason for all this care is that the film, when returned from the lab after being processed, was wound very loose. If the roll wasn't carefully supported on both sides with the metal flanges, the film would uncoil and spill all over the floor. That, in fact, did happen once. Fortunately, I was able to get it all back together again without mishap.

The next step was to mount the picture and magnetic soundtrack in a motion picture film synchronizer. A film synchronizer is a mechanical set of wheels with film sprockets around its perimeter through which the picture and sound would pass so as to maintain perfect synchronization. Because the picture runs at 90 feet per minute and the magnetic soundtrack runs at 36 feet per minute, a 2½ to 1 gear box between the two units was used to maintain frame accuracy throughout the length of the roll. At the beginning of every recording, a set of synchronizing marks are recorded in the picture area of the 35mm or 16mm film along with an audible tone on the magnetic sound track. These marks and tones are applied by the operator prior to the start of the program so the editor has a reference mark to be used later to synchronize the picture and sound track. It was a simple matter to unwind the beginning of the film to locate the group of synchronizing bars recorded in a short burst, then listen for the audible tone.

When each was located, the beginning and end of the synchronizing bars and tone were marked with a white grease pencil to make them easier to see. The track and picture were then placed in the synchronizer and a matching head identifying leader was spliced onto the picture just ahead of the beginning of the program. The exact frame where the picture was to be placed in the projector gate was identified as "Picture Start," printed as part of the standard leader spliced onto the head of the program film. This was known in the industry as an "Academy Leader." A large full frame "X" was inked over the Picture Start frame to make it easier for the projectionist to find. The magnetic soundtrack was marked simply by placing a large "X" on the corresponding synchronizing frame with about a two-inch black line on either side of the "X" to make it easier to see.

In order to determine the exact frame at which the half-hour changeover would be made on programs that were an hour or longer, I would roll the 35mm through the film synchronizer along with its corresponding 16mm magnetic soundtrack. I would always have to roll down to near the end of this large roll of film, some 18 inches in diameter, and locate by picture and word cues the changeover point I had noted during the original recording of the program earlier that evening. Most changeovers occurred at a camera switch rather than at fade outs.

Since we were editing magnetic soundtracks along with the picture, I found it awkward to have to twist the magnetic film upside down so the sound pickup head could play back the sound. I thought if this pickup head could be positioned so that it was mounted inside the sprocket wheel, then no reversing of the magnetic film would be necessary. In 1952, I had the Moviola company, makers of film editing equipment, build me two units. They were so successful that I applied through RCA, then the parent company of NBC, for a patent on this device. Since the RCA attorneys did not understand the device, they told me it was not patentable. However, a few months later, the Moviola company saw the advantage in this device and started building them. Today, they are still being used worldwide but I lost out on a patent because some attorney didn't want to take the time to investigate the patent application.

Whenever possible, I would go up to the film projection studio and tell the director the exact time when the changeover punch marks would be coming up along with the word cue at the actual switch from one reel to another. I was able to do this accurately because the film synchronizer I used to roll the picture and soundtrack together had two timers on the unit. One was a standard footage counter of the type used in the motion picture industry. The other was an hours, minutes and seconds counter that gave me to-the-second timing information for the director in the film studio. The director had to watch for the changeover cues as they flashed on the screen (in ⅙th of a second) so he could start the second projector for the second half hour. If a cue was missed, then there would be an interruption of the picture and sound, generally a slight overlap of a few frames just seen. If the director anticipated the changeover too soon, the program would be upcut by several frames. This was only a problem if there was continuous action or running dialogue at the transition point. But the crew we had rarely missed a beat and perfect changeovers were the norm, not the exception.

On one occasion, a one-hour program called *Saturday Night Revue* was delayed at the lab in Hollywood and didn't get back to NBC Burbank until minutes before air time. We were all on pins and needles because we really didn't want to run the soft image quality 16mm film backup print if we could avoid it. I notified the projection studio of the problem and asked them to be prepared for anything. They loaded the 16mm backup film on the projector just in case.

I carefully laid out on the editing bench all the items I would need just as a surgeon might have his instruments ready for an operation. Jim Nabors came flying through the door and handed me the film about five minutes before air time. I quickly synchronized the picture and sound-tracks for the projectionist but didn't have time to roll the film down to the end of the half hour reel to punch changeover marks on the film.

I gave the soundtrack to my assistant, who shot up the stairs to the studio. I finished splicing on the startup Academy Leader and ran up the stairs with the film clamped to my chest. It was two minutes to air time. Everyone was nervous. As I was running up the stairs, someone was coming down. I screamed, "Out of my way!" and bumped into him. He fell part way down the stairs with me yelling "Sorry!" as I leaped up the steps two at a time. I reached the projection studio less than a minute before air time. I handed the large 35mm reel to the projectionist who threaded it onto the projector. He had it almost threaded but not yet on the take-up reel when the director punched the start button. The projector started and the program hit the air right on time. But the projectionist was unable to get the end of the film threaded onto the empty take-up reel and it spun wildly at a high rate of speed.

Since these were very heavy aluminum reels about 18 inches in diameter, trying to stop such a spinning reel could do much damage to one's hands. The end of the film started piling up on the floor and I grabbed it as soon as I could to prevent any more dirt from getting on the print (this film would later be used to make release prints for delayed syndication). I said, "Put another take-up reel on the bench over there and start winding the film on it." Since the bench was about ten feet away from the projector, we had four people feed the film in sort of a "bucket brigade" fashion over to the film rewind bench. We stood there for the full half hour slowly feeding the film onto the reel as it came off the projector.

Just before the half hour ended, I remembered that I hadn't had time to punch changeover marks on the film. Oh oh! I got someone to take my place feeding the film and tried to remember where the changeover was. Fortunately, the second half hour was intact and the head leader was spliced at the correct point. Since I had watched the original recording a few hours earlier, I knew the program, but I would have to guess when to tell the projectionist to start the second reel. I watched the program and something told me to yell *"Now!"* The second projector started. After several seconds went by, I yelled to the director, *"Switch!"* It was a perfect changeover and no one at home ever knew there was a problem. We do need some luck in our lives from time to time. After the program aired, back in my editing room I carefully rewound the film. As I came to the beginning of the roll, I applied a special cloth (called a "cleaning velvet") saturated with a cleaning solution which kept the film clean and prevented any surface damage.

One time when we were recording *The Texaco Star Theater* with Milton Berle, the phone rang a few minutes after we finished. I answered it in my usual manner, saying, "Editing room, Art here." The voice on the phone said "Hello, Art, this is Milton Berle in New York. Did you see my show tonight?" I said yes. He told me there was a sketch in which he was not supposed to get out of bed until after the fade to black, but he started to get up in his nightgown and didn't want the audience on the West Coast to see that. I told him that I didn't have the authority to cut that out. He asked who did and I told him I thought that John West (at that time president of NBC on the West Coast) might be able to help him. I gave him back to the operator. A few minutes later, the phone rang and it was John West. He said cut it out and I did. So the West Coast audience never did see his goof.

Another problem that occurred from time to time was a film break in the 35mm negative at the lab. When this would happen, we would have to synchronize the 16mm backup print with the 35mm negative and run them down in a synchronizer together to the break in the film.

This was necessary because the network did not want to stay on the relatively poor quality 16mm backup copy any longer than they had to. I would splice and add blank film stock at the break point on the 35mm film until I found a frame-for-frame picture match with the 16mm backup print on the 35mm negative. I would then splice the 35mm film back together with the blank film stock acting as a filler for the missing material. Sometimes the break would only be a few frames long but at other times it could be many feet of film. When the program went on the air, I would tell the director where to switch away from the 35mm film to the 16mm protection copy (to cover the film break) and then where to switch back again.

The reason for always making a 35mm negative picture was that, after broadcast, very often the 35mm negative would be used to make 16mm reduction prints of a higher quality instead of the lower quality 16mm prints. A separate 16mm magnetic soundtrack was also recorded and it would later be used to make an optical printing soundtrack negative.

One of the programs I recorded was the daily Dinah Shore 15-minute variety program, which was recorded in Studio D at the Sunset and Vine studios. Whenever I had time, I would go up to the set and "shmooze" with the crew and even Dinah. This was one way I used to make myself known to people. Later, I edited many specials with Dinah's director Alan Handley and with Bud Yorkin (at that time the associate director on *Dinah*), who also became a very successful and famous director. Many years later, I would see Dinah Shore at the Board of Governors monthly meeting of the Television Academy and we became good friends. When I was editing television trailers for NBC, I would be sent to her home to record her narration for television promotional trailers. She often told me how she appreciated the high technical quality of her recorded programs since she knew they would be syndicated all over the country. Dinah gave the recording crew a large autographed photo of herself thanking us for our contributions to the success of her program.

The time zone delay kinescope process was quite successful and was used primarily to record and broadcast delay prime time programs such as *Your Show of Shows, Milton Berle, Perry Como* and every NBC show sent to the West Coast seven days a week from 8 P.M. to 11 P.M.

The time zone delay process was used from early 1952 until 1956, when videotape came in and essentially removed the need for 35mm recordings (videotape was of much higher quality). Obviously, videotape did not have to be processed and could be rewound and played back within minutes. Even though the use of kinescope recordings for delayed broadcast was coming to an end, it still was a viable tool used later in the editing of videotape programs, a process I'll describe later in this book.

CHAPTER THREE

My Fledgling Career

Enzio Pinza, the famous opera singer, starred in a television special which was shot in San Juan Capistrano, a small community and tourist attraction south of Los Angeles. I'm sure you've heard that the swallows come back to Capistrano every year. The black and white cameras were located in Capistrano and the television signal was sent back to Hollywood via a microwave signal and was recorded on 35mm kinescope film. The negative was developed and a film work print was made. The program was edited in the basement of NBC in Hollywood in a very large storage room, which was adapted to accommodate extra editing benches because there were two editors assigned to this project due to the constricted time frame for completion. We also had a producer's office in our editing room with two desks and other equipment.

Shooting in a remote location severely limited the amount of coverage I had for editing since there was only one feed to the Hollywood studios. All the camera switching was done at the location during production. But there were many takes and *mis*takes. My job was to piece together some 100 separate shots into a coherent and continuous flow. Today, camera feeds from the studio or a location are often split so that several different camera angles are sent to individual recorders, allowing greater flexibility in editing. But in this case, because there was only one feed, I tried to communicate with the director, telling him there was a potential problem with several sequences and that he should consider shooting extra footage to give us coverage for those areas in question. However, due to the fact that they were losing daylight fast, I was only able to get a few of the needed shots. I still had a problem with other areas of the program.

Since a new commercial film processing lab opened up across the street from NBC, we decided to duplicate one of three generic shots we

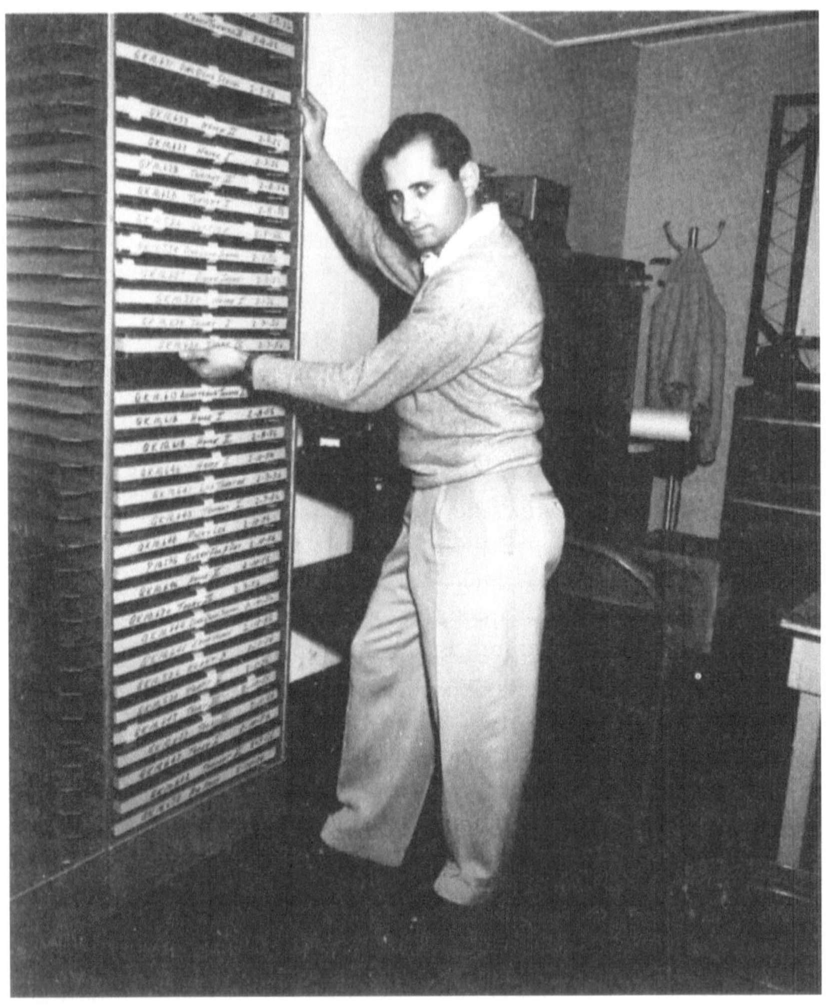

Author at rack of 35mm kinescope films, 1953.

felt we could use in editing. This would make the editing smoother. Since we were in a time bind, we had the lab assign a special crew to follow through on this project. We selected the material and hand delivered the negative to the lab with instructions as to what shots were to be duplicated. Within 12 hours, we had our duplicates and were able to complete editing without any further problems. After work print approval, the negative was sent to a negative cutter who matched the original's camera negative to the edited work print. Once this was done, the negative was delivered to the lab for them to make two release prints, one for New York and the other for Hollywood origination.

Since television is on a very specific schedule, programs must air on time. They cannot start even one second early or late, especially when commercials are to be integrated into a program as it airs. Completed programs are timed before broadcast to know exactly where to insert the commercial. Today computers do this work, but in the 1950s it was all done manually. As soon as we had the program completed and approved by the producer and the network executives, I timed every act to the second. These timings were given to the network coordinators to let them know exactly how many commercial spots there were and the exact time each was to start and end.

To maintain the proper running time of the program, we inserted film material called slugs or spacers between acts in the commercial break positions. These slugs were timed to match the length of the commercials that were to be inserted later. If this is not done, commercials may be clipped or run into program content, especially if the error is significant. When this happens, sponsors may ask for a rebate, something the networks frown upon.

Even though the editing was relatively simple, the unknowns (When will the film get back from the lab? Will we miss the air date?), coupled with the long hours, put quite a strain on all of us. Many family problems originate from this type of work and some people become alcoholics simply because they cannot handle the stress and long hours.

For one reason or another, the lab ran into some difficulty in getting both prints out on time. The first print got out of the lab on time and was air freighted to New York the day of airing in New York, but the second print was delayed. We were quite concerned about whether or not the second print would be delivered to Hollywood in time for broadcast that evening. In a desperate measure, we decided to prepare the edited work print for the Hollywood origination of the program in case the second release print didn't arrive in time for the Hollywood airing.

The work print was in pretty good shape except for some surface dirt and the white grease pencil marks used to indicate dissolves and fades. We had to manually go through each foot of film and, using a special cleaner, remove every trace of grease pencil. There were very few scratches so, after cleaning, we projected a few of the reels to see how they looked. Fortunately, the cleaning removed nearly all the dust and dirt marks. Because the grease pencil marks were used to indicate optical transitions, by removing them, all the indicated effects were simply shown as cuts. As the air time approached, we decided to load up the first of six reels of the work print on the projector just in case, since the lab had not called to tell us the status of the air print.

When the air time approached, we started the West Coast broadcast using the work print on the air. Just before halfway through the hour program, the second release print arrived. The projectionist hurriedly threaded the new print on the projector and at the half hour mark switched to the clean print and finished airing the program with the good print. Thank goodness this never happened again. My nerves wouldn't take it.

In late 1953, the new NBC Studios were just completed and we were in the process of starting to move the entire Hollywood facility to Burbank. I was assigned to edit a *Hallmark Hall of Fame* special that was being shot at the Burbank studios. I was at work that day in Hollywood but not feeling well at all for I had a bad cold which had lingered on for more than two weeks. I wanted to go home but my boss told me I had to go to Burbank and handle the project since he had no one to cover for me.

Reluctantly, I got in my car and drove the eight miles to the Burbank studios. I was sitting at the control room console with my head in my hands when the director walked in. He looked at me and told me I looked white as a sheet and told me to go home. I said I couldn't because my boss told me to stay. The director said he was in charge in the studio and ordered me to go home. That was fine with me since I really was feeling quite ill.

I had severe pains in my stomach and thought I might have pneumonia. I called my doctor who, wouldn't you know, was on vacation. His office referred me to a doctor by the name of Sharp, who was covering for him. I called Dr. Sharp and he said even though it was late, he would wait for me. I got in my car and drove to Beverly Hills, a drive of more than an hour and a half at that time of day through heavy evening traffic. When I arrived, Dr Sharp put me on the examining table and proceeded to check my stomach. When he pressed on my lower abdomen, I screamed. He discovered that I had an acute appendicitis and told me to get to the hospital as quickly as I could since time was of the essence. He would call ahead and reserve a room for me. Maybe it was because I was in such agony that I did not hear him say, "Take a cab." So I struggled to my car and drove to the hospital.

Unfortunately, the Hollywood Presbyterian Hospital was an even longer drive from Beverly Hills. I drove down Sunset Boulevard east towards the hospital. It was very painful to even switch my right foot from the gas to the brake because of the intense pain. In the middle of the infamous Sunset Strip, my car started making funny gurgling sounds. I looked at the gas gauge and was startled to find it reading empty. Just then the car quit. Fortunately I was on a downhill grade and neatly coasted into a gas station. Those were the days before self-serve. The attendant walked over to my window and said, "Howdy, sir. Fill 'er up?" I gasped, "Gimme … two … gallons … I'm on my way to the hospital … with an acute appendicitis attack. *Hurry*." That attendant was petrified but gassed the car in a couple of minutes. I handed him the money and said, "Keep the change."

I drove down Sunset Boulevard to the hospital and parked my car in the lot. I could barely make it to the lobby and walk over to the admissions office. It appears that if you are ambulatory, you are not considered an emergency. But as the woman was taking down my insurance information, I started to sink to the floor. Quickly, a nurse arrived with a wheelchair and took me up to a room. They finished taking the information they needed much later.

In my room, I was prepped for surgery. All this time, a group of interns were hovering over me taking notes as the doctor asked me dozens of questions. Finally, I was given a sedative and wheeled into the elevator and into the surgery room. I expected it to be all white but everything was green. I remember the doctor telling me to hold out my right hand. I felt something cold like ice water on my hand. It was sodium pentothal. The doctor said to count to a hundred. I opened my mouth. "One," I said, and was out like a light.

The next thing I remember was waking up in bed feeling pretty good, like I had just had a good night's sleep. A nurse was standing over me, adjusting the needle in my arm. I asked her if they had decided not to take out my appendix. She said, "Oh, no, it's been out for four hours." I got a strange twinge as I gingerly lifted the sheet and saw this huge bandage over my stomach. I called my boss the next day and told him what happened. His only response was, "When are you coming back to work?"

During my recovery, I felt no pain, except when they brought in another patient (suffering from acute athlete's foot) and he started telling me dirty jokes. Every time I laughed, I thought I was going to blow a stitch. I told the nurse, "Get this guy out of here before I kill him." I spent the next week recovering and then went back to work. The day before I was to be released, the doctor came in and checked the dressing. He grabbed a chunk of skin and twisted it. I yelled and said, "That hurt!" He said, "You're fine. Just checking."

When color television was being developed in the early 1950s, both RCA and CBS were vying to be the first in color broadcasting. The FCC was waiting to give approval to the first one who would build a practical black and white compatible color television system. An interesting and true story in the development of color television by RCA in their Princeton, New Jersey, laboratory was in the way some of the engineers got rid of their boredom. One day they were photographing a bowl of bananas set up in a room several doors away from where the color camera was set up. The bananas looked great, so the staff went out to lunch. When they came back, however, they were horrified to find that the bananas were bright blue. So they adjusted all the color controls until the bananas were yellow again. But everything else around the fruit was the wrong color. They were mystified until one of the staff went to the room containing the bananas and discovered that while they were all out to lunch, someone had replaced all the real bananas with blue ones! Even serious engineers have a practical joker side.

Until 1954, all commercial broadcasting was done in black and white. Within a few months, the first color receivers became available. The first units had a 15-inch flat screen, were only made in console models, were very heavy and very expensive (a hefty $1,500 each). Since RCA built very few of these color sets, we had one set up in one of the studio rehearsal halls. It was mounted on a pedestal surrounded by heavy blue drapes so that only the cabinet and screen was visible. Every time there was a color broadcast, executives and others who were available were ushered into the room and sat quietly, waiting for the program to start. Sometimes just prior to the start of a color broadcast, the receiver would come on for a minute or two with a black and white picture, fade to black and then up would come a beautiful color picture. I'm sure that was done to enhance the effect of color. You would hear a loud gasp from the audience as the effect of a real color broadcast sank in. Remember, there were but a handful of color receivers in the world and those in attendance felt they were privileged to be able to view magnificent color before the public eventually did.

In 1954, I lived in Westwood, California, near UCLA in a duplex apartment with my roommate Arnie. There were two girls living above us, Mary Lou and Dotty. Mary Lou had a friend visit one day and she introduced her to me. The minute I saw her, I knew I was going to marry her. Her name was Deloise, but everyone called her Dee. On our first date, I took her to the Smoke House restaurant in Burbank, across the street from Warner Brothers studios and a stone's throw from NBC. After dinner, we drove over to the studio. NBC had just gotten their new color cameras and were setting up but had no live references to adjust for flesh tones.

The engineers asked Dee if she would mind sitting in front of the color cameras as a model so they could adjust the cameras. She was a natural as a model. One of the NBC secretaries known as "Pixie" joined her and they both sat in front of the cameras for several hours. I would guess they were the first unofficial NBC color girls.

Dee and I dated regularly but the drive to her home in Long Beach and back was getting to me, especially after working long hours in Hollywood and Burbank. One day about six months later, on a date at Point Dume in Malibu, I said, "What would you say if I asked you to marry me?" Dee said, "I guess I would say yes."

We were married in June 1954 and recently celebrated our forty third anniversary. We have two fine children, Robert Paul (our oldest) and Lori Ann (three years younger). When our children were little, I had their portraits taken by the NBC photographers in their famous photo gallery where all the NBC stars were photographed. Both our children are in the television business. Lori is a specialist in digital tape recording and telecine transfer. Robert is a skilled videotape editor who followed in my footsteps and has taken over the editing of all the Bob Hope comedy specials, with more than 90 under his belt at this time. He has also been nominated for two Emmy Awards. I may be a bit prejudiced but I think Robert is the best videotape editor in the business and Lori the best expert in complex digital tape transfer technology.

Even though live color broadcasts were available in 1954, videotape was still being broadcast in black and white. The RCA engineers had not yet figured how to record color on videotape. An interim system was developed using an ingenious method of recording and reproducing color pictures on black and white film. Although the process is much too technical to describe in detail, this brief description should give you an idea of how this system helped bridge the gap between black and white and color videotape.

In order to capture true color on film without the long processing time of regular color film, a method developed in the 1930s by Eastman Kodak called lenticular film photography was modified for use in motion picture films. The purpose of this was to be able to break apart color into its three primary colors, red, green and blue. This process translated black and white film from the three primary colors into shades of gray, black and white. When combined through three special color filters and a lens system, they would reproduce exceedingly good color images. The special film base onto which this was photographed was the key to the success of this method.

During the process of film manufacture, a special roller embossed tiny rows of minute lenses across the width of the film on the plastic side. These lenses, or "lenticules," were embossed or stamped across the entire width of the film. Imagine a circular rod slit lengthwise and put on a flat surface. Now imagine thousands of these half rods back to back across its width of film. That is what lenticular film looked like. Of course these lenses were almost invisible to the eye but could be seen under a microscope or be felt by dragging one's fingernail across the surface of the film. Since the lenticules had to break apart the light into the three primary colors, the film was put in the camera gate backwards. That is, instead of the emulsion facing the lens, the embossed celluloid side faced the lens since the light first had to go through the lenticules before exposing the film.

Three five-inch individual high intensity kinescope picture tubes of the same type used to record black and white kinescope films were mounted through a beam splitter lens system, allowing defined percentages of light to go to each picture tube. Each tube was fed one of the three primary color signals but only as a black and white image. Even though the three images were in black and white, each tube represented the correct densities of each of the three primary colors. For example, the blue tube had the lowest density since blue is not a high brightness color.

Imagine that each of the three signals was recorded and directed to each lenticule. The mirrors and lenses were so angled that each portion of the three colors was exposed in a 30 degree area under each lenticule. Every lenticule on a given frame had these three exposures, all in different densities corresponding to the amount of color in the scene. We are talking *real small* image area.

To reproduce these three black and white images in color, a set of red, green and blue filters were attached to the front of the projector lens.

They recombined the three images into a color picture. I've used this demonstration in lectures and people are amazed to see brilliant color from black and white film. The reason is that there are no color dye images on the lenticular film to affect color reproduction. It worked very well and NBC was the first network to broadcast color images from a recorded television picture before the advent of color videotape. However, by late 1957, both RCA and Ampex had both developed color videotape.

When videotape and color television came in during the mid–1950s, producers were anxious to find better and faster ways to edit. The first videotape recorders in those early days were black and white but producers were clamoring for color. RCA came out with the first color videotape recorder called the TRT-1. It was a monstrous machine taking up five huge electronic racks, drawing more than 5,000 watts of power, costing more than $115,000 and containing 470 electron tubes. I know because I frequently had to dust them.

I began videotape editing as soon as the NBC Studios moved from Hollywood to Burbank. I was one of the first tape editors since I could make more good tape splices than the other guys, partly because of skill and some luck. When editing videotape, there were no visible images on the tape itself, only gray bands and other funny little marks made visible by applying a solution of very fine iron powder to the oxide of the tape. This, in effect, left an image of the magnetized signal on the tape. Each television frame was defined by little gray pip markers on the edge of the tape (one-quarter inch) apart called edit pulses.

We faced a serious problem in that sometimes we could make perfect tape splices but at other times the picture would roll vertically for a few seconds. This was completely unacceptable. The problem we soon discovered was that the edit pulse markers on the videotape were positioned in two places on each frame, one at the beginning of a frame and another in the middle, with each marker identical to the other. It was impossible to know merely by looking at these pulses if we were cutting the tape at the end of a frame or in the middle. If we accidentally made a splice at the wrong frame marker (in the middle of the television frame), then the picture would flip and roll as it tried to stabilize itself. Since there was no way to know if we were always splicing at the end of a television frame, the NBC engineers devised a method of eliminating that extra pulse in the middle of the frame so we would only be able to see the single frame mark pulse indicating only the end of a television picture frame. Now we could be assured that every time we made a tape splice, it would play correctly.

In the early days of television recording, the videotape recorders (called VTRs) were quite cumbersome and expensive. The first ones, made by Ampex, were in black and white. The heart of each machine was the rotating video head, spinning at 14,400 RPM and costing $4,000 each. It cost $1,200 just to rebuild one when it was worn beyond the point of producing quality pictures. Depending how much use each head got, one could expect a head life of between 100 and 200 hours before the unit needed to be rebuilt. You could not still-frame the picture since the design of the video head would quickly saw the tape in two pieces if an attempt was made to bypass the video head playback mechanism. That's why all editing was done "on-the-fly," meaning that the operator would have to use his or her reflexes to quickly press the stop button when an edit point was desired. Since the machine didn't stop immediately, there was a delay of about ten frames or so depending on the particular machine involved and, of course, the person's reflexes.

The editor would then have to calculate how many frames from the point where he or she hit the stop button to where the edit would be made. Using black felt markers on the back side of the tape, edit points would be tentatively marked. Then the tape would be played back a few more times to verify that the mark on the tape would stop at the same place every time. It took a lot of skill and patience to be a videotape editor in those days. It was also very hard on my feet since I was not able to sit in a chair while editing.

The tool we first used to splice videotape was a 12-inch-long machined aluminum block with a two-inch wide slot cut lengthwise in the middle of this block. In those early days, the terms "off-line" or "work print editing" were not in the television vocabulary. All editing was done "on-line" (that is, directly cutting and splicing the master tape). This was somewhat risky because once the videotape was cut in the wrong place, repairing it was a chore. Sometimes the repair would lurch as it went through the video head, causing an unwanted picture shift or movement.

I should point out that the videotape signal on the tape, once developed, was not easy to describe. You could not see an identifiable picture image, just a bunch of evenly spaced lines across the width of the two-inch-wide tape. To give you an idea of what was recorded on the tape, I'll briefly describe the kinds of images the editor had to be concerned with. Along one edge of the tape was the soundtrack carrying the pro-

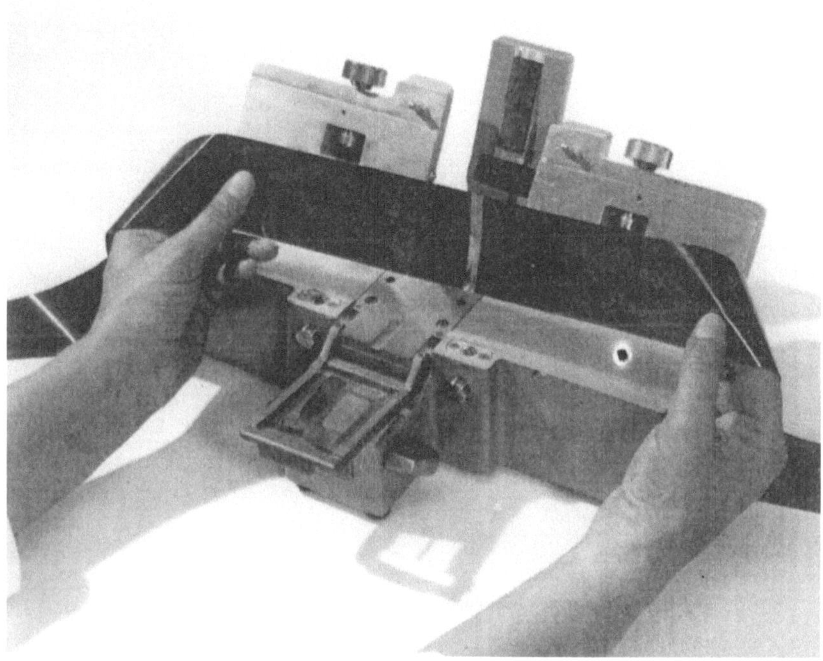

Hands holding 2" spliced videotape.

gram sound. On the opposite edge was a secondary audio channel mostly used for recording time code, voice tracks or other cueing type of information not heard as part of the program sound. Next to this was the control track (analogous to film sprocket holes), used to maintain a constant tape speed.

Filling up the rest of the tape width were the video signals. Videotape in the U.S. and many other countries records television pictures at 30 frames per second. As the tape runs its linear length, each frame is recorded as a signal one-half inch long. Therefore, 30 TV frames would occupy 15 inches of videotape length. Within each half inch video frame on the tape, there are 32 striations or tracks corresponding to two television fields (or two half pictures), one odd and the other even, making up one complete television picture frame. Each track is five thousandths of an inch wide and the unrecorded space between each track (known as a "guard band") was ten thousandths of an inch wide. All this editing was done without the aid of a microscope, just the naked eye.

As a point of reference, the guard band was the only place you could

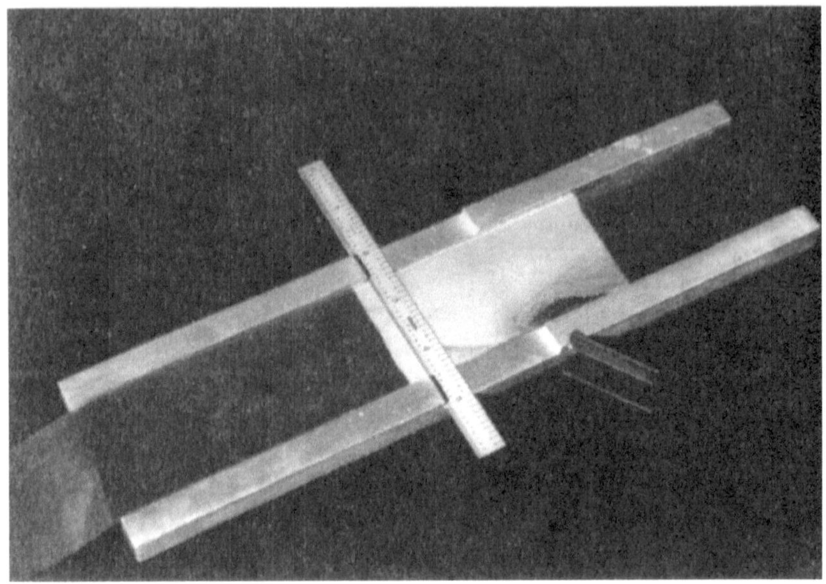

(Alternate) 1st crude 2" videotape splicer, 1956.

make a cut in the tape. Otherwise, you would cut into one of the video tracks and cause a picture breakup. To show you how difficult it was to make a splice, the guard band was about the thickness of a human hair. I had to make a cut down the middle of this guard band, essentially like splitting the a human hair lengthwise with every cut. Remember, this was all done without the aid of a magnifier or microscope. If this cut wasn't made accurately, then the guard band would not be maintained at ten thousandths of an inch wide and the edit would lurch or jump as it went through the video head. We are talking critical spacing on every edit on the tape.

Nevertheless, even after the image was made visible on the tape, I had to carefully position the tape against a splicing guide and then using a stainless steel ruler and a single edged razor blade, make a single swift cut at the point indicated by the frame pulse marker. Believe me, this was no easy task since there was no way to repeatedly make razor blade cuts with precision in exactly the same place on the tape every time. Since the outgoing frame of a cut had to be spliced to the incoming frame of the next scene, the guard band must be exactly ten thousandths of an inch wide.

We soon discovered that this crude splicer was getting us nowhere.

What we needed was a more positive way to hold the tape in the guide so it would not slip. Eventually, hold-down pads were added to the guide, but they proved to be more trouble than they were worth because once the tape was held in position, you couldn't reposition it easily. So Ampex came up with what we felt was the answer. A splicer with hold-down doors for the tape and knobs that controlled rollers that would allow us to move the tape precisely where we wanted it to go. They also added a glass guide positioned so that you could run the razor blade across the width of the tape through the glass cutting guide and make repeated cuts with great accuracy. This was almost what we were looking for except for one thing: Looking for that extremely small edit pulse was very hard on the naked eye.

Finally, a fellow named Smith invented what we felt was the ultimate videotape splicer. It had hold-down doors, knobs that would precisely move the tape even one-thousandth of an inch and a guillotine-type tape cutter that all but eliminated the need for the razor blade guaranteeing sharp, accurate cuts every time. But the *pièce de résistance* was a 40 power microscope mounted so that you could see this tiny edit pulse as a giant mark on the tape. What a relief at last!

Another problem that surfaced was that the soundtrack on the videotape was offset 20 frames ahead of the corresponding picture frame. This is because the sound head could not be physically mounted at the same point as the video head for mechanical reasons. This posed a problem in editing because even though the sound was in lip sync with the picture during playback, any attempts to make tight and very short edits in less than 20 frames would induce a phenomenon known as "lip flap." This becomes quite noticeable because the mouth does not produce the correct sound as it should since the sound head offset was not taken into account when the tape splice was made.

Savvy producers, noting this problem, quickly learned how to record extra sound and picture overlap during production so that the picture could be cut on the frame desired and not run into this undesirable lip flap effect. It was quite easy to do, especially when using prerecorded soundtracks for musical numbers since there would never be any variation between takes because the sound being played back for each take would always be the same. Cuts, even between words, would not be detectable. Although this technique worked very well, it was time-consuming, especially for the director who had to plan to shoot these overlap shots during production and for the editor who had to carefully mark the tape prior to splicing it so that the edit would not lose sound or picture continuity.

However, in order to convince more producers and directors to use the NBC Studios and post-production facilities, the engineers in Burbank developed a more sophisticated method of editing videotape using a 16mm kinescope film as a work print. I was one of the team that developed this new process. It was called the "Double System method of editing videotape." Today, we call it off-line or work print editing.

On-line videotape (editing at the VTR) continued for several years even after the development of this new off-line editing process. For one thing, off-line editing was more costly because of having to make a work print copy of the tape on film as well as conforming the videotape to the edited film work print. Second, even though it was more flexible, it was more time-consuming because of the two-step process. I would like to point out that the terms "off-line" and "on-line" came from the computer industry and were absorbed by television soon after. Literally translated, off-line means "away from the terminal" and on-line means "at the terminal."

Basically, a copy of the program master tape was recorded in one of two ways. If facilities were available at the time of production, along with the master videotape, a 16mm kinescope positive image picture and a corresponding magnetic sound track were recorded to provide a work copy to be used by the NBC editors. If the kinescope recording equipment was unavailable during production, at some convenient time later that day, a transfer made from the recorded videotape master was used to make the work picture and magnetic sound track. In either case, the 16mm film work print would be edited using conventional film editing equipment and techniques. The 16mm magnetic sound track transferred from the production videotape was in all cases considered to be a sound master and was eventually used to create a final composite mix of all the sound elements needed for any given production.

We needed a method of accurately correlating each frame of the edited film work print to the uncut production videotape. An ingenious method was devised that simulated a crude form of time code. A master roll of 16mm magnetic film 72 minutes in length was assembled from several elements. First, a frame-accurate audible tone or "beep" 400 Hertz in frequency was generated and made into a loop so that a one-frame long beep would be placed every 24 frames apart on the master tape. In between each beep, a voice would count off the minutes and seconds. A man's voice was used for the minutes and a woman's voice for the seconds. This voice track was dubbed the "Talking Clock." Technically speaking, we called this track ESG or "Edit Sync Guide."

This ESG talking clock reference code was applied during production simultaneously to the cue channel of the master videotape, the soundtrack area of the picture work print and to a cue track on the magnetic sound track. The kinescope work print was then edited in a conventional film editing fashion. However, once the work print had been approved and was ready to be conformed to the master videotape, a photographic or optical film reader was used to read the ESG voice information from the work print sound track and to generate a frame-accurate log which the editor would use to match each tape edit to the edited film work print.

Readers who are technically minded might ask how a film work print running at 24 frames per second could be correlated with a videotape running at 30 frames per second. The trick was to create a special ruler 15 inches long and divide it into 24 equal parts. What this did was to provide the editor with a means of finding a corresponding tape frame from a log generated by the edited work print. In order for this to work, we had to design and build a special videotape sound reader that could be used on any conventional film editing bench equipped with film-type rewinds.

The edit log generated by reading the ESG time code information from the work print was used to edit the original studio recorded tape into an edited master. By listening to the videotape cue track as it was pulled through the rewinds over the videotape sound reader head, I could hear the ESG information being played back. When I found the appropriate time code, I used the nearest beep as a guide to locate the exact edit point. I would then apply the carbonyl iron solution to the area on the tape to develop this beep which, when displayed, looked like a short gray rectangular bar on the tape. Placing this special 24 frame ruler on the tape starting at this visible beep, I would count down to the frame with the 24 frame ruler as indicated on the edit log. Both ends of every edit would be located frame-accurately in this manner and the cut made.

In 1958, NBC Burbank began using this new process to edit the first Fred Astaire special. As you might expect, all of us involved in this first project were somewhat apprehensive. We made a number of small tests using segments from NBC productions. All this was kept confidential and well away from producers and others who might put pressure on us to start using this process before we were convinced that it would really

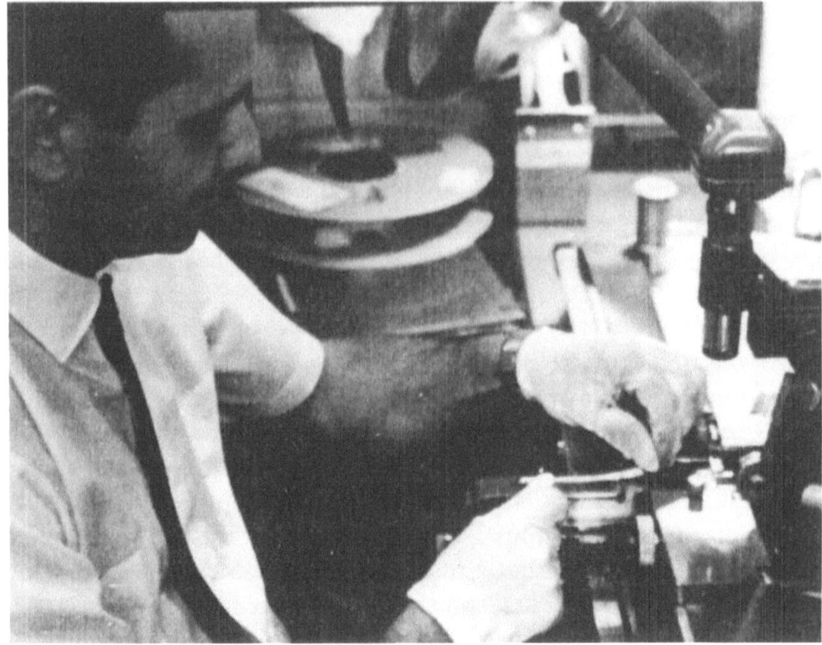

Author splicing 2" videotape.

work and that it was essentially "bullet proof." Although everything worked fine in tests, we didn't want to blow the Astaire project. As it turned out, our fears were unwarranted because the editing and completion of this Astaire special went off without a hitch. The system worked so well that at one point in time, I was editing programs for many outside producers.

Without going into a long dissertation, suffice it to say that this method of editing videotape programs was so effective and accurate that many producers from other networks came to NBC to shoot and edit their programs. Because of this trend, on one occasion I remember seeing my screen credit as editor on three different programs on all three networks on the same evening! I may have set a record of some sort.

The next year, I edited a special called *The Pontiac Star Parade*. It starred Gene Kelly, Donald O'Connor and Carol Lawrence. Gene Kelly was the producer, and Greg Garrison, later director of the Dean Martin TV series, directed. However, Kelly wanted to be involved in the editing process. (I later found out that he was a perfectionist.) Kelly and I got along well and had a great time editing the special, but it was demanding

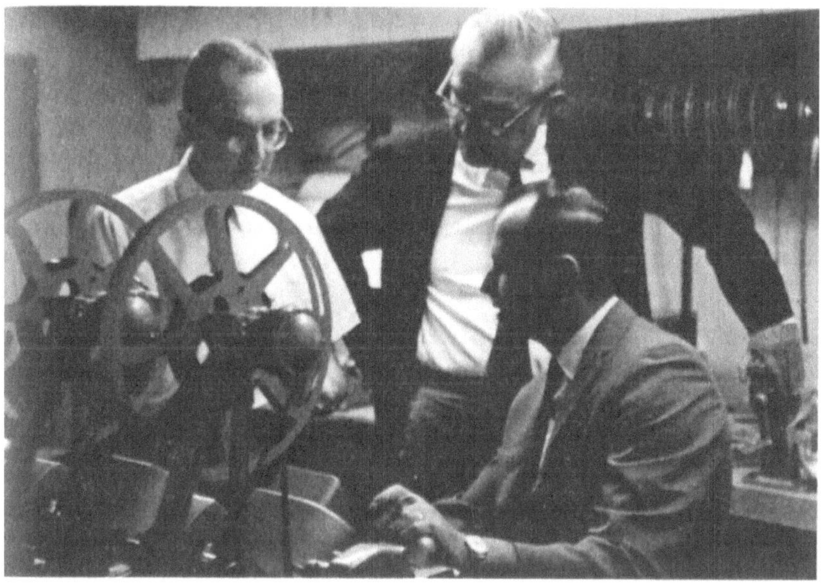

Author (seated), Director Alan Handley (center), and Editor Craig Curtis.

work. I worked with Kelly for three weeks, 20 hours a day. Working long hours continuously takes its toll on anyone, even a young fella of 29. One evening as we were cutting a bar room sequence, I realized I'd forgotten to call my wife to tell her I wouldn't be home for dinner (*again*). I asked Kelly if I could stop for a moment to call her. He said sure and continued to view the edited barroom sequence.

I called my wife and apologized for not calling sooner. She asked me where I was. I told her I was in the basement of NBC where I always was, editing the special. "Why do you ask?" I inquired. She said she heard noises in the background that sounded like a bar. I told her no, that was just one of the sketches I was working on. She didn't believe me. I tried to convince her but to no avail. The reason she wouldn't believe me is that she thought it was one of my friends, another NBC editor and former USC cinema student by the name of Craig Curtis, who was somewhat of a practical joker. My wife knew of Craig's delight in playing practical jokes and thought he was up to something. Gene Kelly was sitting next to me and heard my conversation with my wife. He turned to me and asked, "Doesn't your wife believe you?" "No," I said. He said, "Let me try. What's your wife's name?" I said it was Dee. Kelly said, "Give me the phone." He picked up the phone and said, "Hi Dee, this is Gene Kelly.

Don't you recognize my voice?" Dee said, "No." She still thought it was Craig Curtis playing a joke on her.

"Is this Craig?" she asked. "No," Kelly said. "This is me, Gene Kelly." Then he said, "Wait a minute, let me sing you a little song." He sang her a few bars of "Singin' in the Rain" and she finally realized that it really was Gene Kelly. She was a little bit embarrassed but Kelly assured her that yes, her husband was really working on his special and no, they were not in a real bar.

Although Kelly was a perfectionist, I learned a lot from him. The special was quite successful and he was pleased with the end result and appreciated my efforts. I received a nice thank-you letter from him after the program aired.

Another incident occurred during the editing of this special when Greg Garrison was sitting in my editing room, somewhat bored. He was smoking a cigarette and threw it into the waste basket. Unbeknownst to me, the basket was filled with lots of loose paper and some pieces of rubber. Eventually Garrison left and I continued to work. Soon I smelled a foul odor and looked back to see flames coming from the trash basket. I ran over and stomped out the flames, but the smell of burning rubber drifted up through the ceiling and into the tape room directly above. After I put out the fire, I went back to work. Soon my boss came running down the hall with a large fire extinguisher and a frightened look on his face. I told him what happened and he dropped the extinguisher and ran after Greg Garrison with anger in every step he took. He eventually caught up with him and gave him quite a tongue lashing, but it just seemed to roll off Garrison's back.

From 1951 through 1960, I worked on many of the *Colgate Comedy Hour* specials. Since these programs were essentially shot as a one-hour episode, my part was done prior to the broadcast recording of the show. These shows included Dean Martin and Jerry Lewis, Abbott and Costello, and Danny Thomas as guest performers.

One of the *Colgate Comedy Hour* programs was an Abbott and Costello special that required some trick special effects. The producers wanted a sequence to be speeded up to look like it was part of an old-time comedy routine. There were only two ways to do this. One was to shoot the sequence on motion picture film at 12 frames per second; later projecting the film at 24 frames per second would double the speed. This was costly in terms of hiring a union film crew, shooting it on a sound stage and then preparing it for projection during the recording of the live program feed to the East Coast.

The other way I recommended worked just as well and cost almost nothing compared to the first method. I suggested that we shoot the sketch on 35mm kinescope film in real time, meaning at 24 frames per second. After the film was developed and printed, I took the print to the lab and had them perform a function called "skip printing" (printing every other frame onto a new piece of film). When that film was developed and printed, all the images were running at twice the speed of normal motion. The cost savings were great because no additional crews were needed; the only extra cost was for the skip printing. In the early 1950s, we wrote the "rule books" and had to be inventive to find ways to get things done quickly and efficiently without straining the program's budget, which wasn't very much to begin with.

From time to time I would get a prized show to edit, but generally I was not happy with my lack of advancement at NBC. I used to come to work dressed in jeans and an old leather jacket. People spoke to me but I was just another guy working day to day, rarely seeing much daylight since my hours were so changeable that often I would go to work in the dark and come home in the dark, I sometimes ate my lunch in the editing room. It was quite frustrating and often depressing.

On Christmas, 1959, I was talking to our neighbor, a wonderful lady by the name of Virlee Barnes. I told her about my concerns and how I was not making any progress in my career even after eight years with NBC. She listened to me intently and then gave me a little book to read. It was called *Your Invisible Power*. It was a sort of semi-religious self-help book. I wasn't really interested but I decided to read it anyway. What did I have to lose except maybe an hour of my life to read it?

I read it through and found that there were some interesting things I was willing to try. The first thing I did was change my attitude about work and people around me and try to be more outgoing. The second thing was to drop the jeans and leather jacket and come to work every day dressed in a suit and tie. I started this the day after New Year's and I cannot tell you how this affected other people and made life easier for me. Not only that, but every day when I walked into the studio, most people started saying, "*Hi, how are you?*" even though I didn't know their names. People started to treat me much better. I even felt like I was getting a better share of good specials to edit.

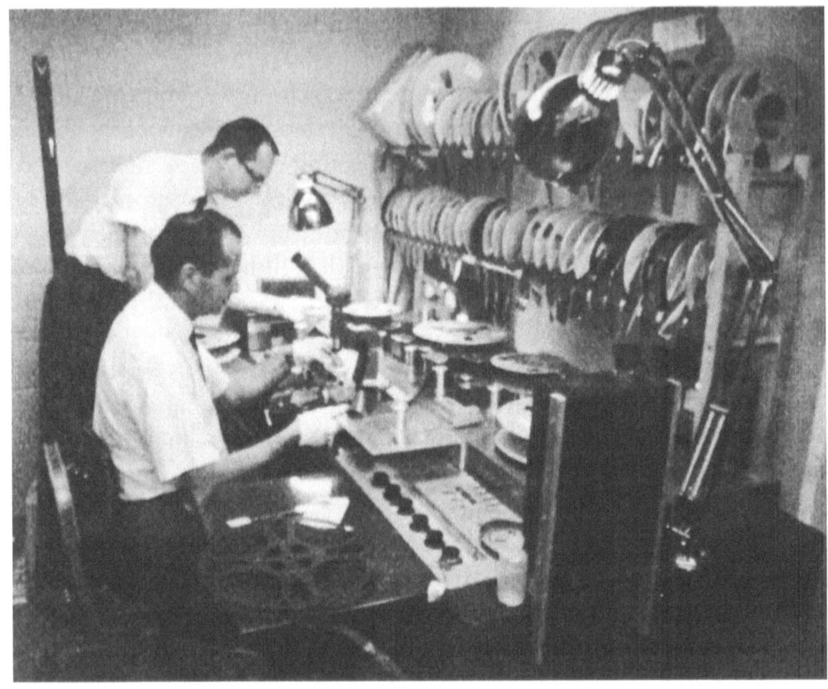

Author (foreground) and Craig Curtis editing on special NBC edit console.

One of the most famous directors I've worked with was Franklin Schaffner, director of such movie hits as *Patton*. We edited a special called "The Richest Man in Bogota," a well-known H.G. Wells story. Schaffner told me that he was starting another project and had to be done with this show the next day. He asked me if I minded staying until it was finished. I said I didn't mind. Actually, I was quite used to long hours in the editing room.

We started at 8:00 one morning and finished editing at 8:00 the next morning. To help pass the time, Schaffner brought in a bottle of whiskey and sipped it throughout editing. He offered me some but I declined, saying that if I had even a small drink, I might not get through on time. From time to time I would ask his opinion about an edit but generally I plodded along and completed the work print in about 22 hours. We had only one disagreement during editing. In one scene at the end of the program, one of the actors shot an arrow. The next edit was the arrow hitting another actor. I timed it so that the arrow had a slight delay before it hit. Schaffner said to tighten up the edit; as soon as the arrow left the frame, he said, let it hit the other actor immediately. I mildly protested, saying that the two actors were supposedly some 50 feet or more apart and that the arrow was a slow-moving projectile, not a bullet. We discussed this problem for a few minutes and I gave in since he was quite adamant about the timing. I put the completed work print on the projector and watched it straight through. Schaffner turned to me, said, "Great," and left.

Working with many talented directors and others gave me the opportunity to ask questions and to learn skills that I would not have gotten otherwise. At the time I was editing at NBC, few of the NBC television production staff had any knowledge of motion picture production. As film producers learned of the success of NBC's film style videotape editing system, more and more film producers convinced their directors and others to shoot on tape and edit in the television medium without having to compromise the continuity or storyline of a television program just because it was shot on tape instead of film.

Once the word got around, many former film producers decided to take a chance and direct and edit television programs on tape instead of the familiar film format. I don't know a single producer or director who, after working with the NBC editing system, wasn't satisfied or who did not feel good about the end result.

Television editing has come a long way from the days of splicing tape and cutting film. Today, the majority of programs, even those shot on motion picture film, are edited using very sophisticated electronic computers and digital storage devices, many of which were not even a glimmer in the inventor's eye in those early days. Speed and economy are two of the most important products of this new technology. A third, creativity, is enhanced even more because of the electronic tools the editor has to work with to help him or her massage the images into a more coherent product without compromising anything. In fact, digital technology has brought forth many new tools such as "morphing," a process which melts one image into another, causing a complete change in a smooth transition that amazes viewers.

In 1959, we were in contract negotiations which broke down and all the engineers went on strike. However, I was not aware of it because as usual, I was in my editing room in the basement of NBC and no one told me we had gone out on strike. For some reason, I kept on working and even skipped lunch (which was unusual for me) and did not go upstairs to the main videotape room until around 2 P.M. that afternoon. When I walked into the room I was startled to see management people running all the equipment. My boss, who was running a videotape machine, yelled to me, "What are you doing here?" I told him I was just going out for lunch. He yelled at me, "You are on strike! Either get on a tape machine or get out on the picket line." I said "Bye!" and raced outside. Apparently everyone forgot that I was in the basement editing and no one called me.

During the strike, which lasted a week, I was looking for work since we didn't know at the time how long we would be out. My friend Craig Curtis asked if I would like to make a few bucks shooting newsreel footage of the submarines being installed in Disneyland. I thought it would be great fun as well as profitable. We first had to drive to the Todd shipyards in San Pedro, California, where the subs were built. There we shot footage of decks being welded, exteriors being painted and other interesting features of the submarines under construction. One submarine was already loaded onto a large flatbed truck which we were to follow to Disneyland.

Side streets were chosen so as not to disrupt traffic on the freeway. We were given a route which included all side streets. The truck with the submarine on it left some 30 minutes ahead of us since they would be traveling slower than normal speeds due to the oversize load. Meanwhile, we continued to shoot footage of the subs in the shipyard. Curtis was driving and I was going to shoot film of the truck going down the side streets.

We took off and followed the route given us by the Disney people. However, we could not find the truck. We stopped at a nearby gas station. I asked the attendant, "Pardon me, but did you see a submarine drive by here recently?" The guy gave me the funniest look, as if I was on something. He just shook his head and walked away. We tried a few more places but each time they thought we were nuts. Finally, we decided to get on the freeway and drive directly to Disneyland in hopes the truck would just be getting there. As it turned out, the truck found it too difficult to negotiate those narrow streets and went on the freeway anyway, getting there well ahead of us. The submarine was lifted by two huge steam shovels and gingerly lowered into the lake over a period of an hour. All in all, we did manage to get some good footage which went on the air the next evening.

Early on, I became friends with the NBC photographers since their studio was around the corner from my basement editing room. Often they would give me outdated film and paper since they knew I had a darkroom at home. On one special occasion, they invited our family to the studio one Saturday to take pictures of our two children. Our daughter wasn't too cooperative and cried most of the time, but we did get some treasured pictures from some of the best photographers in the business.

One of my hobbies is photography and I pursued that often in my spare time. I frequently got assignments to photograph various subjects on 16mm color film. I did a job for a company selling film shorts of the Hearst Castle but was unable to get permission to go into the main grounds and photograph the interior. I did the next best thing. I bought a number of high quality color photographs (mostly 8 by 10 inches or larger) and, using my movie camera, zoomed and panned the photos to create the illusion of movement. The client was very pleased that I was able to circumvent the bureaucracy running the castle and still get acceptable pictures of the place.

However, my most memorable assignment was to capture the blazing fire falls from burning embers pushed over the canyon wall from 3,000 feet atop Glacier Point down to Camp Curry in Yosemite National Park. It had never been done before even by commercial photographers since the sensitivity of color film in 1960 was not deemed adequate to shoot fire showers at night. I felt I could do what the client wanted by performing some photographic sleight of hand.

The fire fall ceremony was originally conceived to entice visitors to stay in the park an extra day. It began in 1871 and continued on and off until 1968 when it was abolished by the park service because they felt it was an artificial attraction not in keeping with the national park's idea of preserving America's wonders in their natural state. There was an established ritual for this majestic production. The guests in Camp Curry were told to be silent so the voices from Glacier Point could be heard. Then, at the right moment, a voice bellowed the call, "Helloooooo Glacierrrrrrrr!" The call wafted up 3,000 feet and could easily be heard at the top. Then the firemaster roared back, "Hellooooo Caammmp Currryyyy!" From the valley floor came the order, "Let the fire faaallll!" With that, the firemaster pushed a half a cord of burning fir bark over the cliff, forming a 1,000 foot stream of glowing embers.

In order to insure that the rock walls lining the valley floor would be visible and that the trees and other outcroppings would be seen in the background, I had to double expose the film. If I shot the rock walls in daylight, and superimposed the fire falls over the walls, it wouldn't look natural. The first thing I did was to put the camera on a solid tripod and lock it down so that it wouldn't move at all. I framed the area from which

I knew the fire would be falling and took an exposure reading. I then closed down the camera lens by two stops, effectively underexposing the film by that amount and making the rock wall look underexposed. I then rewound the film to the beginning so as to be able to add the fire falls later that evening. My wife and I stood guard over the tripod and camera for about six hours so that no one would accidentally bump into it and ruin the shot. It wasn't as easy as I thought because our two little ones, one two and the other five, were constantly under foot and I was afraid they might accidentally bump the tripod.

When it got dark enough to see the fire falls, a voice on the valley floor at Camp Curry began the show by shouting to the firemaster atop Glacier Point. At that time, I again started my camera, superimposing the background shot earlier that day against the fiery ashes falling down the rock wall. But there was one problem. The color film I was using was not fast enough to expose the faint sparks from the flaming ashes. I had to run the camera at one third normal speed, effectively increasing the exposure time; I was hoping to get enough light on the film from the burning embers. I was quite nervous about getting the right exposure and was anxious to see the film developed. It was three days later when I finally got a color print back and was disappointed to see that somehow the fire fall image was not superimposed where it was supposed to be and the background was a little too light. Somehow, the tripod was bumped. I was determined to get that shot right since no one previously had been able to capture that spectacular sight.

I was fortunate to be able to get two consecutive weekends off, a rarity for me, and I decided to drive all the way back to Yosemite to reshoot the falls. What made it even more difficult for us is that we had to bring our children with us again since we had no baby sitter. That meant that one of us had to guard the camera and the other had to entertain and carefully watch the kids to prevent them from bumping the tripod. This time I made sure we found a location with fewer people around and one that also gave me a better view of the fire fall area. I carefully took an exposure meter reading and adjusted the camera iris slightly more underexposed than before, filming the side of the granite cliff from where the fire would emanate. That evening, with my legs numb from sitting in a cross-legged position most of the day, I was anxious for the fire falls to begin. Once again, the voice from the top of Glacier Point shouted the words "Let the fire faaallll!" and I started the camera several seconds before the first embers became visible.

Since I had to be at work the next day, we decided to drive home that evening, a 300 mile drive and a six-hour trip. It was difficult because both kids were tired and cranky and we were both exhausted, but it had to be done. The next day I dropped off the film at a nearby lab and asked if the processing could be expedited so that I could know the results sooner. I picked up the film after work the next day and was overjoyed to see the results. It was spectacular and the client was very pleased. The image of the mountain in the background was perfect so that you could just make out the pine trees part way up the side, and yet when the fire came down, it too was brilliant and looked almost like the way I envisioned it. Even though it took two consecutive weekends to get the shot, it was worth it. The film I shot more than 35 years ago is still sold as part of a travel video today.

CHAPTER FOUR

The Bob Hope Years

The high quality television recording cameras used in the zone delay kinescope process proved themselves by recording images of good-enough quality in the early 1950s to be considered "broadcast quality." These cameras also provided NBC with a means of making film prints of television programs for distribution. The producers of the Bob Hope comedy specials were the first to discover that recording and editing their programs on 35mm kinescope film would be less expensive and faster than shooting them on regular motion picture film. Furthermore, the recording process enabled the quality of the recorded picture to be somewhat improved by means of electronic enhancement techniques over that of a live broadcast.

Since I was a USC film major, the word got around NBC that I was an experienced film editor. In 1951, NBC had only a small group of in-house film editors whose job it was to integrate film commercials into film prints so that the program could run straight through without having to remotely roll the commercials into the program from a separate source. However, the group of people who did the commercial integration, although labeled "film editors," had no experience in editing episodic or full length television programs.

It has long been network policy to prepay for air time to run a commercial. You can see why television stations try very hard not to screw up a commercial. If the commercial does not air or is interrupted in any way by technical difficulties, the station either has to refund the money paid by the sponsor or provide a "make good" airing at another time slot. If a make good is required, then the station loses money it would have made by running another commercial in that slot. Therefore, the film department of networks provided a service of physically splicing the commercials into the film program in advance so this situation would not occur.

The film editors integrating these commercials into film programs were members of one of two competing film unions known as the IATSE (International Alliance of Theatrical and Stage Employees) and NABET (National Association of Broadcast and Electrical Technicians). As a television engineer, I was a member of NABET. An NLRB (National Labor Relations Board) decision ultimately gave NABET the right to edit kinescope film as well as motion picture film. The IATSE group could only edit motion picture film and not kinescope film. Kinescope and regular motion picture film are both edited using the same equipment and techniques. The only difference is in the method used to record the images on the film itself.

Although I spent four years learning editing at USC and took every editing course available, I was somewhat apprehensive about big time television editing. Within a month of starting work at NBC, I was asked by the producer of the Bob Hope comedy specials if I would be interested in being an assistant editor on Hope specials. I soon found that I was able to edit small segments of the specials and felt quite comfortable. Bob Hope was at that time shooting between six and eight comedy specials a year. The shows were shot on 35mm kinescope film and used conventional motion picture editing equipment and techniques. All the Hope specials were done in black and white until 1958, when they switched to color.

The process used on Hope and many other productions shot at NBC was called "stop and go recording" because the program was shot in chunks rather than scene by scene and take by take. A show would record for several minutes then stop when either a goof by one of the actors or a technical problem occurred. There were an average of 50–60 stops in each hour program which had to be edited to gain story continuity. It was simplified editing compared to what other film editors were faced with. Opening and closing credits and other art work was put in at the time of production so there were rarely any optical or other special effects to be added later. The editor's function was to cut together the segments shot in the studio. It really was a lot of fun because I began working with directors and other talented people and learned a lot, especially from those producers and directors who came into television from the film world.

Whenever the Hope show needed a fade-in or fade-out, we found an expedient method of creating such effects. Since we had very little time to get these fades made (they generally took several days in the film laboratory) we decided to make them by using chemical bleach. The film

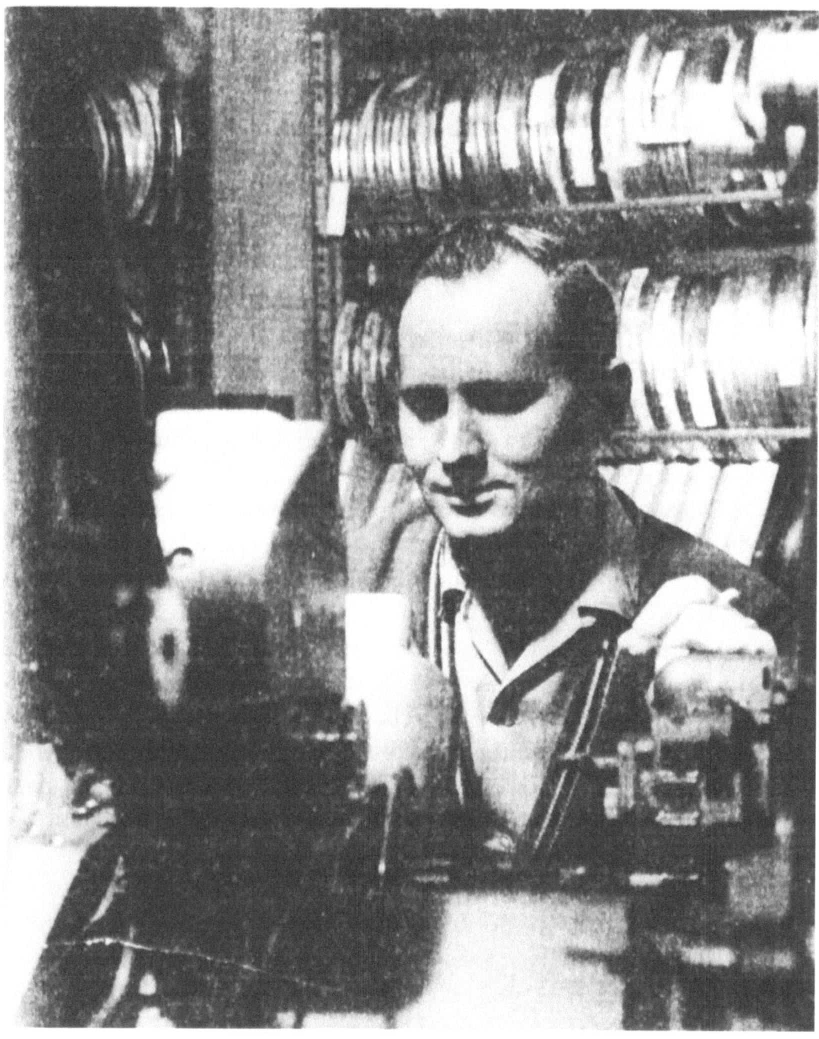

Author editing Kinescope film work print on early 1965 Bob Hope special.

lab was right across the street so it was quite convenient to have the lab make the fades while we waited. For example, the original camera negative would be accurately cut at the point of the end of the fade-out and brought to the lab. The remainder of the film reel would also be brought along since the negative had to be kept intact except where the fades were required because the work print had not yet been approved. A white grease pencil mark on the outside edge of the film next to the sprocket holes would indicate the exact start point of the fade. This mark was not affected by chemical bleach used to make the fade. The cut end of the film would be hand dipped up and down into a vat of photographic bleach until just the right amount of density change was achieved. The film would then be washed and dried and returned to us in less than an hour.

I began editing Bob Hope specials starting in late 1951, but because of NBC policy, film editors did not get screen credit. I worked on and edited more than 65 Hope specials during a nine-year period. Then in 1960, with a contract change, film and tape editors were finally given screen credit and recognized for their talents as film editors had been for decades in the film industry. This was influenced in part by a new and more accurate way of editing videotape developed by NBC (detailed in chapter three). I was so busy that I often edited one program a week every year I worked at NBC.

During my 17 years with NBC, the total number of series, specials and other projects I edited with and without screen credits was in excess of 1,100. This does not include some 3,000 commercials and promotional trailers. After I left NBC, I edited another 300 programs, 200 commercials and other short projects as a freelance editor or on staff during the next 21 years until I retired. At least 80 percent of my working time was on overtime, not just an hour or two a day but anywhere from four to seven hours of overtime a day, often for weeks on end (and especially when working on specials). It seemed as though I was always working and away from my family, which is the primary reason I eventually resigned from NBC.

It took my first nine years with NBC to be accepted as the head television editor for Bob Hope. From 1958 onward, I was considered part of the "family." Then, from 1960 to 1968, I edited more than 50 Bob Hope specials including several Vietnam Christmas specials. During the period of 1964 through 1968, I took a yearly leave of absence from NBC for the month of January to edit the annual Christmas show specials from Vietnam on 35mm color film. I'd like to tell you about a typical Christmas show editing scenario. This one won an Emmy Award as the "Outstanding Variety Special" for the television season 1965-66.

Shooting began just before Christmas at the first of 13 army bases in Vietnam. Every few days, the exposed film was delivered by Air Force jet to Los Angeles for processing. I started working on the show on January 2. Assistant editors were on hand to synchronize the picture and sound so the staff could view the film and take notes. On average, the crew shot in excess of 150,000 feet of 35mm color film for each special. When you realize that all this material had to be edited down to 8,000 feet for broadcast length in less than two weeks, you can see what a monumental task lay ahead of us.

The Bob Hope office rented a suite of rooms on the lot at Universal Studios in Burbank. We spent the first two days looking at every foot of film. It took two 12-hour days in a projection room. There were usually four cameras, each on a different angle, running at any time during the shooting of a sketch or other material, plus several "wild" or roaming cameras shooting audience. I'm sure you can understand why at the end of each day, we were blurry eyed from staring at the screen. During the viewing, Hope and the director would consult and select sketches to be timed and edited later.

An interesting sidelight when we started to edit was that several large signs with large white lettering on black backgrounds were posted in all the rooms for the editors to see. One said, "We traveled 30,000 miles to get these laughs. Don't cut them!" The other sign stated emphatically "Every shot that is asked for exists." The second one was in reference to trying to locate a shot that someone thought was recorded on film. (In some cases, the cameras weren't rolling so the shot in question was never filmed.) Sometimes we had discussions about a shot the producer or director swore was shot on film. But we pointed out that after viewing every foot of film, if it wasn't on the screen, it was never shot. Every foot of film was logged in a book (including the contents of each shot) before editing began, so this situation of thinking we had a shot when it was never filmed only happened at the beginning of editing.

My primary job was to edit all 13 monologues from about 10 to 12 minutes down to three minutes each, depending on the location and the number of funny jokes used. Bob Hope, as the executive producer, was solely responsible for show content. I was given a marked script outlining those jokes to be left in and those to be edited out. The decision to keep certain jokes in was first made during the initial screening the day after New Year's. Then an editing script was marked and given to me. From then on, it was up to me to edit those 13 monologues and maintain the joke timing. It was most important to keep enough space so that laughs could be added later without covering up the next joke.

One day my assistant editor noticed that Hope wanted a portion of one joke removed where he flubbed a line. The only way to make the edit

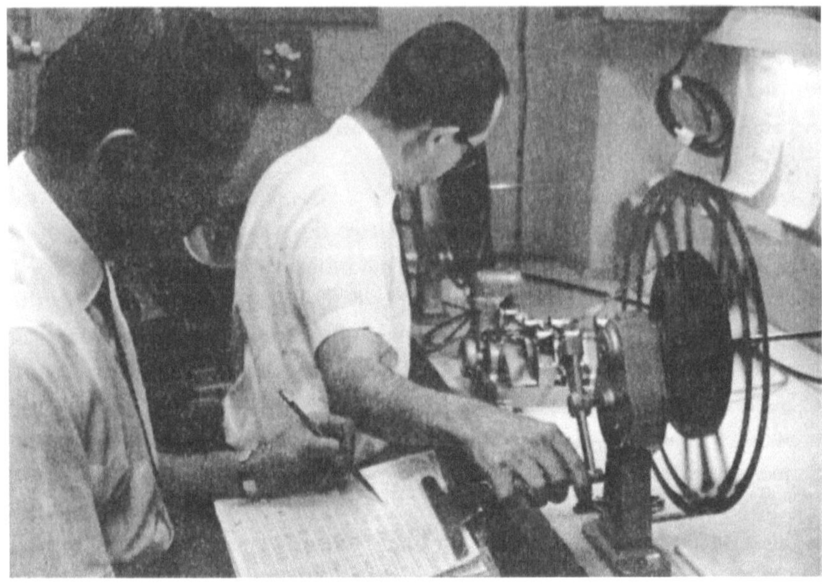

Author (foreground) and Craig Curtis checking edit log on Hope special.

work was to join the material on either side of the deleted material together with an audience reaction shot such as a laugh or applause. But in this unique case, Hope wanted the joke to play in the way he indicated. In other words, he did not want to use a cutaway of the audience. Instead, in a somewhat unusual fashion, Hope insisted the joke play without a reaction to better improve his timing. I carefully looked at the picture frames on either side of the edit, selected the best place to make the edit and spliced the film together.

My assistant came into the room just as I was preparing to view the edit. As I played it for the first time, Hope's head jumped slightly at the edit point. My assistant said, "Hope will never accept that edit." I said, "You wanna bet?" We bet five dollars and a few minutes later, Hope came in and I showed him the edit. Hope said, "Great." My assistant handed me the money, shook his head and walked away. One must understand that Bob Hope sometimes edits his television programs just like they were radio shows. That means that the jokes came first even if that meant the picture jumped. That's why he gave me the "Jump Cut Award" in 1965, which I'll explain later in this chapter.

In addition to editing the monologues, I also edited the promotional trailers for the show. That's why I worked as much as 20 hours a day for two weeks. As a matter of fact, we never left the editing room to eat or sleep. Cots were provided so we could catch cat naps. The best food was brought in, and we had everything we needed to keep us going.

After the picture was approved by Hope, the negative cutters would get the first of nine edited ten-minute reels of film. When the work print had been approved by all, the picture was "locked," meaning that no more picture changes were to be made, period. While they started to cut the camera negative to match the edited work print, my secondary job was to go to the sound mixing studio and stand by in case there were any sound problems that needed fixing. Remember, the picture was approved and could no longer be changed but the sound could be modified (eliminating an unwanted sound, adding a forgotten sound effect, etc.). The sound facility where we mixed the multiple soundtracks put a blanket for me on top of the piano in the sound studio where I would sleep until a change was required. Then someone would nudge me awake and I would fix the soundtrack and go back to sleep until the next wakeup call. I might have to make as many as a dozen sound changes during the mixing session.

One year, we had a near-major disaster. The editing device (called a Moviola) had its sound heads magnetized somehow and nobody knew it. When the ten reels were run through the Moviola before the start of the sound mixing session, the entire soundtrack was magnetized so badly that every foot of it had a very high "hiss" level and had to be replaced. We had to go through the editing script and find the scene and take number of each edit used in the program. The master soundtracks are recorded on quarter inch magnetic tape and then transferred to 35mm magnetic film to be used for editing and sound mixing. When the transfer process was finished, the master quarter inch tape was stored in a vault. We then told the sound facility what we wanted and they had to re-record all the material onto new magnetic sound stock to replace the bad tracks.

It took four of us working 24 hours a day to replace every foot of soundtrack with a new copy made from the original material. However, every edited splice on the bad track had to be made on the new, clean track and we had to carefully check each reel to see that lip synchronization was maintained. We had two sound readers mounted side by side, one for the bad track and one to listen to the new material. I would then find matching sound points such as the same word on both tracks, put them in a sprocket-driven film synchronizer and run both down to the next physical splice on the old track. Then I would listen to the bad track, find a word as a reference point and listen on the new track for the same sound. Since there were two magnetic sound pickup heads (one for the old track and a second for the new material) connected together, a discrepancy between the two tracks would produce an echo. Once found, I would match them and splice the new material together, running them in sync for a short time to see that lip synchronization was still maintained and continued until I found the next physical splice on the edited sound track. This process continued until all nine reels had been replaced with clean sound track. It took two 24-hour days to complete this task. As each reel was completed, it was sent back to the sound mixing studio, so the delay really only cost us a little less than a day.

During the editing of the Christmas special, my average day was 9 A.M. to about 6 A.M., seven days a week for two consecutive weeks. We had an air date to meet and there was no way we were going to miss that. This program aired on NBC on January 15, 1966, and won an Emmy for Hope as the best outstanding variety special of 1965-66. I was awarded a Certificate of Contribution for the program. I also edited six other Bob Hope comedy specials in 1966.

Hope did several other specials through the years, one in particular from Acapulco. This was also shot on color film. I should point out that there was a special reason for my taking a leave of absence from NBC to edit the Hope specials shot on 35mm film. That was because I belonged to the NABET union at NBC and I had to work under the rules of the IATSE Editor's Guild outside of NBC. I was given a temporary waiver to edit these shows only for the duration of editing and post-production. Many years later, after leaving NBC, I joined the IATSE and eventually was elected to the Board of Directors of the Motion Picture and Videotape Editors Guild.

The Bob Hope special shot in Acapulco was typical of the Christmas shows but without the urgency of a two-week air date after shooting. There was one unusual incident that involved Barney McNulty, Hope's cue card man. Barney carried his 8mm movie camera around with him wherever he went, sometimes to the annoyance of the staff. The crew was somewhat miffed at Barney for taking pictures of everything since the camera was hardly ever turned off. To teach him a lesson, the Hope staff chipped in and gave him a free flight on a para-sail, a parachute towed behind a speedboat, in hopes that Barney would drop the damn camera.

When the crew returned to Hollywood, Barney's film was developed and he showed it to the director who was so impressed with some of the footage that the producers had portions of the 8mm home movie film blown up to 35mm and edited into the final program. This little incident obviously backfired on us and we never could complain about Barney McNulty and his camera again.

Whenever I worked on a Bob Hope special, I would always be taken out to lunch and even dinner if I worked long hours. My friend and co-editor Craig Curtis and I and a group of seven or eight people (including the writers) would take over one of the local restaurants. I never spent any money of my own because Silvio (Sil) Caranchini, Hope's associate producer and a longtime friend of mine, would take us to the finest restaurants in Burbank. There were two favorites, Sorrentino's and the China Trader, both within a block of each other. These meals were something I looked forward to because many times Hope's writers would join us and we would often spend our dinner breaks telling jokes.

Every Christmas, Bob Hope would give gifts to the crew. They included briefcases, transistor radios, silverware and a host of other useful items. In addition, I received personalized script books, T-shirts, high-quality jackets and other memorabilia. The only unusual thing about Christmas was that all the cards Hope sent out arrived sometime in January, well after New Year's. I'm sure this was due to the fact that Hope was overseas most of the month of December and spent the first two weeks of January editing the overseas special.

Hope wasn't the only funny man in my working life. Craig Curtis loved practical jokes. One evening we went to dinner at Sorrentino's restaurant in Burbank. Mort Lachman, Hope's head writer, had just gotten a new Chrysler Imperial and asked if I wanted to drive it to the restaurant. I was delighted. There were six of us in this big luxury car and as I drove towards the restaurant, I felt important, very important. Since there were few parking places, I had to drive around the block until I spotted a large enough opening where I could park this long car. As I started to back into the space, I heard a loud thump. I was petrified! I thought I had hit a car where I was attempting to park. I was sweating, afraid I'd end up paying to fix the dent on Mort's new car. I looked behind me and saw Craig Curtis laughing loudly; he had lowered the rear window behind me and thumped his hand on the side of the car to make me think I had hit the other car. Craig was always the practical joker.

Craig and I worked on many Hope shows together and he was always trying to play jokes on us. There was a time when we had a power failure at NBC. I was working in my basement editing room on Hope's monologue when all the lights suddenly went out. I had no flashlights, candles, not even a match. It was really pitch black because there were no emergency lights in the basement. I was trying to figure out how to get out of the basement and locate the nearest exit or at least find a source of light to help me find my way out. Having spent many years in the basement, I kind of knew which direction to head, but with no lights it was impossible to determine how much wall there was before I came to a hallway.

I slowly and gingerly edged my way out of the editing room using both my hands to feel along the wall so I would know when I came to the end of a wall. I moved several feet and found an open door, so I knew there were two more doors before I could get to the main hallway. I inched my way along the wall and suddenly felt something soft and a chill went up my back! I didn't dare to feel around because I didn't know what it was. I quickly backed away.

Then I heard breathing and I was petrified because I thought I was the only one down there. I said, "Who's there?" No answer. I was getting more and more anxious. I said "Damn it, who's there?" Then I heard a maniacal laugh, one I had heard many times before. It was Craig Curtis. He scurried down the hall with me after him. Finally, I saw a sliver of light and caught his shadowy figure running up the stairs. I ran after him and yelled for him to stop, but he disappeared. I finally saw him as he saw me again and started to laugh. I think I chased him up and down every hallway in NBC. Eventually I caught him and we exchanged a few words. I wasn't really mad at him, just ticked off because he had tricked me and I wasn't able to get back at him.

I worked hard on every program not only because I enjoyed it but because my philosophy has always been and still is to do the best job I am capable of doing no matter what the circumstances. Even though I was often exhausted, I still kept pushing myself forward many times, working a 20-hour day simply because there were many changes Hope asked for. These changes had to be made so that Hope could review them the next morning. His schedule was so structured that he had only so much time to view the changes before going on to his next meeting.

When editing Hope's specials, the monologue was always edited last so it could be used as "pad" to get the show to the exact length for broadcast. Often Hope would do about 15-20 minutes of jokes which I would cut down to 8-12 minutes depending on what we needed to get the show to time. The monologue was always shot with two cameras, one a head-to-toe long shot and the other a medium waist shot. This was to allow me some flexibility in cutting. Hope would view the monologue after it was shot and determine which jokes to leave in or take out. He would then mark my script and cross out the jokes he wanted me to delete. Often he would rearrange jokes to play better. However, he never took into account the problems I would face in editing.

The biggest problem was that his facial expression or his hands or some other body movement would not match from the end of the last joke to the beginning of the next after deleting or rearranging one or more jokes. For example, Hope might be looking to his left at the end of a joke and in the next incoming joke he would be looking straight ahead or to his right. When cutting those two shots together, the image would jump as his head lurched from one side of the screen to the other. In other cases, in the outgoing joke, Hope would be smiling and the next incoming joke he would be deadpan. This made for some very difficult editing. The mismatched edit was known as a "jump cut," a term still in use today. When I was editing the monologues, I asked Hope many times to allow me to use cutaways or other reaction shots to smooth out the editing and he just didn't want to do that. I guess he felt the laugh timing would suffer if too much of a delay occurred between the end of one joke and the beginning of the next. Now, however, audience shots are routinely used as cutaways to avoid these bad edits. Maybe my son Robert, who now edits Hope's specials, convinced him to use audience cutaway shots to make the monologue look smoother and less jumpy and made editing the monologue much easier because of this change.

One day I told the producer that I would like to make a Bob Hope puppet doll with strings that I could manipulate to avoid all the bad edits. I've often felt that Hope edits his monologue like a radio show and that the pictures are incidental to the soundtrack. In spite of the problems I encountered, the results seen by the viewing audience did not appear to detract from the laughter. I would ask my wife to watch the monologue as it aired on NBC and to let me know if she saw anything unusual. She would watch the entire monologue and never noticed any picture jumps or edits. It just goes to prove what Bob Hope told me one time; sure, the image may jump for a second, he said, but if the audience laughs, they will ignore even the most horrendous picture jump. He was right, but it really bothered me since there was very little I could do about it.

In order for Hope to keep his monologue as fresh as possible by including the latest news, he would often wait to tape it until one or two days before the show aired on the network. This put a lot of pressure on all of us. I remember Hope calling Sil Caranchini in the morning, saying he wanted to tape his monologue that afternoon. Sil had to scramble to not only find an available studio but an audience as well. Sil would also have to find a crew and videotape machines to record the monologue. This was no easy task on such short notice.

On more than one occasion, Sil could not find a suitable audience and he had to round up one wherever he could get them. Sometimes Sil would ask a game show producer to ask their audiences to stay a little longer after their program was over just for Hope's last-minute monologue. More often than not, these last-minute audiences were thrilled to be part of this project. Hope always needed an audience for timing his jokes. In some cases when a show audience could not be found, Sil would ask anyone at NBC who wasn't busy to come to the studio and sit in the audience while Hope taped the monologue. Since there were often only a couple of dozen people available on such short notice, I was asked several times to be in the audience. Hope knew I was a good laugher and I was seated directly under one of the audience pickup mikes. You can always identify me by loud and sometimes raucous laughter.

There were times when the monologue was shot the day the program was to air on the network. It was heavy pressure time, to say the least. In that case, there was no time to make a film work print and have the flexibility to edit the monologue on the editing bench. We were forced to edit the videotape directly, a very dangerous practice; any mistakes could be disastrous since the master tape could be damaged or even ruined beyond repair. I dreaded cutting the tape under these conditions. For one reason, picture edits could not be made on the same frame as when I was editing the film work print.

To briefly explain why this happens, I must point out the placement of the sound with respect to the video head requires a physical displacement of the two devices of ten inches because the two-inch videotape has the soundtrack and picture on the same piece of tape. This is known as single system editing. The industry standard tape format requires that any picture has its corresponding sound track physically displaced ahead of the picture. This is because the sound head cannot be placed directly opposite the video head from a mechanical standpoint. It was established that 20 frames (ten inches) ahead of the picture head would be where the sound head would be placed. You can see that if I were to make an edit based on the sound cut, the picture would be 20 frames behind the sound edit. A problem known as "lip flap" was inevitable where the lips would move even though there was no sound coming from his mouth. It is quite annoying to say the least. Fortunately, having to edit in that manner was rare. On the other hand, editing with a film work print meant that I had a separate picture and sound track to work with and every edit was made straight across so there was no lag or "lip flap."

Not only did the tape have to be cut and the show brought to time, but the laughs had to be added before the show could be completed. Since there was no time to do it the normal way (that is, to bring the monologue to the sound studio in Hollywood to add laughs), we brought Charlie Douglass and his laugh machine into the NBC tape room, a practice generally frowned upon by the competing unions. He would set up his machine and augment the studio soundtrack to make it sound as though there were 600 people in the audience instead of the dozen or so actually recorded on the soundtrack. Even my laughter wasn't good enough to fill in all the jokes.

I mentioned earlier the term "jump cut," especially as it applied to editing the monologue. The term actually originated in the early days of motion pictures, when film would break in the projection booth of a theater while it was running. Many times, the projectionist would splice the film back together losing several frames. When this spliced image was projected, if there was any movement on the missing frames, the image would jump at the splice point.

I think the worst jump cut I ever made was on a Hope sketch where an actor was on the left side of the screen and Hope wanted to eliminate the joke told as the actor walked across the room to the opposite side of the screen. Since I had no reactions or cutaway shots of the other actors in the set, all I could do was to splice the shot before the actor started to walk across the set to the shot after he had finished the joke and was standing on the other side of the stage. I played the edit and groaned. But there was nothing else I could do. I showed the edit to others and they also shuddered at how the actor jumped from one side of the screen to the other. When the show aired, I asked my wife to watch the sketch and see if she noticed anything odd. As the edit went by, my wife laughed and I lurched in my chair. I asked her if she noticed anything unusual in the sketch and she said no. Hope was right again.

In 1965, I asked to get off the Hope show only because I had been working long hours and my family life was suffering. I spoke with Sil Caranchini and told him I needed a rest. Sil told me that if I wanted to get off the show, I would have to talk to Hope directly. I didn't want to do that and I said that it was not my place to talk with the star. After several weeks, however, Sil told me that Hope wanted to see me. He was in his dressing room putting on makeup. I went in and Bob said, "I understand you want to get off the show. What's the matter, don't you like me anymore?" I told him that I liked and respected him very much, and then told him my concerns about my home life. Hope said, "Look, if I can work 24 hours a day, so can you." I said, "Yes, but your hourly rate and mine are quite a bit different." Hope said, "Don't be funnier than the comedian."

Hope told me how he took cat naps wherever and whenever he could —on planes, in busses or wherever he got a chance. He also said when he was at home, he went into his office, put his feet up and napped. I explained to him that we had two little children and the minute I walked in the door, they demanded attention. Then he told me that he had a small cottage in Palm Springs and if I would call his secretary, Miss Hughes, she would give me the key and I could stay there as often as I wished. I told him thanks very much. However, even though it was a nice gesture, I never did take him up on his offer.

About a month later, we were shooting another Bob Hope special. I was in the control booth upstairs in Studio One at NBC in Burbank. Hope had just finished a sketch with Dan Blocker (of *Bonanza* fame) and Bing Crosby when Hope asked for the boom mike to be brought down so he could talk to the director without the audience hearing him. He pulled the mike towards him and said, "Send Art Schneider down here." I was startled. What the hell did I do now, I thought? His agent and his producer told me that Hope wanted to see me down on the stage right now. I said, "I'm not going. I'll see him after the show." His agent said, "When the star calls, you go *now*." Each of them grabbed me under an arm and dragged me down the stairs to the stage. I remember saying as I stumbled down the flight of stairs, "I don't have any makeup on!"

They opened the stage door and pushed me to the edge of the set. Hope looked over at me and said, "Ladies and gentlemen, we have a fella that has been working with us for many years down in the basement of NBC fixing my mistakes. And tonight we would like to honor him with the first Bob Hope Show Crossed Scissors Award for Jump Cutting Above and Beyond the Call of Duty with Seeing-Eye Clusters." With that, his producer shoved me onto the stage and orchestra leader Les Brown played a fanfare. Hope said, "Art, now's your chance to say a few thousand words." I said "Bob, I'm speechless." Hope said, "That's the first time since I've known you!" He presented me with a beautiful gold plaque with the information neatly engraved on its surface; I have it hanging in my office today. I guess editing all those specials and making the monologue edits work in spite of Hope's image jumping all over the screen really paid off.

In 1986, I was in the process of writing my first book on editing, *Electronic Videotape Editing and Post-Production.* I needed a foreword for the book and asked Sil Caranchini if I could get Hope to write a few words. About a week later, I got a copy of what he had written, but it wasn't signed. Sil told me to come down to the studio that next week while they were taping and he would get Hope to sign it.

At NBC the evening of show taping, my wife and I stood outside the studio in the special ticket line. Soon an usher came out and asked for Art Schneider. I held up my hand and she asked, "Are you Jump Start?" I laughed and told her that I was Jump Cut, the nickname Hope gave me. We followed her into the studio and sat near the front close to the stage. Just before the start of taping, Sil stood out in front of the audience and said, "May I have your attention, ladies and gentlemen? Tonight we have a special guest with us in the audience. His name is Art Schneider and he has been the videotape editor on more than 50 of Mr. Hope's television specials going way back to 1951. Stand up, Art. Please give him a nice welcome." And with that, I stood up and was greeted with a warm round of applause which made me feel something special since, other than Bob Hope, no one had publicly acknowledged my work before. Halfway through the taping that evening, Sil told me to come with him and said Hope was ready to sign the paper. We walked to his dressing room and he spoke briefly with me as I told him about the book. I gave him my pen and he signed one copy. Then I asked him to sign a second copy in case it got lost on its way to the publishers. He laughed and signed the second copy.

Hope's willingness to write that foreword—which was very complimentary—really shows his generosity and loyalty to the people he works with. He has been generous in other ways by treating me, in a sense, as part of the family. His son Kelly worked with me for a time after I left NBC when I opened a post-production business with George Schlatter, the producer of *Laugh-In,* as one of the partners. Kelly also went with us

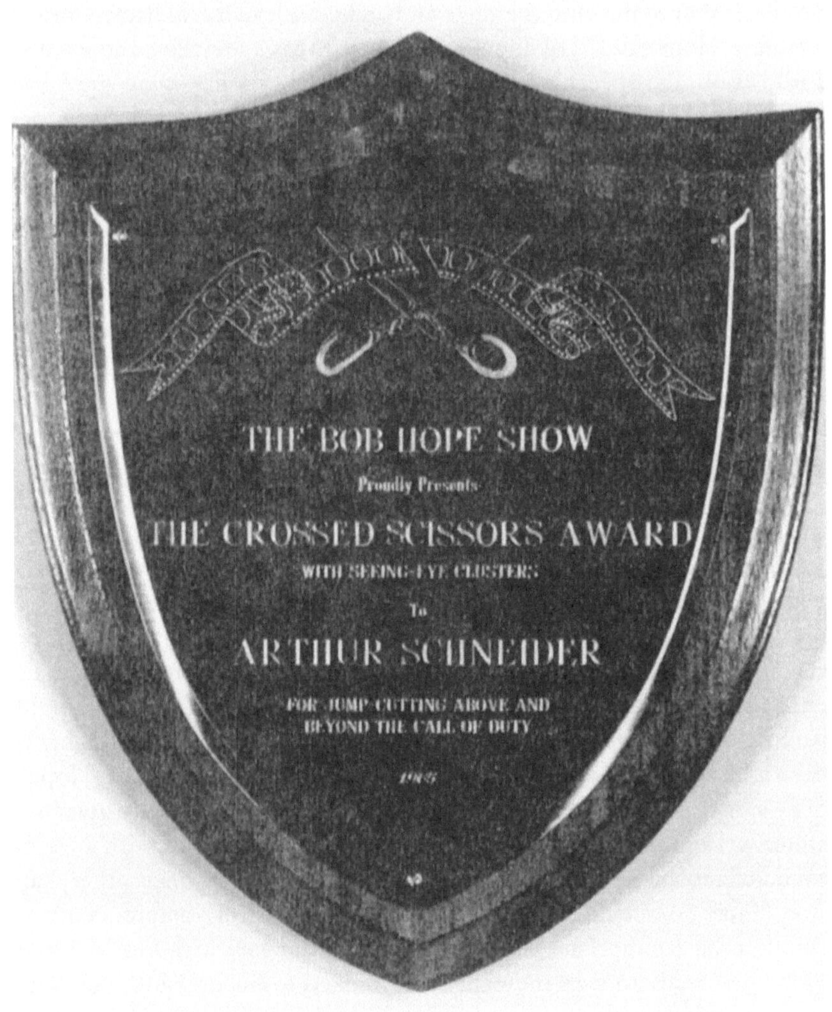

Jump cut award plaque.

as a still photographer when we were shooting environmental films on ecology.

In all the years I worked on Bob Hope shows, I had a good relationship with him and his staff became like a second family to me. He never yelled at me although I've heard him yell at others. I asked Sil Caranchini why Hope never yelled at me. He said he only yells at the high-priced help.

Bob Hope's brother Jack was a great man and ran the Hope organization until his death in 1962. I was always involved with Hope's family in one way or another. In the mid 1960s, Hope asked my boss at NBC if his daughter Linda could spend a couple of weeks watching me edit his specials. I had never had anyone looking over my shoulder while editing but I said okay and Linda spent several weeks with me. She was very interested in editing and if my memory serves me correctly, Linda then went to London to a film school to complete her schooling. She now heads Hope Enterprises.

Hope's younger brother George and I became friends and his wife Mary invited me over for lunch one day. She made a large pot of spaghetti which I devoured (including seconds and thirds). Mary was so pleased she said the next time I came over for lunch, she would make a larger batch of spaghetti in the bathtub.

On one occasion, Sil Caranchini called me at home on my day off and asked if I would go over to Hope's house in Toluca Lake to see if I could fix the stereo in their living room. I said I'd rather not since I'd been working many long hours six days a week and I'd like to spend my one day off with my family. Sil persisted and I finally gave in. I drove over to Hope's house and eventually found the stereo system hidden under a false panel in the living room. I quickly discovered that someone had accidentally pulled off a ground wire and that caused a loud hum whenever the unit was turned on. I screwed the wire back in and everything worked fine.

When Sil called me the next day, I told him what I found. I said I couldn't charge them anything since it was a very simple repair. Sil pointed out that I was on my day off and had to drive some 50 miles round trip to fix the problem. He insisted that I send him a bill for the repair. So I sent Hope a bill for $35 and, a few days later, Mrs. Hope sent me a check. I wish other people were so quick to pay their bills.

I remember one year when we had to work on Christmas Day (not unusual for me at all). Bob Hope had delivered a gallon of liquor to our department with his own inimitable label on it: "Bottled by the Hope Booze Works." On the top of the cork was a phone number which we all thought was the number of a hooker. It turned out to be the phone number of Alcoholics Anonymous. When we called, the voice angrily said to stop calling because he had been getting calls from dozens of drunks all night.

Even though it was Christmas, we weren't allowed any alcohol in the tape department because company rules stated there was to be no alcohol on the premises during working hours, especially for anyone involved with on the air broadcasting. We really didn't know how to divide up this gallon of booze so we decided to dump it into the almost-empty water cooler, figuring that nobody but those of us in the department would be drinking from the cooler. As it turned out, a vice president of the network was giving a tour of our department without any prior notice. At the end of the tour, he stooped over to get a drink of water out of the cooler. We were panic-stricken! He took a sip and made the worst face. He spit it out and said to us, "Get rid of this stuff in the cooler. It tastes terrible." Over the course of the evening, we dutifully obliged.

In the early 1970s when I was supervising editor for the videotape division of Consolidated Film Industries (CFI) in Hollywood, my son Robert asked me to teach him how to run a videotape machine. After getting approval from management (this was a union shop), I spent more than 15 Saturdays and Sundays teaching him operational procedures. Finally, I felt he knew enough to get a job on his own. One day soon after Robert had finished his training, I got a call from a friend of mine at TAV (Trans American Video). As fate would have it, they were looking for a night tape operator to make copies of television programs for syndication. After about six months in that job, Robert became an assistant editor and, several months later, a videotape editor, a job he still holds to this day.

In 1980, I introduced Robert to the Hope organization and he started editing the Bob Hope specials. After Robert had a half dozen shows under his belt, Hope told me that he liked Robert's work and said, "At last we have a modern editor!" I would like to point out that between the two of us, my son and I have edited more than 170 Bob Hope specials over a span of 42 years.

I've also worked on other projects for Hope over the years. On several occasions, Hope asked me to edit together clips designed for fund raisers for his favorite charities. At the time, I was working another job and would not get off work until 10 or 11 o'clock. I would then have to drive from Hollywood to his office in Burbank to consult with him about the details of the projects. I would spend at least a couple of hours with him on a one-to-one basis going over lists of material. From time to time, we would stop and tell jokes. He was very funny off-camera and at times I was laughing so hard, I had to stop and remind him why I was there. Then the conversation would get back to the work at hand for several minutes until either he or I would remember a joke, sometimes in reference to the material we were working on.

Bob Hope has a terrific memory as evidenced by the fact that, at one point, I hadn't seen him in 20 years and when he came into the editing room, he remembered me as if it had been yesterday. Considering all the years that went by and the thousands of people he meets each year, it is amazing that he has instant recollection.

During the years I've known Bob Hope, I found him to be generous with his time. In 1984, I asked him if I could have a photograph taken with him, myself and my son Robert as sort of a second-generation father and-son team who worked on most of his television programs. I tried to set up a photo session with Sil Caranchini but, because of Hope's intense schedule, all Sil could do was to get him in the hallway for a brief moment outside the studio where the show was being taped. One evening between tapings, Sil asked my son and me to come down to the set. He took us out in the hall to wait for Hope. In a couple of minutes, Hope appeared and shook our hands and asked how we would like the photo. I told him and he stood between my son and me with his arms around our shoulders and we were able to get three good color slides of the three of us. Later, I had two blowup color prints made and had Hope autograph my copy. He wrote, "Next, the grandchildren."

At one point, I was writing an article for one of the television trade magazines and they asked me to use the color slide of the three of us on the cover of the magazine. I called Sil at NBC and told him what the magazine wanted. The next day Sil called me back and said that NBC would approve of the use of the photo in the magazine but they wanted $1500 for the right to use it as a cover picture in a magazine. I was flabbergasted. I couldn't afford that kind of money and I knew the magazine wouldn't spring for it either. However, there was no charge for the photo if it was used inside as part of an article, and that's how it was finally used. Bob Hope also gave me autographed copies of two of his many books, "Five Women I Love" and "I Owe Russia $1200." So I have a lot of cherished Bob Hope memorabilia.

When a renowned entertainer such as Bob Hope reaches his ninetieth birthday, the whole world sits up and takes notice. Hope has been entertaining audiences for decades, and in 1993 he completed 55 years with NBC. During World War II, Hope traveled around the world entertaining troops of many nations. During the Vietnam conflict, his annual

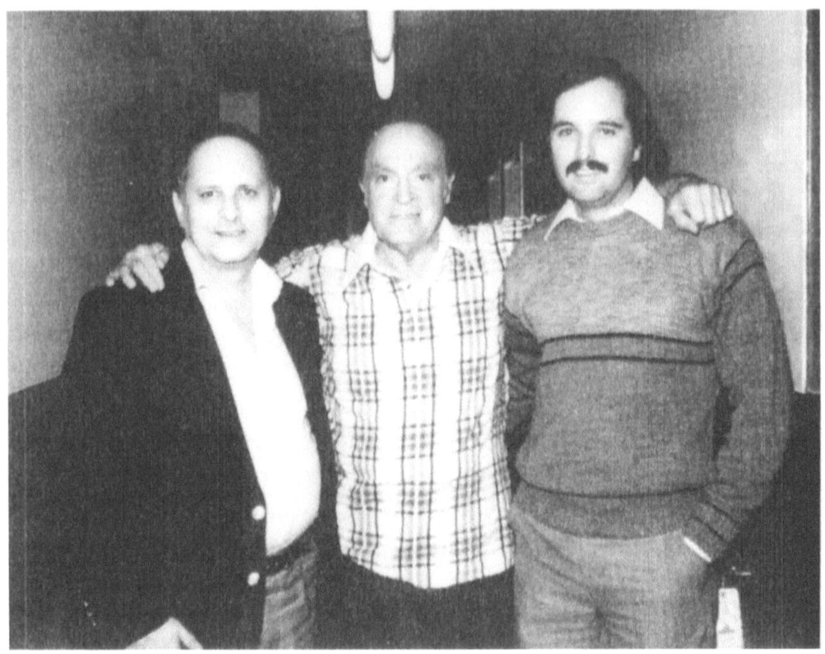

Left to right: Author, Bob Hope and author's son Robert ("Jump Cut, Jr.").

Christmas visits to the G.I.s were welcomed not only by the troops but by the many parents who were thrilled to be able to see their loved ones in faraway places even if it was only on television. What made this three hour birthday program so special were the many friends and entertainers who attended.

About a week before the taping, my son Robert called me and said the Hope office wanted us to come to the taping with our wives. It was a black tie affair, and because I hadn't worn a tuxedo in about a dozen years, I was somewhat apprehensive. Since we now live about 300 miles north of Burbank, I told my son that I would give him my measurements over the phone and that when my wife and I got to Los Angeles on Saturday, I would pick up the tuxedo.

The culmination of Bob Hope's first 90 years was the three-hour special that aired on NBC on May 14, 1993. Several weeks before that date, Robert started editing hundreds of clips from Hope's movies and television specials as well as highlights from more than five hours of goofs collected by myself and my son over the years. I've asked Hope to someday do a special on just these goofs which I know will be hilarious.

My wife and I decided we would drive down to our son's home early Saturday afternoon since the show taping would not begin until 5:30 P.M. Two days before the taping, I received a telephone call at home from a woman in the Hope office asking me to come to the NBC studios Friday morning at 9:30 to rehearse. Rehearse? For what? I thought we were only going to be guests in the audience but I told the woman I would try to get to NBC in time for the rehearsal the next day. My wife and I went to bed early and left at 2:30 A.M. the next morning. We drove all night and got to our son's home at 8:30. I dropped my wife off, drove to Burbank, and managed to get to the studio just in time.

After the six-hour drive, I was dressed very casually in old jeans when I walked into NBC Studio 11. Soon people I knew began to show up; I hadn't seen many of them in more than 25 years. What I soon discovered was that I, along with a small group of other people Hope had worked with over the years, were going to announce ourselves on the show and say a few words about their association with Bob Hope during the taping the next day. I was among the few privileged people who would get to be on stage to show my appreciation for this great entertainer.

We went through the rehearsal several times, making changes each time. Even though our lines were supposed to be ad-libbed, the writers were there to offer funny lines for those of us who might be tongue-tied. I was talking to one the participants, longtime joke writer Hal Kanter, and we reminisced about some of the funny "war stories" when we worked on the shows in the past. (The next night, when we were all dressed in our tuxedos, Hal Kanter walked over to me and said, "You cleaned up real nice.")

The day of the show, I went to the rental shop to try on the tuxedo my son had rented for me. To my surprise, it didn't fit. The jacket was too small and the trousers would have split if I had worn them. I guess over the years I expanded in the wrong places. In a way, I guess I edited in a few pounds and was unable to delete them! The moral is, don't rent a tuxedo over the phone. Fortunately, the needed alterations were made on the spot and I came away with a well-fitting tux.

Several weeks earlier, selected clips were edited together and they were to be integrated into the show and shown to the audience on the night of taping. Instead of using a single large-screen projector to show these clips, a multi-screen device made up of two vertical rows of four projection television monitors was used. When connected together with another group of eight monitors, they would allow the viewing of an image made up of 16 monitors (4 wide by 4 high). By using special electronics, the television image can be manipulated into an almost endless variety of different split images or recombined into one which can then be rapidly switched to any one of the individual screens, creating a very interesting montage effect.

The evening before the taping of the program, the opening segment was shot outside the NBC Studios in Burbank. The street in front was blocked off to traffic. Lights, cameras and other equipment filled the front of the studio. There were even cameras on top of the building, shooting down on the whole procedure. At least a dozen news cameras were lined up like ducks. The event was preceded by newspaper and television ads asking people to show up for the taping of the opening. I think they over-did it since crowd control was a major effort which included NBC security and the Burbank police department. I would say that there were at least 2,000 people in attendance that evening. I couldn't get close enough to get my video camera into the area and had to settle for shooting profiles of the stars through the crowd.

Jay Leno, star of *The Tonight Show*, told jokes and introduced Bob Hope. The Thunderbirds were to fly overhead as a salute to Hope but apparently got mixed up and flew over the nearby hospital instead. The opening ended with Hope being presented with a plaque that read "NBC Bob Hope Studios" and which would be added to the existing NBC building complex. When Hope accepted the plaque, he quipped, "Does this mean I now own a piece of the studio?" Then I heard very loud explosions which startled everyone in the crowd. It was fireworks going off less than 100 feet away from where we were standing. I thought we were being bombed! The noise was so loud that my ears were ringing for a while.

The night of the taping, we arrived at the NBC Studios and our car was valet-parked as we walked up the red carpet to Studio 11. Directly behind us was Zsa Zsa Gabor and around us were many of the biggest stars in the television and motion picture industries. Ginger Rogers and many other famous personalities (including Lassie the dog) were gathering at the studio entrance.

Studio 11 had been transformed into a nightclub. There were about 50 tables seating 12 people each. We found our numbered table and sat down. Each table had a centerpiece of cut fresh flowers and 48 glasses along with eight pieces of silverware for every guest. There was hardly any room for the dinner plates. Just before the taping started, I was told that toward the end of the program, an escort would take each of us who was to go on stage down to a holding area next to the stage. Needless to say, I was quite nervous. When the show began, we all got involved and enjoyed ourselves. Johnny Carson opened the show and more than two dozen celebrities followed honoring Bob Hope that evening. Then a lady tapped me on the shoulder and said, "It's time." "Already?" I said. I was taken down to sort of a "green room," an area where guests wait to go on. Then another escort asked me to follow her up to the wings of the stage and wait for our cue from the stage manager.

I was told to walk to the wings and stand by. I walked up the short flight of stairs adjacent to the stage and stood next to some of the world's greatest entertainers and statesmen. I stood shoulder to shoulder with former President Gerald Ford (and his two Secret Service bodyguards), Walter Cronkite, George Burns and John Denver. I was more nervous standing back stage with these people than I was when I finally got on stage and said my lines. In addition to the celebrities, there were 12 of us on the stage who were longtime associates of Hope, six on one side and six on the other. When I was cued by the stage manager to go up to the microphone, I spoke my lines. The rest of the people did their thing and it went off quite smoothly, especially since most of us were amateurs.

Then President Ford did his tribute to Bob Hope and we all sang "Thanks for the Memory," with special words to Hope's theme song written for the occasion. Since we did not know these new lyrics, they were put on huge 60-inch monitors with letters eight inches high so that the words could be seen by everyone on stage some 100 feet away. This was followed by the audience singing "Happy Birthday to Hope" while 50 or so waiters brought lighted birthday cakes down the aisles toward the stage. This ended the taping and we all went back to our tables to enjoy our catered dinner.

Later on that evening, my son Robert, his wife Sharon, my wife Dee and I went to Bob Hope's table so that our wives could finally meet him after all these years. I asked Hope if he would tell my wife that I really was working all those late hours on his shows. He laughed and nodded yes. The evening was wonderful because it brought back fond memories of working on the Hope film and videotape specials. I saw many of the old clips I had edited as far back as 1951, along with my old friends, directors, writers and many of the members of Hope's production staff.

When that evening was over, Robert had his work cut out for him. The program had lasted more than three hours and was taped using six separate cameras. However, the estimated running time indicated that the show was about 45 minutes too long. This is where careful editing brings the show down to time, which is one of the primary functions of an editor—to make the program look like it wasn't edited and have it come out on time. Robert's daily schedule was open-ended, a general start time but no stop time each day. Several days prior to taping, Robert had worked 17 hours a day for a week editing selected clips. After the taping, Robert put in 100 hours of editing on this special in the first week. You must have great stamina to be able to work those long hours and then drive home safely (Robert lives 25 miles from Burbank and travels the freeways daily).

To say the least, I was pleased that I was asked to participate in Bob Hope's ninetieth birthday celebration and to say a few words as well. I learned later that because the show was long, my lines were cut along with those of several other people. However, my son left a close-up of me on camera as we all sang "Thanks for the Memory" on stage.

All in all, this experience is one I will never forget. Having been associated with Bob Hope for more than four decades has been a rewarding experience and has given me memories and friendships few people are lucky enough to share in a lifetime. As editors on a majority of all those Bob Hope comedy specials, Robert and I share many memories of editing more than 170 Hope specials. We even shared father and son screen credit on the 1988 Persian Gulf Christmas Tour. Bob Hope, thanks for those memories.

CHAPTER FIVE

On the Go at NBC

I never lacked for anything to edit. When I wasn't editing syndicated programs for distribution, I was assigned to other projects (even in the early days when we were in cramped editing quarters in the basement of NBC Hollywood). I often edited local news stories for our local affiliate. I would work with news writers and edit segments shot on film as well as edit\kinescope film material from our archives. There were two news programs every day, one at 5 P.M., the other at 11 P.M.

Nearly everything I edited was on 16mm. However, every so often we would get some 35mm footage that had to be integrated into the rest of the news stories. We had a 16mm projector connected to a separate 16mm sound reproducer since most of the stories had some kind of separate soundtrack. After being edited, the stories would be assembled on a reel in the order they would be used on the air. A second reel containing only 35mm footage would be threaded on the 35mm projector. However, we could not connect a separate sound reproducer for the 35mm projector. In nearly every case, however, narration was written to be integrated into the story. So the writer would rehearse the script to be sure it fit with the story and did not cover up any sound dialogue within the story itself.

Quite often, the writer would have to rewrite his narration in order to satisfy time requirements. But by viewing the film as he read the narration, he could easily see where he needed to modify his script. Once these changes were made, a second rehearsal was made to verify all the changes. Sometimes it was a real pain because the only story that needed to be changed was at the end of the film reel. Since we did not have a film projector that was reversible, it meant removing the film from the projector, rewinding the film, threading it back on the projector along with any associated separate soundtrack and running the film through all the stories until we came to the right one. When there were as many as a dozen stories on one reel of film, it was obviously a time-consuming effort to rehearse only the last story. After going through the experience of winding through all the film several times, eventually we convinced the writers and the on-the-air talent to be more careful with their segment timings.

Everything we did in the way of news editing was in black and white until the late 1950s when news color film was introduced. NBC Burbank purchased a custom-designed color film processor which was installed in the basement of the main technical building. This enabled us to develop color film and return it to the news department within about an hour or so, depending on the amount of film that was shot. The film was a color reversal, film the same kind as used in color slides but in a 16mm movie format. No work prints were made but this original film, after developing, was used by the editor to cut all the news stories. Cement splices were used in editing and sometimes these splices would break on the air, forcing the anchor person to ad lib the rest of the story.

In addition to the color film shot by news staff cameramen, color film was processed for other cameramen selling their news stories to NBC. These freelance cameramen were called "stringers" and were paid by the story. Freelance photographers were often used since the NBC cameramen could not cover every breaking news story in the Los Angeles area. NBC also maintained a 16mm black and white film processor used for processing 16mm kinescope programs for the making of delay broadcast programs for distribution as well as work prints for the double system method of videotape editing described earlier.

In 1954, the entire NBC Hollywood operation moved to the newly completed Burbank Studios. Not only was facility space increased ten-fold, at last I had my own editing room. No more cramped quarters working in "closets" and nowhere to hang my hat—literally. Now I had plenty of room to edit, store materials and even a desk with an intercom (which never did work quite right).

There was a period from about 1957 to 1960 when I was heavily involved with the NBC promotion department. We used to make promotional spots for the network shows and most were edited on 35mm film and reduced to 16mm for release. Even though we had videotape facilities at our disposal, the complexity of some of these spots was such that only a photographic optical lab could create these special effects. All

the major shows (*Bonanza, Wagon Train* and others) were heavily promoted, which I know contributed to their success and in many instances
saved them from being canceled.

I worked with promotion department writers who were responsible
for all the programs on the West Coast. When a request for a promotional spot (or "promo") came in, I would often go with the writer to the
studio where the series or special was being shot and we would spend a
day or two looking for material we felt would be useful in promoting it.
By contract, the show's producers paid all the costs in obtaining the material such as duplicating costs for both the picture and soundtracks. Gen
erally we would produce a series of 10, 20, 30 or even 60-second spots
from one batch of material. We would also go to screenings of edited
work prints of some shows to select appropriate footage.

The rule was to make a spot so good the audience will want to see
it. We used the most exciting material from action shows and the most
provocative dialogue from what are known as "walk and talk" dramas
where there was very little if any action. If a program turned out to be a
dud and we had to promote it anyway we always used the only good stuff
we could find in a series or an episode. Viewers would tune in but would
be disappointed to find that none of the excitement in the promo was to
be found in the show, but that's how we kept some shows alive months
after they should have been canceled. After all, you have got to get the
audience's attention. Our motto was to "Hit them over the head with a
two-by-four to get their attention." It almost always worked except in
those rare cases when the show was so bad, we couldn't even find enough
palatable material to make a decent promo. During the three-plus years
I worked for the NBC promo department, I made more than 3,000 promos, several of which actually won awards for creativity. The reason I was
able to make so many spots in that length of time is that many were one
simple shot; there was no complex editing involved, it was just a matter
of adding titles. In that way, I could edit as many as a dozen short and
easy spots in a day.

It wasn't always that easy because when complex optical effects were
called for, it would often take a week or two to complete them because
of time required in the film lab. Most of the promos I did were on 35mm
film and eventually reduced to 16mm for most of the TV stations in this
country and Canada. In addition to editing the picture and creating the
titles and special optical effects, I had to build soundtracks with music,
sound effects and narration. I had to be a sound mixer, often blending in

several tracks to make a smooth composite so that the music and sound effects did not overpower the narration and production sound. After the soundtrack was completed, it was sent to the lab to make an optical printing negative.

When completed, the spot contained all the titles and other optical effects blended into a composite duplicate negative by the optical lab. The soundtrack and picture negatives were then synchronized and sent to the lab for what is known as a 16mm first trial print or answer print. After approval by the promo department for content and by me for technical quality, the lab was told to make the release prints. Often a promo order would call for upwards of a hundred release prints, one for each of the NBC affiliates. These bulk prints would come to us on large 1200 foot rolls. I would have to break them apart, tape down the end of each print, stuff them into already addressed envelopes, lick them shut, stamp them and deliver them to the promo department office. It seems like a lot of work and sometimes it was but the effort was worth it because I learned a lot about optical effects by dealing directly with the optical lab. I also learned specialized phases of production and post-production, concepts and ideas I would not have discovered had I not been able to do all the things I've mentioned.

From the day we received our first broadcast videotape machines, all editing was done mechanically—that is, every picture edit we made was a physical cut and splice on the tape itself. It was not only time-consuming but tedious as well. Furthermore, it required great skill to make a tape splice that would play through the video head without a breakup of the picture. Even with the double system method of editing videotape using film as a work print, I always ended up conforming and splicing the master tape segments together into an edited master videotape. In addition, when editing tape, it was being cut apart and spliced and that tape, once spliced, could not successfully be reused again for a new recording since previously-made splices on old stock frequently ended up in the middle of a picture frame, causing a momentary "glitch" or picture disturbance.

Then in early 1963, Ampex came out with the first computer controlled electronic videotape editor, "Editec." Before Editec, early electronic editing was somewhat of a hit-or-miss proposition. Edits were made by physically cutting and splicing the tape or by electronically making edits by manually transferring information from a playback VTR to a record VTR which created an edited master tape, but on a hit-or-miss basis since each edit was made by cueing up the record VTR and the play VTR and simultaneously starting both machines together. The record button was then pressed when the operator thought it was the right spot to make the edit, a process editors often called "kamikaze" editing.

The accuracy of each edit was determined by the operation or start-up time of each VTR, the accuracy of where each tape was cued to prior to the start of the edit, and of course when the editor punched the record button. Editec improved reliability of each edit (as well as productivity) by giving editors the capability of creating an edit point quickly. Remember, less than a decade had gone by since the first videotape recorders were introduced in 1956. Editec, or for that matter any form of electronic editing, is called "transfer editing" and is how all videotape editing is done today. The physical splicing of videotape was eventually dropped in the early 1980s in favor of electronic or transfer editing.

Editec was a programmable computer module that enabled editors to precisely locate edit points on either the playback VTR machine, or the record VTR machine allowing frame-accurate edits to be made. A single frame audio tone was recorded at the point the editor wished to make an edit. These edit points could be erased and re-recorded and moved a frame at a time either forwards or backwards with relative ease.

One of the first uses of Editec was to animate on a frame-by-frame basis in color. I spent weeks at the tape machine with a headset glued to my ears listening for cues from the studio director to record each frame. It took about 20 seconds from the time I pushed the record button until that single frame was recorded. Then the director would change animation cells and tell me to record another frame. This process went on for about three weeks. The result? Thirty seconds of color animation generated from 900 animation cells, probably the very first animated material done directly on videotape. The color looked great but the animation had a "shimmy effect" due to an aberration in the color television camera. That is, each frame was randomly shifted slightly to the left or right, producing a horizontal "shimmy" effect on the screen as the frames rolled by at 30 frames per second. These early cameras were never designed for the rigors of electronic animation. So, after three weeks of work, we decided to scrap the animation project. Today, however, videotape animation is a piece of cake with all those electronic quirks resolved.

I edited many television specials in my career, in particular a number of Jack Benny specials. One of the guests was a tiger by the name of "Sarang." The segment with the tiger was shot on 35mm color film away

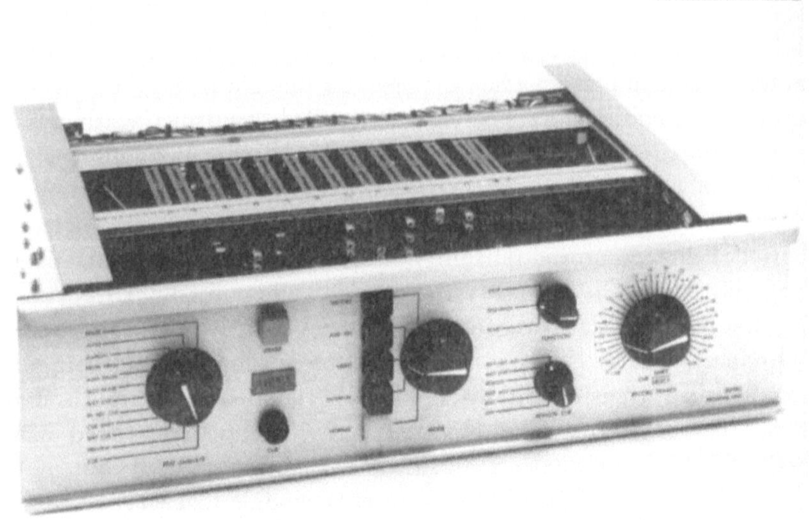

Ampex Editec control panel (courtesy Ampex Corp.).

from NBC, I suspect at a local zoo since it was somewhat difficult to transport a wild tiger into a studio to do tricks. The segment involved Walt Disney and the tiger. Generally, the film, shot by an outside production company, would be contracted out to a post-production facility. Since there was a problem with unions in this case, the director wanted me to edit the film rather than subcontract it out. The director was some sort of joker. He said as they finished shooting the segment with the tiger, "That's a Sarang wrap!" Even my jokes aren't quite *that* corny.

As I pointed out earlier, our union, NABET, had jurisdiction over both motion picture film and kinescope film. I was one of the few editors at NBC who had 35mm film editing experience and I was asked to edit this ten-minute segment. When it was finished, it was shown to Walt Disney for approval. He thanked me for doing a good job, which made me feel great, coming from the master himself.

Prior to the 1964 political elections, I did a lot of editing for national as well as local candidates. However, the ones I remembered most vividly were a series of TV spots for Barry Goldwater. As it turned out, the Democrats were editing in the next booth alongside of my equipment. Since there were no walls between us, I could hear all the sound from their editing session quite well. Editors were not assigned to edit by their political affiliation. We were assigned by the needs of the producers. An interesting experience relating to political editing in those days of physical splicing of videotape resulted in a moment I will never forget.

For several years, there was an incompatibility problem between videotape that was recorded on one VTR and played back on another. This was due in part to the mechanical design of the video head. To temporarily get around this problem, whenever a prime time special was recorded (including series such as *Laugh-In*), when the recording was over, the video head would be removed from the VTR and placed in a box and stored with the tape until the next time a recording or playback was needed. This procedure guaranteed optimum playback quality for on-the-air broadcast or for making duplicate copies. However, this posed some serious scheduling problems as well as making it necessary to maintain an adequate supply of quality video heads. At $4,000 per video head, this could end up being an expensive temporary fix. Because of this incompatibility problem, we sometimes ran into unusual situations where we could not get a particular tape to play back properly. This is a case in point.

As I became more experienced, I was being asked by producers and directors with whom I had worked in the past to be their editor on various projects. It really was an ego trip. I was assigned to edit what we would now call a one-hour political "infomercial." The edited program (comprised of live interviews and historical film clips transferred to tape) was to be broadcast live to New York by NBC at 5 P.M. that same day. There were dozens of reels of two-inch videotape from which to select footage. I should point out that all the edits I was to make were physical edits, not electronic edits, which made this job even more difficult. The director and I started work at 8 A.M. that morning. We were doing fine until about two in the afternoon, when I asked the director how much more we had to do. He said he had only a few more cuts to make then add the credits. Fine, I thought. We'll make it with plenty of time to spare.

Around three, I was getting concerned because we were still editing and nowhere near ready for the credits. At four I told the director we were only an hour away from air time for a network broadcast. Normal procedure is to make one protection copy for local programs and often two or more for network releases. There would not be enough time to make even one protection copy of this one-hour program; this puppy would have to go on the air to the East Coast with no backup. We would be making the backup copy at the same time the program aired to the East Coast, a very dangerous procedure in those days.

Finally I spliced on the credits and rewound the tape. There were so many physical splices in the videotape, they sounded like a series of tiny machine gun bullets as they passed through the video head during rewind. I would estimate that there were in excess of 150 splices in that one-hour program. It was now less than ten minutes to air time. I was sweating bullets as I ran across the room to set up the machine assigned to playback this program. I put the VTR in *play* and looked at the pictures. They were awful. There were multiple bands of color from top to bottom of the picture. Obviously the video head that made the recording was nowhere near compatible with the video head I selected for playback. I was editing on an Ampex brand VTR and ended up playing back on an RCA VTR. These two brands of VTR used video heads that were not mechanically compatible. In other words, you could not put an Ampex video head on an RCA machine or vice versa. I rewound the tape and went to another VTR. The same thing happened. Even though we had 24 VTRs in the area, most were assigned to record or play back previously scheduled programs or to record programs from one of the four studios in the building. There were only three unassigned VTRs at my disposal. What's worse is that the minute I finished editing on the Ampex machine, it was reassigned to record a program, so even that VTR was now unavailable.

Now I was worried. Here we were, about five minutes from air and I couldn't find a VTR that would play this tape. I should mention that advertisers pay for air time in advance and that was true for political programs as well. NBC didn't want to lose this program since they would have to refund a quarter of a million dollars. At that moment, my boss walked in, white as a sheet after hearing about my problem. He asked me if there was anything he could do to help. I was so frustrated that I said, "Just get the hell out of here." He quickly disappeared.

I was frustrated, angry and puzzled as to why I couldn't get this damned tape to play. I went to another VTR and found that the pictures looked acceptable. I wasn't going to be that fussy with only minutes to spare. I put on my headset and contacted the studio through which this program was being fed. The director screamed that he didn't see any pictures from my tape machine. I thought he was going to have a heart attack! I couldn't stand the yelling in my ear so I told him, "Look, when you see my color bars, you'll know I'm rolling this tape. If you don't, then there is nothing more I can do. Put up a standby slide." With that I tore off my headset and began to set up the machine.

I thought I was home free but then another problem arose. One of the special color amplifiers quit working. There was no time to find another VTR. I screamed at the top of my lungs for maintenance. A maintenance man came running up to me and I told him what just happened. He scratched his head for a second and then ran back to get another electron tube. He pulled out the suspected bad one and replaced it with the new one.

In order to allow sufficient time for the proper setup of these complex VTRs, NBC procedure was to start all tapes 90 seconds ahead of the beginning of the program in order for the operator to be able to set up the color, brightness, contrast and other controls to match certain FCC and broadcast standards. This is easily done under normal conditions, but when you just lost an amplifier and you are seconds away from going on the air, all bets are off.

While the maintenance man was installing the tube, I had to start my VTR anyway because it was 90 seconds before air. I had cued the tape to the 90 seconds pre-roll point since I would then have that time to make all the necessary adjustment. The VTR started and I put my headset back on to talk to the studio. I told the director that the tape was rolling but he saw no pictures because of the faulty amplifier. I told him, "If at five P.M. you see pictures, fine. If not, put up a standby slide and fake it." The other problem I faced was that I had no idea if my splices would play on this machine since the heads and the electronics not be compatible. What if the splices broke up and the picture flipped at every splice? What if, what if….all kinds of things ran through my mind. Even though the VTR was now running and in a playback mode, I could see no pictures because the tube just replaced took about 30 seconds to warm up. People were screaming at me from all sides *and* over the headset. The viewers or even the broadcast technicians at NBC in New York had no idea what was happening in Burbank at that moment. Everything I did to make that tape play was by instinct and years of training.

The clock was ticking away. Pictures slowly began to appear, and I finished setting up the tape using the color bars as reference. Color bars ended about 28 seconds before program start but by the time the replacement tube had warmed up and the amplifier was again operational, there were only about ten seconds of color bars remaining for me to use to finish setting up the playback tape. The TV screen went dark as the color bars ended and the clock ticked away the seconds—five, four, three, two, one. Up came the NBC peacock and all those in the room applauded out of thankfulness. Another tape operator on another tape machine was recording backup copies for the West Coast as the edited program was being broadcast to the East Coast.

Everyone heaved a sigh of relief as the program went off without a hitch; even the splices played perfectly. I apologized to everyone for getting so excited. The color came back to my boss's face. A few minutes after the program went off the air, the director and the producer and his wife came in to thank me. She gave me a big hug and a kiss and was thankful that the program went off so well, but I was ready for a change of underwear!

I was frequently assigned to be a tape operator on what are called remotes (an assignment that takes you out of the main studio). I used to go to baseball, football and golf games as a tape operator to provide instant replays for the sports department.

In July of 1964, a crew from NBC Burbank was assigned to go to Atlantic City, New Jersey, along with several other crews from other affiliates to cover the Democratic national convention. We were to record, playback and edit news segments for the Huntley-Brinkley NBC daily news program. We were to be gone for two weeks in July and August, one of the hottest and most humid months on the East Coast. As it turned out, the day I was leaving was the day we were going to have a new swimming pool installed in our backyard. The problem was that we had poor access to the backyard and the pool would have to be dug by hand. That worried me. My wife was left at home with two small children and also had to be responsible for dealing with the pool contractor.

The trip to New Jersey was my first commercial jet ride on a Boeing 707. By union contract, we had to fly first class. My hotel room was right on the boardwalk within walking distance of the convention center, but it wasn't very nice, and I really preferred to work than to come back to that dump of a hotel room. As it turned out, I did spend up to 22 hours a day editing once the conventions began. When did I sleep, you ask? Anywhere and anytime I could. This meant taking cat naps in empty offices or in any other area where the noise level was low enough to allow me to get a few minutes of shut-eye. I never got more than a couple of hours of sleep during the entire convention. The first couple of days were orientation days, getting to know who we would be working with, setting up work schedules and just trying to get the lay of the operation in general.

I walked into the convention center and was somewhat awed at the vastness of this huge auditorium and the massive amounts of television equipment everywhere.

The third day, I began editing news clips to be used the following day. It was a grueling job for we ended up working much longer shifts than anyone ever anticipated because news stories were coming in faster than we could edit them. NBC had several news crews at the convention center as well as roaming crews working out of cars with portable black and white videotape recorders mounted in their trunks. Those so-called "portable" two-inch VTRs were monstrous machines and only a car with a large trunk would be able to carry them.

NBC brought a dozen very expensive studio-type VTRs from New York to use to record, play back and edit the numerous stories on a daily basis. When a news producer was assigned to edit a story with me, we would gather the material (some recorded by other tape operators) as well as record material on my own VTR from outside sources.

Sometimes we would be able to take breaks while waiting for a news producer to get his material ready to edit. There was food everywhere for us since we rarely had time to go out for a decent sit-down meal. When I would have an hour or more between stories, I would either try to take a nap, find something to eat or wander around the basement of the convention center out of boredom. One day, I found several unused offices. I went in and discovered phones on the desks. However, I never saw anyone go in or out of these offices. I picked up a phone one day and dialed my home phone number in Los Angeles. To my surprise, my wife answered. It was a direct line! Wow. Now I could handle any problems relating to the new pool being built (and there were quite a few). My wife was so relieved that I was able to talk to the contractor. Every day I called home to see how the pool was coming along. It made my job easier, too, since I didn't have to worry about how things were going at home.

Editing many news stories every day, seven days a week, was difficult and very tiring, but I did enjoy it and made many new friends, especially those editors from NBC New York. Often the topic of conversation was how much money we were making every day. I figured out that by the time the convention was over, I'd have enough overtime and other monetary fringe benefits in two weeks to pay for the pool in cash.

My most unusual editing assignment was a news story concerning Hubert Humphrey going to see the President. The news item itself wasn't as interesting as what happened after I edited the story. I loaded the story onto the tape machine and cued it up on a ten-second start mark, the usual procedure. There was no automation in this somewhat temporary facility in the convention center basement. In those days, all equipment was started manually by the operator. I put on my headset and called the director to tell him I was standing by, but got no answer. The Huntley-Brinkley evening news program had just started, so I switched my monitor to watch the entire news program as it was being broadcast live just to see what other news there was that day. I kept calling the director but got no answer. The voice of another tape operator on a machine nearby, also waiting to run his story, came on. I asked, "Have you been able to contact the director?" He said, "No."

Then I heard David Brinkley say on the air something like, "We now take you by videotape to a story of Hubert Humphrey visiting the President." I said to myself, "That's my story!" and I pushed the *play* button. Suddenly I saw my story on the air! How about that! As soon as the story ended, I heard a click on my headset and a voice said to me, "Who told you to run that story?" I said, "No one. I heard David Brinkley describe my story and since I could not contact you, I felt I should roll the tape." The director chewed me out and said, "Don't you ever roll a tape unless I tell you to. Is that clear? I'm going to report you to the union." I was dumbfounded. Here I saved this guy's butt and he had the audacity to reprimand me!

I reported the incident to my supervisor. A couple of hours later, in came a group of engineers, the director and the union steward. They all came up to me and I expected the worst. The union steward told the director, "Go ahead, tell him." The director profusely apologized for the remarks he made and thanked me for rolling the tape on my own initiative, preventing an embarrassing moment for the news department. I don't know what really made me roll that tape but I'm glad I was cleared of any wrongdoing. When the convention was over, I took a needed two-week vacation and enjoyed our new swimming pool.

A mix-up of instructions and timing errors got me my first helicopter ride. NBC had a good reciprocal working agreement with the other networks. On one occasion, ABC contracted with NBC to record and edit a program called the "Deb Star Ball" since ABC's facilities were tied up. I was assigned to record the program and to stand by in case editing was required. Because there was only a two-hour turnaround time for the tape to be delivered to ABC so they could air it, NBC hired a small helicopter parked in the back lot to take me and two videotapes directly to ABC after I finished editing.. As the crow flies, ABC is only about five minutes away, but by car it was a good half-hour at that time of night.

I was to get videotape editor credit on the program and my credit was recorded during the production on the end credit list by ABC. I watched the entire program and it went off without a problem except for one thing. End credits in those days were white letters printed onto a black cloth roll and mounted onto a motor-driven drum that could vary its speed. This device is called a crawl machine, I guess because the credits crawl up the screen. The studio camera is pointed at this machine photographing the credits. When the credits started to roll up at the end of the program, my name came up but somehow it got stuck in the center of the screen because the crawl machine jammed. My name was on the air for almost two minutes, probably the longest screen credit anyone has ever gotten. Maybe I should contact the *Guinness Book of World Records.*

As it turned out, there was really nothing anyone could do about it because of the short turnaround time, so they decided to let it go as it was without any editing, even though I received air credit as videotape editor. I rewound both recorded tapes and was escorted on a golf cart through the halls of NBC, out the artist's entrance to the back lot where a helicopter was waiting. I got in and strapped the two program tapes on my lap since there was little room in the cockpit. The pilot asked me if this was my first helicopter ride. I foolishly told him it was. He started the engine and lifted off with a blast that took me by surprise. As my heart dropped down to the pit of my stomach, the pilot turned to me and gave a smirk as if to say, "Gotcha!"

We climbed to about 400 feet and I looked down as we passed over Forest Lawn Cemetery. I counted several opened graves , which made me very uneasy because this little helicopter shook like it was about to fall apart and I wasn't ready to fill one of them. After a few minutes, we landed safely in the back lot of ABC in Hollywood and the pilot said, "You know your return flight to Burbank is already paid for." I said, "No thanks, I'm going back by car." I drove back to Burbank with a friend.

Because I was involved with editing in television's early years, I had the privilege of participating in several important "firsts." One of those was the first instant replay. The NBC sports department had long wanted to be able to show replays of great football plays right after they happened. Even though sporting events of all kinds have been broadcast for decades, it wasn't until 1965 that the first instant color replay was provided to national viewers on network television. This project was planned for the New Year's Day Rose Bowl game in Pasadena, California.

I should point out that today, instant replay is provided by very sophisticated electronic equipment on digital disks and by other means so that any game play can be replayed.

Prior to this game, there was no way to easily record a game play in color and almost instantly play it back mostly because of hardware limitations. The desire was there, but videotape equipment was cumbersome and expensive and was not designed for what the sports producers wanted to do. The NBC sports department, in cooperation with the engineers in their Burbank studios, came up with several plans, including a "Rube Goldberg" contraption which was tried out before any commercial use of it was attempted. First a large four-by-eight-foot wooden box was constructed two inches wide to allow loose videotape to accumulate at the bottom of the box. The end of the tape was then threaded onto an adjacent VTR. The box was sort of a buffer to store the tape until it was needed instead of letting it fall on the floor. That didn't work because as the tape piled up on itself, the weight of the tape pressed down on and wrinkled the layers of tape beneath it, making it useless. That idea was quickly scrapped.

The next attempt was to go from one VTR to another and skip the dreaded plywood box. Two quadruplex VTRs were placed side by side. A game play was recorded on the first machine and the end of the tape was fed through the transport mechanism of the second VTR. This kind of worked, but the delay (about 25 seconds) was too great and there was danger of tape damage as the tape was fed from one machine to another. It also required two tape operators who had to keep in sync with one another to avoid tearing the tape. Another bad idea.

The design that eventually was used (and remained functional until more sophisticated hardware came along) was the simplest solution of all. In the NBC remote production truck used at sporting events were two RCA color VTR standing upright side by side. I innocently suggested, "Why not use the two VTRs already installed in the production truck to record each football play, rewind the tapes and play them back in real time?" This was easier said than done, for several reasons. First, the director wanted to save each play we recorded. That meant we had to use 90-minute videotapes which were very heavy and hard to manipulate. Second, there was no guarantee the VTRs would be able to produce pictures that would become stable quickly enough to use on the air. No one had ever attempted anything like this before. Here I was, pioneering again in television.

Since I was in on the development of this technique, I became one of the first operators in the sports department tape truck. The 90-minute videotapes were also required because the director wanted to be able to record coach and player interviews prior to and after the game in addition to the anticipated 200 or so plays of the game. I was in constant communication with the program director and the technical director in the adjacent truck in order to be able to get the cues to roll my replays. Each time the offensive team would go into a huddle, we would start to record. When the play was over or the ball was dead, I would stop and rewind the tape. Since the tape reels were mounted vertically one above the other, the supply reel being on top, I would grab the supply reel with all my strength and rewind the tape to the beginning of the play.

Two tape operators were assigned to the remote truck. Each was to operate a machine with a different camera angle (assigned by the director). The procedure was to start recording a few seconds before the ball was snapped and stop recording as soon as the ball was dead. But how would we be able to know where to start the play? We decided that at the point the ball went into play, we would put a short but very loud audio tone on the sound track and crank up the speakers so we could hear the tone even over the loud noises in the truck. When the ball was dead, we would hit the stop button, grab the upper supply reel and rewind the tape. This tone was recorded each time we started recording the play so that we could tell precisely where to cue up the tape for the replay.

The supply reel of tape at the beginning of a game weighed some 30 pounds, and grabbing the edge of it with all my strength was hard on the muscles—especially when you consider how many times during a game I would perform this function. Because of the force needed to rewind the tape, the videotape would sometimes be stretched to the point where it would no longer record video. At the end of each game, we would throw away a $250 roll of tape.

During rewind, the loud tone would come on as we neared the start point of the play and would stop at the beginning of the play. It was somewhat hit-or-miss depending on how strong we were and how quickly we stopped the tape reel at the end of the tone. As soon as the tape stopped, we would put the machine in play and the director would switch to it on the air. Depending on the length of the play, we would average eight seconds from the end of the play to the start of the instant replay. This was incredible. The director was overjoyed. It worked so well, I was assigned to many more remote ball games before more sophisticated equipment became available. This led to replays at the 1966 first annual Super Bowl football game, a project I initiated as an instant replay "expert."

Needless to say, that was the fastest two hours I ever spent watching a football game. The only time I could take a breather was during half time. I really couldn't enjoy the game because I was concentrating so hard on the mechanics of the equipment and listening carefully for the director's cues.

The next generation of instant replay hardware was the helical scan VTR that had the ability to playback at variable speeds and freeze-frame a single frame for long periods. Current technology has the video recorded on hard computer-style disks that can replay in less than a second and perform all the creative functions that were limited by our old technology of 1965.

Another technological innovation of 1965 was a color process known as Chroma Key, developed by NBC. With Chroma Key, a foreground image on one camera is combined with a second image on a different camera. For example, the foreground camera photographs the image of a person standing next to a fence with a wind machine blowing his hair as though he were outside. Behind this person is a blue background. By itself, such a scene means very little.

Now, on another camera in another studio or anywhere else, project the image of an ocean scene with sea gulls and a few clouds in the sky. By using the electronic Chroma Key device, only the blue background of the first shot of the man at the fence is replaced by the ocean scene from the other camera. All of the rest of the picture remains unchanged. Now the two images are electronically combined to make the audience think the man is really standing near the ocean.

One of the first uses for this ingenious process was in the NBC daily series "Matinee Theater." The name of the episode was "The Invisible Man." All of the exposed parts of the actor, his hands and face were wrapped in blue bandages so that no skin was left exposed. When the Chroma Key was inserted into the scene, the actor looked as though he had no head or hands because the blue was replaced by the scenery behind him. To make the actor visible again, he merely unwrapped the bandages, exposing his flesh.

Chroma Key is also used in many other ways. Nearly every news broadcast has the news person sitting at a desk with action video going on behind. The news person actually sits in front of a blue screen and the news story seen behind him is coming from some other source such as a videotape machine. The old Sonny and Cher variety series used Chroma Key quite effectively during the "vamp" segment where Sonny and Cher changed costumes and were combined with themselves to look like there were as many as eight different characters in the set instead of just the two of them. As complex as it was to choreograph, it only took about 45 minutes to composite each vamp segment.

As a videotape operator, I worked nearly every holiday in the year for the more than 17 years I spent with NBC. For example, during the Rose Parade on New Year's Day, I would record each award-winning float on one videotape machine. On an adjacent VTR, I would set up to edit the float segments together. After I recorded a float, I would rewind the tape and mark a beginning and end point for the segment, cutting the tape a few inches ahead of where I was going to edit to the previous shot. I then transferred the cut reel to the machine next to me and made the splice to connect the shot to the previous shot, stopping at a point where I wanted to make the next splice. I cut the tape and brought the supply reel back to the record VTR so as to be able to record the next float. I generally had about a minute or more between floats because they rarely had two award-winning floats back to back.

The toughest part was getting these instant replays of the award-winning floats back on the air seconds after the last float passed by the cameras. Often, as I was splicing the last shot onto the reel, I would hear the live announcer saying, "Here comes a montage of all the award-winning floats." There were some 15 to 20 shots edited together on the reel and I had to carefully and quickly rewind the tape to a start mark so they could be rolled into the live program for all the world to see. I never had time to run all the shots together to see if the splices held together since the whole point of this was for the audience to see an "instant replay" literally seconds after the last float went by. I did this for several years before the real instant replay as we know it today came into being .

Editing material together for a live replay is a tension-filled few minutes during which there is no such thing as "I'm not ready." Fortunately, I did a good job every year (and, unfortunately, I was asked to do it every year). I almost never spent time with my family during Christmas and New Year's. Similar situations occurred on many other special holidays.

Some of the shows I enjoyed working on were the Danny Thomas *Burlesque* specials. Craig Curtis and I worked together on most of them. I remember one in particular with guest star Mickey Rooney that was very complicated. The opening was a musical montage cut precisely to music. Since Craig knew music very well, he cut this opening and it turned out to be the highlight of the show.

Most programs, whether series or specials, would shoot in segments, using a series of camera shots rather than editing every shot together as is the practice on motion picture film. Because a video switcher can be used to switch between several cameras, most directors prefer to use this method since it saves much time in editing. However, this Danny Thomas special was shot single-camera style as though it were shot on motion picture film. In other words, there were no electronic edits made by the technical director in the entire program. All 400 edits were made by Craig and myself.

To the amazement of Craig and myself, the show won an Emmy for technical direction, not editing. The technical director who got the Emmy, the person in charge of the crew and who makes all the electronic switches between the cameras, did nothing but say "Roll tape" and "Stop tape" in this program. It was one of the unfair situations we faced because, I suspect, the Television Academy as well as the Blue Ribbon panel viewing the nominations did not understand the difference between switching cameras in the studio and putting together every shot in the editing room. The edits were so well made that those viewing the program thought it must have been done live! That was a tribute to our skills as editors but it lost us the chance to get an Emmy for that program.

Several years later, because of the number of complaints not only by me but by many other editors who found the practice unfair, a new rule was finally established that allowed editors to include a brief description of any unusual techniques used in editing that would assist the Blue Ribbon panel in evaluating a program nominated for an editing award.

In 1966, I joined the Hollywood chapter of the Academy of Television Arts and Sciences (also known as ATAS) as a member of the category called "Electronic Production," an all-encompassing term that included everyone—cameramen, technical directors, tape operators, video editors and anyone else who had anything to do with videotape or the technical aspect of television productions. In 1977, I was elected to the Board of Governors of ATAS and served in that position for four years. There were 22 categories represented on the Board with two Governors for each. I represented Electronic Production.

I was involved with several other ATAS committees including the Membership committee, the Emmy Awards committee, the Engineering Awards committee and the Library committee. I was also on the Executive committee for two years as the Academy's secretary and treasurer. I enjoyed taking an active part in the Television Academy because it was a chance to meet with friends and to know that my input was taken seriously. For example, the Engineering Awards committee accepted input from companies and individuals who felt they had developed some special piece of hardware, procedure or software that would materially improve production or post-production.

There were about a dozen people on the Engineering Awards committee who had expertise in one field or another relating to production, post-production or the television engineering field. My specialty was editing and anything related to it. If an entry wasn't deemed strong enough to win an Emmy statue, the project was given an Engineering Award plaque, not quite as good as an Emmy statue but still recognized within the industry as a sign of notable achievement. At each of these committee meetings, we were given dinner since the meetings generally started at 7 P.M. and ran until 11 P.M. Maybe that's why I joined so many committees!

The Library committee doesn't sound very exciting, but one of our goals was to get oral histories of people who led interesting lives and to put these experiences on tape. It was not important they be stars but ordinary people who, near the twilight of their lives, would be encouraged to tell of their life experiences on tape, guided by someone who would ask pertinent questions so as not have the person just ramble on. Once recorded, these interviews would be typed into a computer program and eventually bound in book form to be kept in libraries as sort of a research tool.

The one thing I will always remember about being the Academy's treasurer is having to sign checks for the Emmy Awards production, often in amounts of $400,000 or more. It's a shame I couldn't spend any of that. All in all, I was heavily involved with ATAS from 1977 until I left the Los Angeles area in 1988. Otherwise I would have kept on even in retirement. I met and made friends not only with celebrities such as Jean

Stapleton and Dinah Shore but with producers, directors and other well-known people in this industry.

We had many different meeting places for our monthly Board of Governors meetings, from the Sportsman's Lodge in the San Fernando Valley to my favorite, the Beverly Hills Hotel. I would pull up in front of the hotel and my car would be valet-parked as I walked up to the entrance. Entering the plush foyer, I would go to a private dining room reserved just for the Board of Governors. We would be served an elegant dinner and have time to chitchat with friends before getting down to business.

Every year of my membership in ATAS, I was a member of the Blue Ribbon panel, a group of active people judging the nominations in every category of possible Emmy Awards. Most judging was done in August, about a month before the Emmy Awards telecast. Often the judging was held in local hotels or other facilities dedicated to handling big groups. For example, one year we held the judging at the Universal City hotel in the San Fernando Valley. It was generally a long day starting at eight in the morning. First, we checked in and went directly to an orientation breakfast where we were given our room assignments for a particular class of judging. The many questions we had were also answered by the Academy staff. There was never a shortage of food at these affairs and we would grab a table and enjoy our breakfast. Since seating was unassigned, I would sit down at the nearest empty table. Soon friends would appear and often stars who were judging acting categories would sit with us, which made it even more of a delightful occasion. I don't want you to get the idea that I only participated in these events because of the free food. On the contrary, I was really more interested in making connections in the event I ever wanted to change jobs. People respected me for my contributions as an editor and I wanted to stay out front so I wouldn't be forgotten.

The Academy reserved dozens of suites and rooms for the judging. Each room had comfortable chairs and plenty of soft drinks and munchies to keep us happy. There was a television set on a stand along with the video cassettes we were to watch that day. If we had to view a number of long format programs, such as a miniseries or other programs longer than two hours, we would be asked to return the next day to complete the judging.

There would be a short break after each nominated program was shown, but we were not allowed to comment on it. The procedures were so designed as to prevent contamination of the panels by influencing or in other ways trying to alter the result of a vote. Being on a Blue Ribbon panel is something like being sequestered as a jury member in that we were not to discuss the merits of each program. Somewhere around noon or after the last morning program was viewed, we would break for lunch, again getting together with friends. More often than not most of the members on our panel were other editors we have worked with or have known for years. The Academy policy is to have members on each panel who are familiar with that category since it would be unfair to ask someone to judge something out of their expertise (for example, hairstylist judging music). Once the ballots were sealed and sent to the accounting firm, we could talk about it since nothing could then influence the outcome of our votes.

One of the perks of being on the Board of Governors was getting two free tickets to the Emmy Awards every year I was on the Board. For many years, there would be two awards ceremonies, one for the crafts and technical awards and a second for the regular prime time Emmy Award network telecast. Of course we would go to both. The technical and craft award ceremonies were not televised but were recorded on tape. That evening, all the winners would be combined into a single clip which would be shown the next evening on the prime time telecast. At first, the technical awards would be held a week before the prime time telecast. That meant having to rent a tuxedo twice. Then it was changed to a consecutive Saturday and Sunday. That way I could rent the tux for the weekend at the same cost.

In addition, as a nominee, I was also given two free tickets to both the technical awards and the prime time telecast the next evening. All in all, I have been to the Emmy Awards some two dozen times, as a nominee seven times as well as being on the Board of Governors of the Television Academy. The Awards ceremonies have been held at many locations starting at the Hollywood Palladium way back in 1965. More recently, they have been held at the Pasadena Civic Auditorium, an excellent location which has underground parking and a separate banquet hall. I never really liked wearing a tuxedo because I feel somewhat awkward in it. Once I even put the cummerbund on upside down. I can't tie those stupid bow ties so I use those clip-on ties. Those dinky cuff links are hard to button. I swear I feel like a penguin stuffed into one of those tuxes. When my wife and I arrived at the cordoned-off street in front of the auditorium, valets would open our doors and politely help us out and whisk away our car to some unknown destination.

We were then escorted up a long red carpet to the auditorium entrance with the area on either side of the carpet roped off to keep spectators from clogging up the path. Flashbulbs were always going off because often stars would be arriving ahead or behind us as we walked in the door. I remember someone from the crowd asking me, "Are you someone?" I just shook my head no.

We generally got there about an hour before the doors closed. The program was broadcast live to the world at 6 P.M. West Coast time, 9 P.M. East Coast time. During that hour we met old friends and had a drink or two. My wife and I usually had soft drinks only because we really don't drink very often and I didn't want to say something stupid if I had too much to drink. As nominees, we were seated pretty close to the front of the stage.

The technical awards ceremonies used to be just as much a gala affair as the prime time awards with a live orchestra, stars as presenters and well-choreographed entertainment so that we all felt we were just as important as those people accepting their awards the next evening. But in later years, I guess costs had to be contained, so most of the frills were dispensed with; and the awards were given out, followed by dinner. It's a shame that the crafts and other technical people are relegated to the status of second class citizens within the television Academy, but that's the way it has always been, not that it's right.

My own first Emmy Award was an example of how I often had the good fortune to be in the right place at the right time for many of my career accomplishments. My friend and co-editor Craig Curtis and I were assigned to edit a Julie Andrews special in late 1965. I had just finished editing another special, *Lorne Greene's American West*, when I was asked to edit the Andrews program. Curtis and I worked with Alan Handley, a director with whom we had both worked on many other television specials. Handley was also the director of the first Dinah Shore television series, which debuted in 1951.

We used the NBC double system method of a kinescope work print to edit the special. Then the edit information derived from the edited work print was used to conform the videotape master. Over a 12-year period, more than 300 series and specials for all the networks were edited by this method. We used conventional film editing equipment and techniques and were able to accomplish far more with this process and be absolutely frame-accurate than with any other editing process at that time. Craig and I were both in on the development of this process since we were USC Cinema students together and had the most film editing experience of any of the NBC editors at that time. Craig and I were sort of the Frick and Frack of television. We edited many programs together and were asked for most often by producers and directors until Craig eventually went into a management position at NBC.

During the editing of the Julie Andrews special, we were heavily involved in all phases of post-production. On one occasion, we needed the sound effect of a boiling cauldron for a sequence. Our sound effects library didn't have one so Curtis and I improvised. We found an electric coffee maker, filled it with water and let it heat up. Although it did bubble somewhat, it didn't have quite the effect we were looking for. I located some straws and decided to try and blow into the hot water to increase the effect.

We borrowed a microphone from a nearby studio and mounted it near the top of the coffee maker and connected it to the tape recorder. Since we were improvising, we didn't have a sound proof booth to keep extraneous noise away from the mike. We told everyone to be quiet for at least ten seconds while we recorded this effect. I told Curtis to start the recorder while I blew into the straw. However, because the straw was wax coated and not intended for hot liquids, it came apart in the hot water. But we persevered. I cooled the straw off under some cold water and then quickly plunged it into the hot water, while blowing into the water. After a number of tries it worked, but I ended up with a lot of soggy straws.

When we had the first work print cut of the program, Julie Andrews was invited to a screening to give us her opinion. She watched for a while and then said, "Stop. You've mixed the colors in that shot." Since our work print was in black and white, it was nearly impossible for us to tell what colors were on the work print. Julie Andrews, of course, knew what she was wearing; we had used another take in which she had changed the color of something she was wearing. We edited in a different take equal in performance and she was quite pleased. The special aired on NBC in November of 1965. It also won a Peabody award. When the Emmy nominations came out the following year, I was surprised to see that there were only two programs nominated for videotape editing, not the usual five. One was the *Lorne Greene's American West* special and the other was the Julie Andrews special, both of which I had edited. I couldn't lose! Now it was just a matter of which one would win. I was elated.

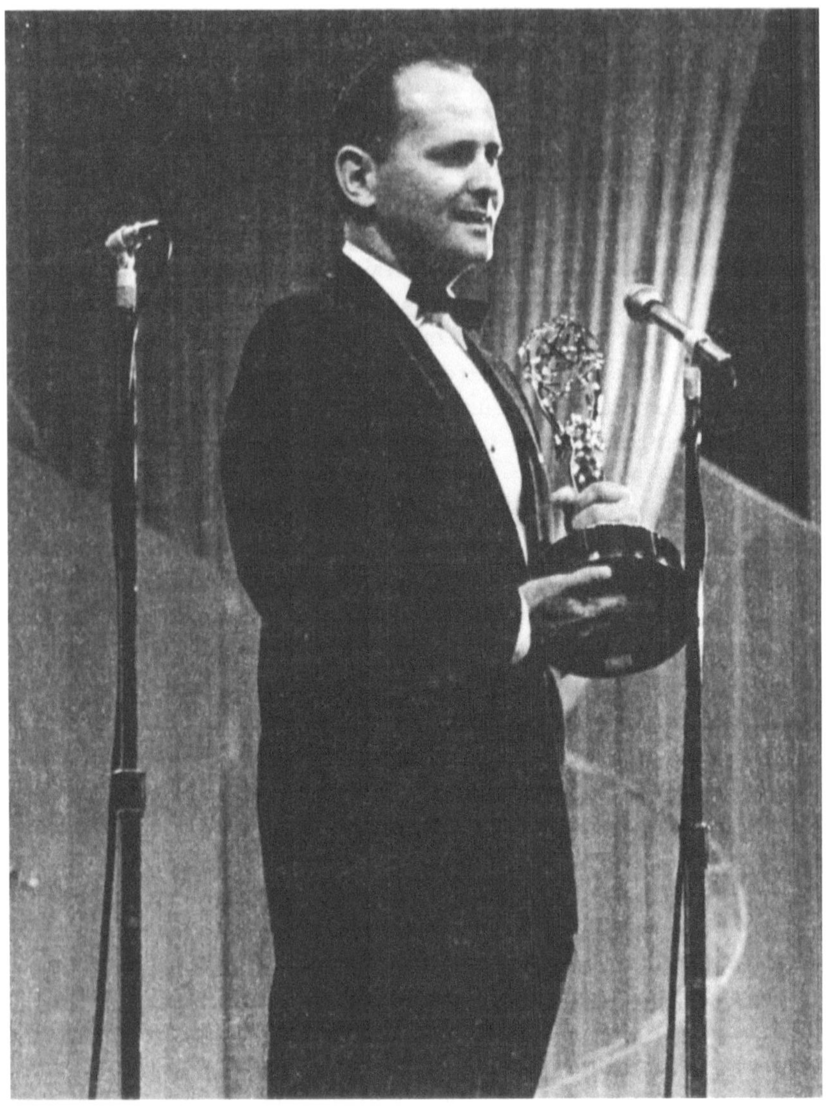

Author accepting Emmy for Julie Andrews special, 1966.

The Emmy Awards were held in the Hollywood Palladium on Sunset Boulevard in the heart of Hollywood. We were seated with our wives at the same table. At our table was my wife Dee, Craig Curtis and his wife Susie, Robert Vaughn, Mary Ann Mobley, director Alan Handley and several other personalities.

As I wrote earlier, the policy of the Television Academy was to only broadcast live those awards relating to the stars and what are known in the industry as "above the line" people. In simple terms, above the line is an imaginary line separating the production budget from the crafts or post-production budget in any production. The crafts people (including camera, sound, editing, lighting and dozens of other skilled categories) are considered below-the-line people. The production side included actors and actresses, producers, directors, writers and musicians. In order to resolve this problem, the Television Academy decided to air only the above-the-line personalities; therefore, the editing and other technical awards were given prior to going on the air with the Emmy telecast. There have been a number of changes in this policy, but the Academy still feels that the viewing audience is more interested in seeing stars than any of the so-called "crafts people." They are probably right. However, crafts people in general have always felt slighted by the Academy in that regard. To give credit to the Academy, the winners were selected just before going on the air and their names and awards were announced and each winner was photographed during the live telecast.

When the nominations for the best edited videotape programs were announced, my heart was pounding. Even though I knew I would win for one program or the other, the excitement was enough to give me the jitters. After all, this program was being seen by millions of people. Danny Kaye was the master of ceremonies. When he said, "And the winner is…. [pause, pause, pause] the Julie Andrews special," the audience applauded and Craig Curtis and I walked—no, I think we ran up to the stage to accept our awards.

I was so nervous on stage with all those stars and other guests looking at me, my knees were shaking. I had a speech all prepared but I forgot most of it and improvised. All I remember is thanking Alan Handley, Julie Andrews and my wife and children. Craig Curtis did a little better because he was a bit more composed than I was. The NBC photographers took several photos which hang in my office today. When we got back to the table, I kissed my wife and gave her the statuette to hold. I noticed that there was nothing inscribed on the silver band around the base of the Emmy. I later found out that I had to return the Emmy to the Academy and it would be properly inscribed and returned to me. This obviously was to prevent anyone from knowing in advance who the winners were.

For every nomination, the Academy gives the nominee a plaque as a remembrance. It is quite an honor just to be nominated since many very talented people never even get that far. My career includes seven Emmy nominations, four Emmy Awards and an A.C.E. "Eddie" nomination. I'll talk about those later in this book.

I also received an NBC Service Award, but the story surrounding that ceremony is rather embarrassing. It happened in 1966, when I was editing a Danny Kaye special. His wife Sylvia Fine was the producer. There was a lot of complex editing and (as usual) I worked a lot of overtime. This particular Friday, however, was the evening of the annual NBC Awards ceremony and dinner held at the Beverly Hills Hotel Crystal Room. This annual event was a tribute to the longtime employees and honored them for their loyal service. However, you were not honored until you had been with the company for ten or more consecutive years and only employees were invited. On my tenth anniversary, I received a plaque for loyal service.

On my fifteenth anniversary, I really wanted to go since I was to receive another plaque and it was a chance to enjoy the festivities. I was editing the Danny Kaye special and I asked to come in early that day so as to be able to leave by five. I even told the staff of my request the day before so there wouldn't be any surprises. At 4:30, I asked producer Jess Oppenheimer to meet me in the hall and asked him if I could leave by five.

He said he would take care of it. Since we were still editing and Jess knew I had to leave, he told Sylvia Fine there was a phone call for her upstairs in the tape room. When she left, Jess said, "Go!" I sneaked out the basement tunnel under the parking lot and left. I don't know what happened when Jess told Sylvia I had gone, but the following Monday she had a strange look on her face and said nothing.

I got to the Beverly Hills Hotel where they valet-parked my car. Because of heavy Friday night traffic, I got there about an hour late. There was an open bar so I had a couple of drinks and then a few more and before I knew it, I had consumed ten drinks in an hour. I was so drunk that my friends had to help me to my table. When I sat down, my face fell into the salad plate and I came up with a piece of lettuce on my forehead. Everyone thought it was very funny but me.

I started to drink lots of coffee at dinner which helped somewhat but did not get rid of the nausea I felt. I got up and started for the men's room, but I didn't quite make it. Halfway there, I barfed on the red carpeting, several times as I remember. After awhile, I was stable enough to go back to my table and attempt to eat dinner. I managed to get through dinner and accept my plaque but by the end of the evening, I was feeling terrible again and didn't think I could drive home. I asked Craig Curtis and another friend, Art Lopez, to drive me home. Craig said he would drive my car and Art would follow us in his car. We started down Sunset Boulevard but a few miles from the hotel, I barfed again leaning out the window this time.

It was one o'clock in the morning when we finally arrived home. I was sitting behind the driver's seat. I pushed the driver's seat forward in order to get out and the seat hit the horn button on the steering wheel. The horn kept blaring and all the lights in the neighborhood came on. My wife came out and found Craig helping me out of the car. They each grabbed me under one arm and brought me inside to our bedroom, where I flopped backwards onto the bed. My right hand hit the nightstand so hard my wife thought the impact broke my hand. I didn't feel a thing. However, the next morning it was quite sore.

The moral to this story is, don't be stupid and try to make up for being late to a party. All I got for it was a fierce hangover for more than two weeks and a lot of embarrassment. That was the last time I ever drank like that. Ever! The following year, I attended this same function but this time the only drink I had was Seven-Up. Several people didn't believe me so I let them taste my drink. That convinced them I was a changed guy.

One assignment I remember fondly is working with director Sam Peckinpah on a special called *Noon Wine*, based on a Katherine Anne Porter story about a drifter looking for work on a farm. It was to be shot near my home in Agoura at a place called the Morrison Ranch. I was able to get my schedule adjusted so that part of the day could be spent on location, meeting Peckinpah and watching the shoot. The all-star cast included Olivia de Havilland, Jason Robards, Per Oscarsson and Theodore Bikel. I arrived early one morning before shooting began. The producer invited me to have a catered breakfast with the cast and crew. As I got in line, a giant swarm of bees took over the food line and caused everyone to scurry for cover. Although I didn't get bitten, I didn't get to eat either.

I spent several days on location taking notes given to me by the director for later use in editing. The following week, I started editing the special. Although I knew who Peckinpah was, I had only seen one of his films (probably his most famous) *The Wild Bunch*. He was a dapper little man and we got along quite well. He told me that he appreciated the fact that I was a trained film editor and not a so-called technician he was afraid would edit his television special.

We started editing and I was able to assemble what we call a first cut very quickly. Peckinpah was pleased that I was able to work so fast, partly due to the fact that we worked long hours in editing (often as much as 20 hours a day). It took me about four days to complete the first cut and then Peckinpah started to play. By that I mean he tried a lot of "what if" scenarios. This process is fine if you have enough time to try various combinations and takes to get the best performance. Although we started editing a little more than three weeks before the scheduled air date, Peckinpah's fervor for improving an already excellent performance was getting on my nerves (although I tried not to let it show).

Towards the end of the third week, I was getting worried because I still had to cut the master tape and we had to mix all the soundtracks for a final composite. I couldn't get Peckinpah to leave well enough alone so I went to my boss and told him of my concern that we would not make the air date if he continued to make changes. Perhaps if my boss went to his producers and explained to them what had to be done, Peckinpah would at least listen to them if he didn't believe me.

We set up a meeting with Peckinpah, his producers Dan Melnick and David Susskind, myself and my boss along with two of NBC's top technical people in an effort to convince Peckinpah to stop making changes in the work print. When Peckinpah directed feature films, he could move a release date back if he felt he needed more time. However, it didn't work that way in television because of the advance publicity required, promotional trailers that had to be made and a host of other technical details that would literally consume most of every day until the actual air date. The meeting with Peckinpah answered a lot of questions he had about editing videotape for television and he reluctantly agreed to finish editing by the end of the following day. What a relief!

Now the finishing work began. Because of the large number of edits and the hundreds of scenes and takes, I had to bring in help to organize the material so we could finish in a reasonable amount of time. (I didn't want to finish the program just hours before the scheduled air time, a problem I faced several times before and didn't want repeated.) Even with the extra help, we all had to work the weekend and, as it turned out, at least 20 hours a day for the next five days to be sure we finished at least one day before the air date.

Directors often schedule themselves too tightly, making commitments to their next project without taking into account the amount of technical work needed to complete a project. They feel that once the show is "in the can," they can safely go onto their next project. This leaves the technical staff cursing the director since he need not be there for the technical completion of the program. Fortunately, I had a good crew working with me; they were used to this kind of craziness and were willing to pitch in to get the job done.

I also acted as the post-production coordinator, assigning tasks to my crew so that the sequence of events flowed in the proper order. My basic task was to cut the videotape master while I supervised the preparation of the music and sound effects tracks. The one problem we all faced was the weariness of long hours day after day. Even though I was used to long hours and complex technical problems, they take a toll on you.

The sound mixing session went well and we transferred the newly mixed soundtrack to the edited videotape. What a difference music and sound effects make to a picture after working with nothing but a production dialogue track! All those watching us transfer the sound back to the videotape were quite impressed with the story, the acting and the beauty of the outdoor scenery. I heaved a sigh of relief when we finished the backup copy and shipped it off to NBC New York. We had completed this complex project the night before the scheduled air date.

Even though this project was stressful, the finished project reflected the skill of all those involved, from the actors to the director and all the other members of this team. After *Noon Wine* aired, I received two letters, the first from producer Dan Melnick, who wrote, "You did a magnificent job on *Noon Wine*. We have made a film to be proud of, and thank you for your unfailing cooperation, patience and thoroughly professional performance. It made a pleasure of a difficult and challenging piece of work."

The second letter was from Sam Peckinpah, who wrote in part, "By this time, *Noon Wine* is history...and good history at that. Needless to say, I am more than grateful for your assistance in making this one of the very finest television performances of the present year. I note that at least one reviewer remarked that 'the videotape editing by Art Schneider was the best this reviewer has seen'—should I write and tell him that we still had three more cuts to go—? Everyone concerned with the production of our show is proud of the results and I feel we have a right to be, but as the director, I must lay a hell of a lot of credit in your lap."

There were dozens of positive reviews on this project including ones from *The Hollywood Reporter*, *Weekly Variety*, the *New York Daily News*, *Time* magazine and the *San Francisco Chronicle*. I was very proud to have worked with this great director and to have him acknowledge my skills as an editor.

Toward the end of the sixties my career took a surprising twist when I began publishing articles on editing and video post-production. I had struggled through my English courses not because I wasn't capable of learning the material but because I wasn't much interested. As an adult, however, I found I enjoyed writing in my area of expertise. My writing "career" began when I wrote a few short technical memos and articles for my boss at work. After getting a number of compliments from him and other people, I decided to write an article on the editing process I helped develop at NBC. The article, titled "The Double System Method of Editing Videotape," was subsequently published in the 1969 summer issue of the *American Cinema Editor* magazine. This was my first published article of any kind and was the beginning of a writing career that is still in progress. To date, I have published more than 65 articles on editing and video post-production. Although I was not paid for my first article, I have done well by selling articles to several trade magazines over the years. At one point, I wrote so many articles for two magazines, *Broadcast Engineering* and its sister publication *Video Systems*, that I was on those magazine mastheads for many years.

Sometimes proofreading errors on the magazines' part caused me some embarrassment. In an article on the editing of the *Laugh-In* series, I wrote, "That was the beginning of one of the most exciting TV series ever produced." Everything I sent in was typed and easy to read but when the magazine came out, I was horrified to see that sentence read, "That was the beginning of one of the most exciting TV series *I* ever produced." I immediately called George Schlatter, the producer, and told him of the error. He just laughed and said not to worry since he knew who the producer really was! Over the years, there were other typographical errors but none that caused me the anxiety that this one did.

Working in Hollywood in the area of editing, I had the opportunity to meet with many television and film stars. The occasions varied from meeting them in a screening room to working with them or their offspring. While in NBC Hollywood, I met such entertainers as Jonathan Winters who, at the time, had a weekly comedy series on NBC. I would often see him in the hallway and say hi. But he never did remember my name. On one occasion, he saw me walking up Vine Street towards the old Brown Derby coffee shop and asked if he could join me. What, me tell him no? Don't be silly. He knew I worked at NBC but didn't really know who I was or what I did. Maybe he thought I was an executive.

When we got to the coffee shop and found a seat at the counter, he started up with the jokes. Within a couple of minutes, he had everyone in the restaurant in stitches. I could hardly eat my lunch, I was laughing so hard. I met and talked with him several other times and discovered that he was one of the most down-to-earth people I have ever met. He was never a put-on or exploited his popularity.

Gordon MacRae, another star I met, was a very popular singer who also had a weekly show on NBC. One day I was starting to drive out of the NBC parking lot on Vine Street when he came up to me and asked if I was going up to Hollywood Boulevard (just a few blocks away). I said sure and he got in. He introduced himself and told me he was going up to the Christian Science Reading Room on Hollywood Boulevard. I asked him if his car was in the shop and he said that he didn't own a car; he said his manager told him he didn't need one at the time. He too was very polite and gracious.

A vaudeville comedian by the name of Pinky Lee had a daily kids' show on NBC, and every once in a while he would do a sketch that required some editing. I got to know him because he sometimes came down to editing. His son Morgan and I would often visit the NBC photo lab, which was around the corner from my editing room. One time our neighbor asked me if she could get on the show. When I asked Pinky Lee, he said sure, no problem, and he even asked her name. My neighbor not only got on the show but won a wristwatch for herself. What a coincidence.

I was sometimes asked to drop off films to stars who would generally preview it at home. In one instance, I was asked to deliver a copy of a 16mm film program to Groucho Marx, who was interested in being a guest on it. I had to bring all the equipment—projector, film, screen and even an extension cord—to his home and set it up. I got to his home in Beverly Hills about ten in the morning and parked in the driveway. I unloaded all the equipment, lugged all this stuff up to the front door in two trips and rang the doorbell. In a moment, the door opened and the maid appeared. I told her who I was. She closed the door in my face

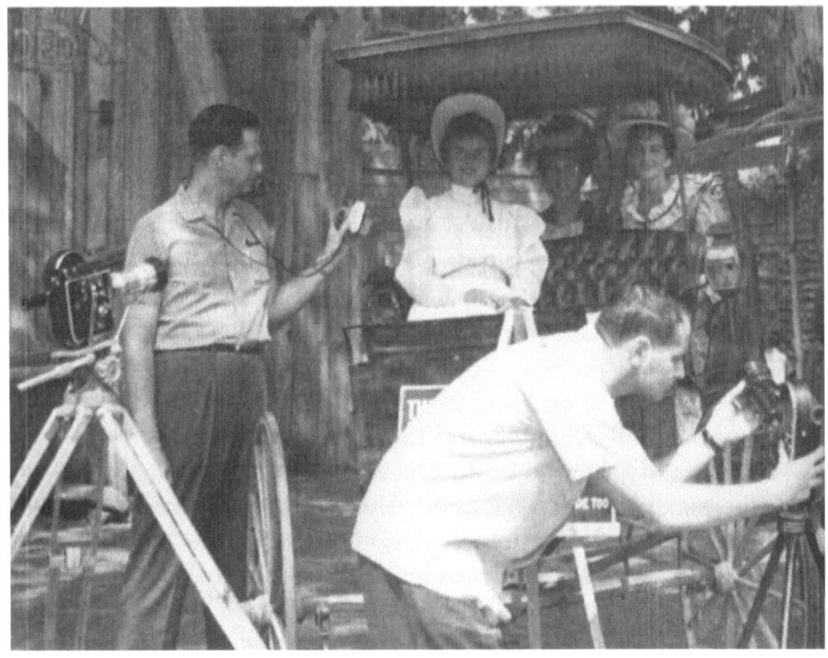

Author (foreground) and friend Don Andrews at Knotts Berry Farm.

without saying anything. I was somewhat taken aback by this and didn't quite know what to do. Should I ring the doorbell again or leave?

About a minute later, the door opened again, only this time Groucho appeared in his bathrobe. He apologized for the incident and showed me to a den where I was to set up the projector. He told me to have the maid call him when I was ready. Then he walked over to the stairway, sat down on a chair lift and pushed a button which lifted him up the stairs smoothly on a special track alongside the railing. I later found out that Groucho had a heart condition and this stair elevator was installed so that he didn't have to exert himself. When I had everything ready, I called the maid and she summoned Groucho. I was all prepared to meet this funny man and be a straight man for his jokes. To my dismay, Groucho never cracked a joke while I was there. After we screened the film, we sat and talked for almost an hour. Groucho showed me some of the photos and awards he'd received over the years but never said even one funny thing. Still, I greatly enjoyed this chance to meet and talk one-on-one with this great legend of comedy.

On another occasion, I was asked to deliver a film to the home of

Red Skelton, one of my favorite comedians. It was after work, and I arrived at his home in Brentwood (a posh section of Beverly Hills) a little after eight. This was in late July and it was quite hot. I drove up Skelton's semi-circular driveway and parked near the entrance. As I got out of my car, I heard laughter coming from the open window directly above the front door. I walked slowly, trying to hear what was being said. I heard Skelton telling someone, "That's funny, write it down." I soon discovered that they were watching Milton Berle on television and "selecting" jokes that they might use on Skelton's show. I rang the doorbell and after a few minutes, the door opened and Skelton appeared. His foyer was quite unusual in that it was decorated all in white, including a white piano and white carpeting. I was almost afraid to step on the carpet for fear of leaving footprints but Skelton made me feel at ease. After exchanging some pleasantries, I left.

When I was supervising editor of CFI in Hollywood, the son of Gregory Peck, Steve Peck, came to work in the videotape division. He worked in all areas since I suspect his dad wanted him to get an understanding of the post-production process. Steve was a great guy, easy to get along with but somewhat shy. He stayed with us for quite some time. He would sit in the editing room and watch while I edited. After the client left, he would sometimes ask questions about what I had done to make a particular edit work.

In 1974, I was asked to show someone a brief two-inch videotape of a child's birthday party. I told management that I would in about ten minutes, as soon as I finished editing a project in progress. As soon as my client walked out of the editing room, I told them to bring him in and I would be happy to run his tape. The gentleman walked in and I was introduced. His name was Ray Bradbury. He was the author of many books and I was aware of his celebrity status. He gave me a two-inch videotape which I set up on one of the tape playback machines and ran it for him several times since it was only a few minutes long. We chatted awhile and he thanked me and as a gift offered me an autographed copy of his book "The Machineries of Joy." I thanked him for his generosity but he repeatedly thanked me for taking the time to show him this special tape.

Another celebrity I worked with was the actor Burgess Meredith famous for many movie roles and for playing the "Penguin" in the *Batman* TV series. He brought in several hours of home movies which had to be rearranged and some material removed. I often gave him suggestions on what to do to improve the material and he readily accepted all of them, which I thought was exceptionally nice of him. When lunch time approached, he invited me to join him but I didn't feel right about intruding on his lunch so I bowed out, saying that I had other plans even though I didn't. I must say he was very cordial and pleasant and that we had an enjoyable day watching and editing his home movies.

In 1965, I was involved with our union while at NBC and I was asked to go to New York for a conference regarding local jurisdiction of editing. It was a last-minute thing and I ended up taking the "Red Eye" flight from Los Angeles to New York which left at 11 at night. Due to contractual obligations, I was "forced" to fly first class. I got on the plane and sat down next to the window. The seat next to me was empty. A few minutes later, a smartly dressed gray-haired lady came to the seat and, with a whisk broom, dusted off the empty seat.

I was somewhat amused by her action but really thought nothing of it. She then deposited a briefcase on the spotless seat next to me. Just before the last call for boarding, a tall distinguished gentleman sat down next to me. After a few minutes, we exchanged pleasantries and found we had some things in common. The man's name was Paul Monash, the producer of the television series *Peyton Place*. One thing led to another and after many drinks, we both were quite relaxed and we started talking about everything under the sun. Monash told me about his private life and all his problems, as if we had been friends for years.

We arrived in New York early in the morning when it was still dark. It was pouring rain. I thanked him for a most enjoyable trip and said I was going to get a cab to my hotel. He told me, "Nonsense. You'll never get a cab at this time of night. Come with me in my limousine. I'll have my driver drop you off at your hotel after he drops me off." Wow! We waited under an awning at the curb and in a few minutes, this long sleek black limousine, about a block long, pulled up and parked in front of us. The driver got out and put our bags in the trunk while we both got in and sat down in absolute luxury. There was a television set, a wet bar, a car phone and even a small refrigerator stocked with all kinds of snacks. We continued to talk (and eat) during the ride into the city. After his driver dropped Mr. Monash off at his hotel, I told the driver where my hotel was. When we got there, the driver grabbed my bags, escorted me into the lobby and directly to the registration desk, where he made sure I was signed in. The driver then saluted, clicked his heels and left. I had never been treated so well and had a great flight with one of the top television producers of that time.

I'm sure I've forgotten many of the people I've worked with over the years, most of whom were pleasant and interesting people. I'm not trying to be a name-dropper but I thought readers would be interested in knowing some positive information about stars that usually does not get in the tabloids.

CHAPTER SIX

Laugh-In

One of the most successful and copied television series in history was a series called *Rowan and Martin's Laugh-In*, a comedy variety series starring Dan Rowan and Dick Martin that spoofed everyone and everything. I was involved in that series from the pilot and well into the series. Even after I left NBC in 1968 to pursue other things, I was involved with *Laugh-In* in other ways which I'll cover later in this chapter. At the time, I had no idea of the impact this series would have on me and the rest of the world.

George Schlatter was a producer of television specials at NBC. For years, I edited many of his television specials including one called *The Colgate Comedy Hour*, a remake of the mid–1950s weekly series on NBC. One day in the summer of 1967, George called me into his office and told me about this special he wanted me to edit, called *Laugh-In*. The script was four inches thick and weighed more than four pounds. He asked me to take it home and read it. In the '60s, almost everything was an "in" of some sort. At the time, I thought *Laugh-In* was kind of a dumb name. That evening, I started reading the script and started to laugh and laugh and laugh. I called George the next day and asked, "When do we start?"

We began shooting the special in July 1967. There was a large amount of material recorded on tape (in excess of eight hours) that would eventually be cut down to one hour. In addition, an outside film company called Group One hired by Schlatter shot 16mm color film segments that would be transferred to videotape which I would later edit into the program. (For example, Bob Collins, the cameraman, would go on location and shoot funny sequences of Judy Carne covered with body paint.)

We started editing the special in August. George and I worked 20 hours a day for three weeks, eating mostly Kentucky Fried Chicken. I put the work print together from the script and showed it to George. He was very disappointed. I think he cried. Needless to say, I was also not happy with the results. The continuity of the program was in chaos. George went back to his office and worked over the script and came up with a new idea. I disassembled the work print and started over, this time with a completely different format. The second cut was a little better, but George was still not happy. Back to the drawing board again. I re-edited a third cut which was an improvement over the second but George was still not happy. Take it apart and redo it a fourth time. Better, but not there yet.

At this point, almost three weeks of 20 hour days had gone by and we were both a little punchy. But George did not give up. We edited a fifth version. I hoped this was the last version because I was getting sick of fried chicken. Also, the film work print was starting to fall apart from so much wear and tear. There were so many patches on the work print that I had to ask for copies or reprints of several elements that were beyond repair. These new work print copies usually got to me in less than four hours provided there was a VTR available to play the tape and a recording engineer to make the new work print. Fortunately, NBC had its own 16mm black and white processing lab in house which speeded up our requests for these reprints.

I put the fifth version of the work print on the projector and ran it for George. He started to laugh right from the beginning and so did I. Even before the program ended, we both knew we had a hit.

It appears that the nickname of "Jump Cut" given to me in 1965 by Bob Hope was really being put to the test with this special. This is the fastest paced program I've ever edited and it set a trend others tried to emulate. The jokes came so fast that if you didn't pay attention, they would be gone and all you could say was, "What was that?" Admittedly, this was a new style of editing for me since all other comedy programs I had edited were paced and timed for laughs in the conventional way.

In 1967, there were a lot of things that were taboo and couldn't be said or seen on television but George Schlatter proved that he could get by without really offending the viewing audience or the NBC censors too often. The censors were hovering over us like vultures waiting to see the next thing George would try to sneak by them. Even an offstage toilet flush was not allowed, but somehow George managed to get that in the program. These things were not dirty but somewhat "risqué" then. By today's standards, they're quite tame.

When we finished viewing the program, we congratulated each other and George knew he had a winner. But before he left the room, I told him there was something missing, sort of a statement or maybe a kind of punctuation needed to cap off the program. He asked me what it was but I had no idea. I said, "Let me think about it and I'll get back to you tomorrow."

I went home early that day for the first time in about three weeks. I told Dee what we had been doing and asked her if she had any ideas. All during dinner that evening, I tried to think of what was missing. I tried to go to sleep, but when you have things on your mind, it is often impossible. I was beginning to think I had been hallucinating. As I tried to doze off, I kind of got a feeling of what was missing. Then, like the proverbial light bulb going on over my head, I knew what it needed.

I couldn't wait to get to work the next morning. I ran down to my editing room without even getting a cup of coffee. That in itself was unusual. I rummaged through the trims I had been saving to be filed away. I found it. It was the shot of Arte Johnson as the little German in the helmet coming up from behind the potted plant saying, "Verrry interesting." As soon as the credits were over, I spliced on this clip and called George. He came over and without telling him what I had done, I showed him the last few minutes of the program. When the little German came up, George applauded and said, "That's it, that's what it needed!" And that's how the little German became the tag capping off every *Laugh-In* program thereafter. I guess this kind of innovation from the writers and others is what made *Laugh-In* the success it was.

Rowan and Martin's Laugh-In special was first broadcast on September 9, 1967 and it started a trend that is still copied today. Even though the special was very successful, I've heard that NBC was a bit leery about putting it on as a series since George did have a number of "disagreements" with the NBC censors. However, in January of 1968, *Laugh-In* replaced the series *The Man from U.N.C.L.E.* It went on at eight o'clock Mondays and became as popular as any television series of its time.

Once *Laugh-In* became a series, the editing hours were very long. I became somewhat punchy after continuous 15-hour days, six days a week, month after month. My regular schedule was nine A.M. to midnight six days a week. (I had Sundays off since I suspect NBC might have gone broke with the union penalties, overtime and "golden hours" I might have accumulated.) As it was, I more than doubled my salary every week for about six months. I was so tired that I slept most every Sunday for weeks at a time. I only saw my kids either before school or for a few hours on Sundays. This was no way to live. But at that time in my life, I was just getting recognized by the industry and I wanted to keep the momentum going as long as I could. I guess my ego was getting in the way of common sense.

There was an incident during one of the tapings where a segment was recorded with a prerecorded soundtrack (one made days earlier in a sound studio). The idea was for the actors on stage to lip sync to that track and make it work. Sounds easy? Not on your life.

When the recorded show material arrived in my room the next day, I started to break it down and began to synchronize all the soundtracks with their associated work pictures. When I got to the segment using the prerecorded soundtrack, the sound was way out of sync with the picture. I scratched my head and said to myself, "What the hell is going on?" I sat there for a moment pondering the situation. All the other pieces were in perfect sync except for this prerecorded number. (It's very easy to synchronize picture and soundtracks with a visual aid such as a slate with clapsticks attached since it is only necessary to find the point where the two sticks just come together and line that up with the sound. I also pride myself in being able to get picture and sound in absolute lip sync by guessing at sync without clapsticks or other aids, often on the first or second attempt.)

Try as I might, I could not find even one word that would match lip sync. I thought that perhaps some of the equipment had failed during the making of the work print and the sound was running either slow or fast. Perhaps, I had somehow gotten the soundtrack confused with a different take. Then again, maybe I had been working too many hours without a break and was punch drunk. The last seemed most likely at the time. I tried one more time to lip sync the picture to the soundtrack and finally gave up.

I called George Schlatter and told him I thought we had a serious problem with one of the numbers. A few minutes later he and associate producer Carolyn Raskin came down and I proceeded to play the segment. "See," I said. "It is way out of lip sync and there is no way I can get it to work." George turned to Carolyn and they stared at each other for a second, then began to laugh hysterically. I said, "What's so funny?" Then George told me the number was deliberately shot that way as a gag on the show but they purposely didn't tell me just to get my reaction. The gag was to have the actors deliberately mouth different words to the soundtrack. It was never meant to be in lip sync but I was the only one who didn't know that!

George had a way of getting around the censors in a very clever way. It was kind of a game with George because he knew how stuffy they could be. In order to throw them off guard, he would have the band laugh at straight lines and be silent during the punchline of a joke. This confused the censors since they couldn't understand why the band laughed at things that weren't funny and didn't laugh at the obviously funny stuff. The censors were always on the lookout for something George might try to get by with. Even when the censors got the script in advance, a joke on paper would not always come across the way it was written on the page. When a joke was shot, the person saying the lines, the inflections and even body language affected the way the joke played. The censors would be on the set every shooting day, their ears pointed upwards in anticipation, always watching with an eagle eye for anything they could delete in the name of decency. George was very clever since he was able to get material by the censors other producers feared to even try.

One day, I received a telegram from the Television Academy notifying me that I was nominated for an Emmy Award for the 1967 *Laugh-In* special. This was my second nomination for an Emmy. The television Academy provided all the nominees with a get-acquainted lunch to let the press meet the nominees. In a ceremony, we were all presented with our nomination plaques. However, this time I had a lot of competition from four other excellent programs and an Emmy for me was not a shoo-in.

Once again the Television Academy presented the technical awards at a special ceremony the evening before the telecast. It was an elegant affair, as much as the main awards ceremony itself. Stars were there as presenters. There was entertainment and a dinner dance after the ceremony, a duplicate of the main awards ceremony. Since the *Laugh-In* special was the most popular show on television that season, people were shaking my hand before the ceremony and congratulating me on my nomination. Dee and I had a great time. When the awards ceremony started, I was getting very nervous and I wasn't sure if I would win even though *Laugh-In* was winning awards in many categories that evening. When they finally got to the videotape editing category, I was shaking in my shoes. The host named the five nominees and said, "And the winner is ... Art Schneider for the *Laugh-In* special." All I remember is that the audience let out what seemed to me at the time a roar of approval. As I got up to go to the stage, people were slapping me on the back and trying to shake my hand. I got up on the stage but I don't remember what I said. I stood there awestruck and speechless for a moment but did manage to thank Schlatter and other key people on the show. Believe me, it was a very short speech. The NBC photographers took my picture once again which I am thankful for since I have another memento of that special occasion. I believe *Laugh-In* won eleven Emmy Awards that evening.

It's difficult to imagine the thrill of such an exciting evening along with being nominated for a total of seven Emmy Awards from 1965 to 1984. In 1968, I was nominated for editing the *Laugh-In* series but for some reason, no videotape editing award was given for any program even though there were five nominees. There was a lot of grumbling from the tape editing nominees and, a few weeks after the awards were over, a gripe session with the Television Academy officers was held at NBC to air our grievances. I felt the least they could have done was to notify us that no awards would be given that night.

When *Laugh-In* first came on, it took people a little time to get used to its unusual format with rapid fire jokes and one-liners. It was not the style of editing I had been used to on shows like the Bob Hope and the Danny Thomas specials. On those programs and others, you usually leave room for laughs. But *Laugh-In* was very different. Jokes were rapid fire and came one on top of the next with no room for laughs. With very careful use of the laugh machine and absolute control over the level of the laughs, the beginning of the next joke came through strong enough so that the audience was able to hear all the jokes through the laughter. It was almost like laughing continuously for one solid hour every week.

Schlatter had a knack of getting famous personalities on the show (usually by some form of trickery) to say one-liners. Few of these people realized how these lines would later be used in context with someone else's one-liner, which made for some very funny jokes. Richard Nixon (who said "Sock it to me?"), John Wayne, Johnny Carson and Jack Benny were just a few of the hundreds of stars George sort of "commandeered" to be on the program. I think George had scouts waiting outside in the main studio hallway in case a star showed up so that he would get that star to say a dozen or so non sequitur lines. The star's expression was often one of pure amazement because they usually did not know what was going on. Several weeks or months later, these one liners would be edited together with other one-liners to come up with some of the most outrageous and funny lines one could imagine.

Because Schlatter was too busy with other things to come to editing on a weekly basis, Carolyn Raskin, a very talented lady, worked with me in putting the series together every week. When I edited the special, I was working by myself. When we started the series, I had another editor, John Teele, work with me since the workload turned out to be more than one person could handle. Here's a synopsis of what it took to put *Laugh-In* on every week.

To make sure that we could intercut videotape segments from week to week, the two-inch format videotape machines had to be set up in a special way. One of the problems we faced is that no two video heads were manufactured exactly alike. To prevent a compatibility problem, at the beginning of each season we would select the two best video heads we could find. After the first day's recording of the new season, we removed the video head from the VTR and stored it until it was needed each week to record new show material. In that way, we would be assured that every recording would match subsequent recordings made week after week for the entire season. Although it was not crucial to the compatibility problem, we also persuaded NBC to let us record each episode on the same two VTRs every week as a little bit of extra insurance. Even though NBC owned 24 VTRs in Burbank, we felt that recording on the same machines every week would allow us to maintain optimum quality.

We went even further to be sure that every physical splice we made would pass through the video head without so much as a glitch. This was especially important since material from the first week's recording could conceivably be used on the last episode of the season, some 25 shows later; a perfect splice was imperative. To insure this, at the beginning of the season, we recorded about ten minutes of industry standard color bars which were used as a reference to set recording and playback criteria for all videotapes. Each week prior to the start of recording from the studio, we would mount the video heads we allocated for *Laugh-In* on each machine. Two VTRs were used, one for the master copy and one which was a backup copy. Both machines were set up to the same color bar standard. After the machines were adjusted, a short recording of new color bars was made on each machine. Then a piece of tape about four seconds long was cut off the standard tape and spliced into the head of the just-recorded new tape for that week.

The newly intercut and spliced tape was played back and we would watch the splice as it ran through the video head to see if there was any disturbance of the video signal or if there was any interruption in the color. This process was necessary because the videotape machines used to record *Laugh-In* were also used on a regular basis to record other programs and from time to time, slight adjustment might be made by other tape operators or maintenance personnel that would change the recording characteristics of the machine. Therefore, we had to be vigilant to be sure that every recording matched every other recording. It was a painfully slow process each week but it was worth all the effort. Bill Gamboa was our chief recordist, a meticulous engineer and a really great guy. He massaged those two machines with great finesse so that I never had the slightest worry about the technical quality of any of our tapes.

More than 400 individual shots were recorded every week but not all of that material would be used in a particular episode. The scripts were often overwritten to be able to use this material at a later date. You can understand that if a piece of tape recorded at the beginning of the season didn't match a tape recorded at the end of the season, we would be in real trouble. Fortunately, the recording and editing staff were very good at their jobs and I never worried that the recorded tapes would not match from week to week.

As an editor at NBC in the decades of the fifties, sixties and seventies, not only did I have to know how to edit, but I also had to be a skilled videotape operator familiar with all the technical stuff needed to record and play back broadcast quality pictures and sound. We were technically called television "engineers" but few of us had engineering degrees. That term only meant that we were assigned to the engineering group within the union.

I've always liked to tinker with mechanical things and learned a lot more about the operation of these $100,000-plus videotape machines than was required of tape operators at NBC. Sometimes in my zealousness to adjust the machines to try and get just a bit more quality out of them, I would misadjust something else and I would have to call for one of the maintenance engineers to come over and fix it. We used to carry tiny green-handled screwdrivers to "tweak" or fine tune the controls on these machines and one time the maintenance group threatened to take away my "greenie" screwdriver if I didn't stop messing with some of the off-limits controls. Because of this temptation, someone had a placard made up and posted it on the walls of the tape room at NBC. It said, "Don't tweak yourself into twubble."

Record-keeping was vital to the success of our editing efforts. During production of each weekly episode, the tape operator would make a log of all the scenes, takes, time code numbers and any other pertinent information needed to locate material. Everything was recorded on one-hour rolls. To insure that we would never lose anything, I used a very simple slating system. The first thing we ever recorded was slated Scene 101. The next takes were slated as 102, 103, 104, etc. For the second roll, I changed the slate to 201 for the first item. Then we continued with 202, 203, 204, etc. The roll number increased by one every time we started a ncw tapc roll. In this way, every scene or take had a unique identifying number and there could be no duplication of slate numbers. By looking through our logs, we could tell when a take was recorded and where it was located on the reel. These logs were our "bible" and were critical to the success of the editing process.

Two master videotapes were always recorded. The primary tape was the one that was eventually broken apart and spliced together to create the edited master tape for broadcast. The other tape was stored uncut in a vault, acting as a backup in case something unforeseen happened to the edited original tape. Fortunately, nothing ever happened to the edited master. However, from time to time, several of the *Laugh-In* production backup tapes would be used to copy selected material for promotional trailers or other uses such as showing outtakes for use on the *Tonight* show. All optical or special effects were recorded in the studio including the opening and closing credits. There were no fades or dissolves added during editing. Each act cut up from black and cut to black going into commercial. On the average, about seven hours of production material was shot for every episode. On every seventh show, the unused ("banked") material was used to create another episode. About the only new material recorded would be Dan Rowan and Dick Martin's opening and monologue. My bookkeeping system was simple and enabled anyone to find material quickly. Two types of banked material would be saved, the 16mm kinescope film work print and its corresponding soundtrack along with the two-inch videotape master of the same material. The work print takes of banked material were kept in boxes or, if they were to be used soon, hung on wire hooks in a fiberboard barrel called a "trim bin." A row of pin type hooks was mounted above the bin to allow the storage of film pieces as short as one frame. After the edited film work print was approved, the primary videotape was broken down by scene and take number and stored on small plastic reels.

The kinescope film work print was developed in the film processing lab in the basement of NBC Burbank. As soon as it was developed, I would synchronize the picture with the corresponding magnetic soundtrack for that reel of film. Then I would break apart each reel into scenes and takes, identifying the slate by writing it on the head of the film and magnetic soundtrack using a white grease pencil. Each one-hour reel would contain as many as 60 takes. I would then roll up these little pieces of film and soundtrack together and temporarily store them on a rack on the editing bench in front of me. Due to the nature of the show, nothing was ever recorded in show order. That's why it was necessary to first break the material apart and later sort it by where it fit into the script. I would also save anything I noted during production or during editing as a candidate for our outtake or "goof" reel. Next I would put all 350 or 400 little pieces in script order, but this did not mean the shots would necessarily *stay* in that order.

I should point out that only during the first *Laugh-In* special and one or two episodes of the series was an audience allowed in the studio. It was felt that the length of the production day was longer than most people could stand. In addition, it took a lot of time to change sets and costumes and the concern was that the audience may not be inclined to laugh after six or seven hours in their seats. Early on, it was decided to add laughs in the sound mixing session where they could be carefully controlled. In order to maintain the quality of the laughs so they sounded as though they belonged to the audience, Charlie Douglass and his associates recorded the laughs in those first few episodes from the same studio where each episode was shot so that the acoustical sounds would match. This worked so well that no one realized that the laughs were "canned."

The work print editing of each one-hour episode took an average of 24 hours (two 12 hour days) to assemble. That was done on Monday and Tuesday of each week. However, my average workday was almost always at least 15 hours due to preparatory work, filling out paperwork and performing other duties. The work print editing is where the pacing and timing were integrated by prudent editing. Sixteen-millimeter film is not the easiest way to edit since the images must either be viewed on a somewhat cumbersome film viewer or inspected through a magnifying glass. I had originally suggested using a 35mm work print since we were already set up for it in editing but it was decided not to do it for two reasons. First, it would require sending the undeveloped film to a lab in Hollywood, potentially causing a delay in its return. Second, the cost using

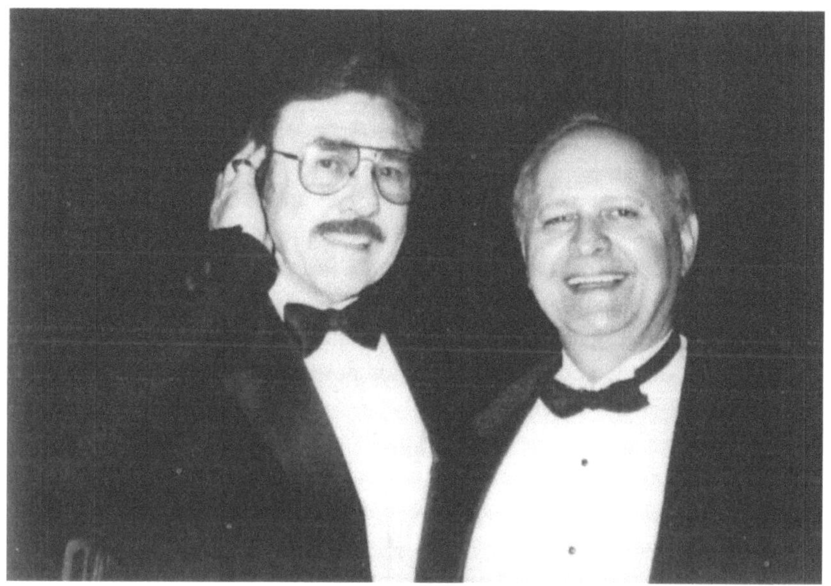

Author and Gary Owens, announcer and actor on *Laugh-In*.

35mm, even as a work print, was about four times the cost of 16mm (which could be processed in our own NBC lab in Burbank). The schedule was so tight that if anyone even hiccuped, it would have thrown a monkey wrench into the editing process. We rarely had a preemption where we could take a breather.

On Wednesday, the work print was viewed by the production staff and changes were made for continuity and time. After the viewing I would make the required changes. Generally these were minor, often just re-arranging the order of sequences rather than re-editing. From time to time the NBC continuity department (the censors) would insist on a change or a deletion but that was rather rare.

Thursdays were used to finish making changes as well as to construct a second soundtrack (called a "B" roll) which contained music, sound effects or narration. This second track was in frame synchronization with the production soundtrack and was blended or mixed with the production sound to create the final composite soundtrack. The B track consisted mostly of music tags sometimes called "lick playoffs" and other things such as sound effects or other specialized sounds that were not practical to add in a sound mixing session.

Friday was the sound mixing day. I would bring the program on two

30-minute reels to Glen Glenn Sound Company in Hollywood where the laughs were added, all the separate tracks mixed and a new composite soundtrack created. This new soundtrack would later replace the original, unsweetened (unmixed) production soundtrack on the master tape. Glen Glenn Sound Company had 16mm projectors that were reversible, enabling the mixer to go back to a just-missed laugh or applause with relative ease.

The fellow who did most of the laugh work on *Laugh-In* was Charlie Douglass, an expert in his field. Charlie had a special laugh machine which he designed and built. There are many separate loops of laughs, applause and other types of sound enhancement material in this so-called "laugh machine." In order to change tapes, he had to unlock a large brass padlock on the side of the box (he didn't want anyone to see what was inside). Every time he needed to change tracks, he would disconnect the machine and wheel it into a corner or behind a curtain so as not to have anyone peek over his shoulder. Sometimes a laugh would be too strong or too weak, so we would stop and back up to just ahead of the area needed to be corrected. Then Charlie would redo the laugh, then continue adding new laughs or go back and modify laughs he had just done. Generally, mixing all the separate soundtracks together and adding laughs took about one eight-hour day.

It is interesting to know how the famous single handclap on the end of every *Laugh-In* series episode came about. One day we were getting ready to mix the sound on one of the episodes when John Pratt, one of Charlie Douglass's assistants, was warming up his laugh machine by playing different laugh combinations. John then played a single handclap. Carolyn Raskin, the show's producer, asked John what that was. John replied that he just used it to warm up the machine and test it. Carolyn said she wanted to use that hand clap. John objected, saying Charlie Douglass didn't want it used on anything. I think that was just a put-on.

Near the end of the mixing session, Carolyn told John to use the single handclap and start it over the Romart production logo and keep it rolling through the end of the NBC chimes and into black. George delivered the show as per contract and NBC now could do anything to it they wished. When NBC previewed the episode the day of air, the executives went ballistic. They said we were desecrating the NBC chimes and they wouldn't allow it to go on the air. George was smart. He delivered the tape only hours before it was to air, knowing that it would be too late to change it. As we all know, the handclap went on the air and from then on everyone waited for the single handclap on *Laugh-In*. I've even heard that other programs have added a handclap to the end of their program, imitating what we had done.

Once the sound mixing was complete, the videotape had to be cut and spliced or conformed to the edited film work print. This was one of the most time-consuming and non-creative parts of editing each episode. Since there were so many quick edits, sometimes ten edits or more per minute, it was a tedious job to locate each edit and carefully splice it together. If a quick cut of less than a second was made on the work print, it would be too short to be able to read the ESG (Edit Sync Guide) voice track time code. Careful notes had to be made of those short cuts during the editing process so that a frame-accurate log could be generated later.

When a cut was very short, I would find the correct voice code before actually splicing the film and note the code on the exact frame. I would then use a very fine India ink pen and write this tiny frame number on the clear edge of film between the sprocket holes and put an "X" on the precise frame where I was about to make the splice. In that way, I would be assured that that critical number would be written in ink on the film itself. When it came time to generate a cutting log later on, I would only need to look at the film at the splice and read the number, transferring that information to the cutting log. Fortunately, short cuts were not an everyday occurrence. Even though this process was tedious, it saved me a lot of time when it came to finding these same cuts on the videotape.

Every Saturday was reserved for preparing the splicing log used to conform the videotape and breaking apart the master tape into individual scenes and takes that would be used to create the edited master tape. The first step was to read the voice ESG track with a photographic or optical sound reader. As I pointed out in the last chapter, the work print film contained the picture and a soundtrack that did not carry the program sound but the custom-designed ESG guide track which provided time code cueing information. I would read the ESG soundtrack from the work print, listening to the man's and alternate woman's voices reading the time code. As I was listening for the ESG time code numbers, I was holding the edges of the film with my fingers so that I could feel the mylar tape as it went by, indicating a splice.

I should point out that there was a one-frame tone applied to the ESG track exactly every one second (24 frames). If a splice came between any set of tones, I would use a plastic ruler we designed which was divided into 24 equal parts. After placing the beginning of the ruler on a tone (which was quite visible on the film in the form of a small one-frame rectangular bar) and noting on which frame the splice appeared, I would write down the code number.

For example, if the code read 27:15 and the splice came six frames after the tone, then the exact frame on which to make the splice would read 27:15 +06 frames. Every splice in the program would be read in this manner. It would take me on the average about seven hours to read all 400 or more splices in a one-hour program. Once the log was finished, I would turn it over to another editor who would cross-check my numbers. This sort of redundant cross-checking of the edit log was mandatory due to the large number of edits and the possibility of errors. In every episode we would find several mistakes, most of them caused by the weariness that comes from working long days. I would then verify these errors and correct the log if necessary.

If I finished early on Saturday, I would spend the rest of the day beginning to break apart the master videotape into small rolls. I usually had Sundays off and would spend the day sleeping. Household chores rarely got done because I was so tired. For nearly six months, my work week was mostly from 9 A.M. to midnight six days a week. It was hard on me and taking a toll on my family. When I accept an assignment and agree to it, I will finish it to the best of my ability. I don't want anyone to ever say that I sloughed off because I was tired.

I felt that the editor who cut the work print should also cut the videotape. The following week, John Teele would edit the work print and I would spend the next 60 or so hours splicing the master tape for the episode I had just completed. The reasoning behind this procedure was that often there were some quirks in each episode. Finding the pieces and locating specific material sometimes from banked material is more easily done by the editor who cut the work print than another editor not familiar with that episode. Finding all the pieces and splicing them together frame-accurately would take about five 12-hour days or so, depending on the number of edits in each episode. Tape splicing was a matter of conforming the tape to a frame-accurate time code log in a manner quite similar to film negative cutting.

After being broken down into small reels, the videotape was arranged in program order on racks in the editing room. Two hundred or so small reels made up any given episode. NBC engineers designed custom videotape readers that could be used on an ordinary film editing bench. Conventional film rewinds were installed with adapters that could accommodate the three-inch diameter tape hubs of the reels. The tape was then wound between these rewinds and passed over the tape reader head. The sound reader would read the secondary or cue channel of the videotape through its back side with the magnetic side facing up so the magnetic developing fluid could easily be applied later to identify a particular edit pulse that identified the desired frame.

Using the editing log I previously generated, I would listen to the production soundtrack for the correct scene and take number and then switch over to the cue channel on the same tape to find the time code number indicated in the edit log. In the same fashion in which I generated the edit log, I would find the nearest edit tone and place a ruler against the tape and run down to find the correct frame number, where I would make the cut. All the tape splicing was done on the bench, not on a videotape machine. I used to average about 15 minutes per splice because much of this time was used to find the material and locate the exact edit point, not in making the splice. To videotape-splice a one-hour episode would take between 50 and 75 man hours, depending on the number of cuts. A heavily-edited episode would often require the use of two or more editors splicing the tape in order to maintain the weekly schedule and make air dates.

After the tape was spliced in conformity with the work print, the next step was to transfer the new composite or "sweetened" soundtrack generated at the Glen Glenn Sound Facility back to the edited videotape master. At the very head of the composite soundtrack and the edited videotape, I would splice a two-minute piece of ESG time code material to act as a synchronizing leader, allowing both the videotape and the composite soundtrack to be matched up frame for frame. Once the two units were synchronized by using this two-minute leader, we would rehearse the entire program before actually transferring any sound back to the edited tape.

We had a dual speaker set up in the sound transfer room. The picture from the playback videotape machine would be seen on a monitor and its soundtrack would be heard on the right speaker. The sound reproducer containing the new composite soundtrack would be heard on the left speaker. A unique device called a "variable speed synchronizer" allowed the composite soundtrack to be sped up or slowed down ever so slightly with no audible change in pitch of the sound. This device let us correct "on the fly" any cutting errors that may have crept in during the tape splicing operation.

To begin the rehearsal of the sound transfer, we would be on an inter-com with the tape operator in an adjacent room. The videotape would be cued up and stopped on some arbitrary ESG time code number on the leader on the videotape approximately two minutes ahead of the program start point. The composite soundtrack would be cued up to the same num-ber and stopped. Since there was no easy way to automatically start both machines at the same time, the tape operator would say over the inter-com, "On the count of three, roll. One, two, *three*." The tape operator would start the VTR and the sound operator would start the sound play-back machine. By listening to both speakers in the sound room, I could hear an echo if both soundtracks were not in perfect synchronization. With each edit, if there was even a slight echo in the two speakers, it would mean a correction in either direction would be needed. This whole pro-cedure may sound somewhat crude by today's standards but it worked flawlessly. The variable speed synchronizer required two full turns of its crank to change the speed of one tape frame. Most corrections were either one-half to one full turn of the crank.

There were times, however, when a cutting error required up to four full turns of the crank, a two-frame error. In order to get the composite track in sync with the production sound (our absolute reference until such time as it was erased and replaced by the new composite track), I had to continually note in my editing script every change at every edit during the rehearsal. There was always the possibility of creating a "wow" in the track, especially if a large correction had to be made during a musical num-ber. The corrections required skill in turning that crank carefully and smoothly so that no wow or pitch change was heard. The easiest place to make large corrections was during applause since that is somewhat akin to random noise and no matter how fast the crank was turned no change in pitch could be heard. The next choice was laughter, but too much cor-rection too fast could change the pitch of the laugh. Dialogue was the third choice and last was music. In order to correct synchronization, if the sound from the left speaker sounded ahead, then the synchronizer knob would be retarded until the sound echo disappeared. I would note in my editing script the number of turns needed to get rid of the echo. This would vary from a quarter-turn to sometimes as many as two turns in either direction, depending on the kind of cutting error that had occurred.

I should also point out that because the kinescope film work print we used to edit the program and create continuity was recorded at 24 frames per second, built-in errors were sometimes encountered since the videotape was recorded at 30 frames per second. On the surface, this sounds like a horrendous problem. In reality, we had developed a sophisticated (for that time) method of converting this 24 frame work print rate to the 30 frame videotape rate with minimal error.

Because of the complexity of the editing process, we all worked long hours. Fatigue was evident on a daily basis. I never became ill or missed a day of work during the editing process and would take extra vitamin C to keep my body's immune system intact. Every so often, I or one of the other editors working with me would make an error and splice the wrong frame number which was out of the realm of the correction process. This would require stopping the sound transfer process, returning to the editing bench and finding the mistake. If the splice was cut too long, it was a relatively easy fix since only the extra frames of the edit needed to be trimmed off to the proper frame and re-spliced. However, if the splice was cut short, the editor would have to go back to the trim reel and find the remaining tape frames and splice it back to the end of the shot. This was the worst possible scenario since splicing additional material onto the end of the shot sometimes made the splice lurch or whip as it went past the video head. Fortunately, errors of this kind were rare, happening only about once or twice a season. When you consider that in a season, we would sometimes average some 5,000 splices, one or two errors of this type is really insignificant.

We would rehearse the entire program in real time, noting all the changes in the script. When we finished, the videotape and the soundtrack would be rewound to the same start point. Once the two synchronizing leaders were in sync, the tape operator would press the sound record button on the VTR, erasing the original production sound and replacing it with the composite sound mixed at Glen Glenn Sound Studios. The same corrections made during the rehearsal would be made during the transfer process. It was even more crucial to pay attention during the actual sound transfer since there would be sound emanating only from one speaker (the old tape sound was now being erased and replaced by the composite soundtrack). As soon as the sound transfer process was complete, we would make three protection copies of the edited program, one for Hollywood and two for NBC New York.

It wasn't until Sammy Davis, Jr., came on the program that *Laugh-In* really took off. His vaudeville routine of "Here come de judge" became a household word for a time. In addition, the Baskin Robbins ice cream company grabbed onto Davis's popularity and came out with a special ice cream called "Here come de fudge." We used to get free samples and it was very good. I remember the time George Schlatter asked Sammy Davis to look at the work print of his debut on *Laugh-In*. Sammy came into the projection room and was introduced to all of us. I ran the program for him and he laughed all the way through the program. When the lights came on again, Sammy Davis was so overjoyed, he did a handstand in the screening room and banged his head on the acoustical tile on the walls with glee. Right after that episode aired, *Laugh-In* became the number one hit on television.

Laugh-In spawned a new generation of toys, sock-it-to-me bats and other memorabilia. There was even a *Laugh-In* comic book. I got a copy of volume one, number one and had it signed by all the cast. It's a treasured memento. A regular segment on *Laugh-In* was the Fickle Finger of Fate Award given to people who did stupid things, especially politicians. Schlatter gave all the crew this award as a memento of the series.

We were always being interviewed by magazines, newspapers and television. A book was published called "Inside *Laugh-In*," the behind-the-scenes story of putting out *Laugh-In* every week. I was often interviewed and gave stories to the old *Saturday Evening Post* magazine. Working with George Schlatter was easy because I had done many other specials with him over the years and we worked well together. I knew George's staff and we were much like any family working on a regular basis. I made many friends, not only with the *Laugh-In* staff but with some of the cast members as well. Arte Johnson, Gary Owens, Henry Gibson, Dick Martin and of course George are some of the people I still maintain contact with.

At the end of the first regular season, I had stashed away dozens of outtakes or goofs which I put together for our beginning of the season party the following year. I made up a reel of funny outtakes for three consecutive years and they total about 50 minutes of the funniest material that never made the screen. Without naming names because I don't want to be sued, let me just say that several of the cast members taught me words I never knew existed. Not all of this outtake reel is dirty, however. There are many very funny things that the NBC censors wouldn't let us get by with, but I saved them for our own amusement anyway. The first year, we didn't tell anyone we had made this outtake reel and during the first annual cast and crew party, we surprised everyone with it. I remember watching the faces of the cast as they saw themselves making mistakes.

One day, Gary Owens wanted to visit the editing room. It was a mess with film scraps on the floor, barrels of film trims filling the room and hardly any space to move around. I explained to Gary the basics of what we were doing, After the explanation, he looked at me and exclaimed, "This show gives me such a headache, I need an Excedrin credit card!"

Before *Laugh-In* started production in the fall, George Schlatter shot another special called *Soul*, a black version of *Laugh-In*. It starred Lou Rawls and other well-known guests. Although it got good reviews, NBC was afraid that it would create too much controversy and did not put it on as a series. I was concerned about being able to handle another series like *Laugh-In* with the enormous amount of post-production and the fact we didn't have enough skilled editors to handle another show of that magnitude.

You may think that working at a big network television facility and editing prime time specials and series is a glamorous job. Well, only about 5 percent of that statement is true. The other 95 percent is plain old hard work and very long hours. The old adage "the better you become at your job, the more clients ask for you" is a true statement no matter what business you are in. Between series like *Laugh-In* and Bob Hope, I often edited specials (sometimes for other networks) since the producers liked our method of editing videotape; it gave them the same frame-by-frame flexibility as a film produced program.

Working nine A.M. to midnight six days a week for six months got to me both physically and mentally. Although by union contract we were entitled to two 15-minute breaks each work day, I almost never took these breaks because once I got involved in editing I did not want to stop until I had finished the sequence. I was often chided for not taking breaks but that was the way I was. At the end of every day I would get up from my editing bench and walk, hunched over, all the way to the parking lot more than a mile away. That may be how I eventually ended up with back problems. The job of editing wasn't physically challenging, but the stress and strain of having to meet network deadlines coupled with correcting technical problems made me very weary. Even though I really enjoyed the job, some of this stress was due to my wanting to do my very best on every production I worked on. That way no one could ever say that I wasn't giving 110 percent. In a sense, part of my eagerness was more ego than anything else. I was one of the youngest engineers at NBC and was on my way to the top (I thought). Telling people I was the editor on *Laugh-In* brought all kinds of questions. (Did I know Dan and Dick? What were they really like?) After all these years in retirement and after more than 700 screen credits, people are still interested in *Laugh-In* and ask me questions about the cast even today.

In October of 1968, at the start of the second season of *Laugh-In*, I was working under tremendous pressure. Even though I had help, the enormous effort of *Laugh-In* began to get the best of me. I had been working my usual 90-hour weeks. One day I came home to find Dee very upset. I asked her what was the matter. She told me that it was difficult managing our two teenage children by herself and that I was never around to help discipline them. She said that I would give unreasonable orders to be carried out and then leave for work, expecting her to be the disciplinarian. Both our son Bob and our daughter Lori were taller than Dee (she is only 5'2") and she had to look up at them. I worked so much overtime and was away from home so often that my kids called me "Uncle Daddy."

I realized at that moment that in a way I was being selfish, more concerned about work than I was with my family. My wife is a good person wanting to please everyone all the time. Although our kids were good, they got into the same mischief as other kids, wanting to stay out and not coming home on time or not telling us where they were going. Fortunately, they never did drugs, alcohol or got involved in gangs. Still, my wife had a tough time keeping them under control. I was very upset when I went to bed that evening. I couldn't sleep because I didn't know how to resolve the problems my wife faced and take the pressure off her.

About four o'clock that morning, I still could not sleep, so I got out of bed and went downstairs and sat at my desk. I thought for a long time about what to do to resolve these problems. There was no way I could stop working the long hours. The better you become at your job, the more people demand of you. They don't want the second best. I must admit I had an ego. I was in the position of possibly winning more Emmys. I would frequently go into the videotape scheduling office to see what projects were coming in and attempt to get myself assigned as the editor. Since I would not compromise my work, I made myself a workaholic, often going out of my way to please the producers and directors I worked with.

I could see no easy way out of this situation. I made one of the most important decisions of my life: I sat down and hand wrote my resignation and addressed it to my boss. After more than 17 years at NBC, I felt it was time for me to change since I really doubted that NBC would. In essence, I wrote that I had been working long hours for almost six months and the trend was not letting up. My resignation was dated the next day.

In part it read, "Although my 17 years with NBC have basically been good ones, I see more of the same long hours away from home and continually mounting pressures. In the past six years, I have worked overtime almost every week in the year. Now I'd like to enjoy life and the things I've worked so hard to get. Therefore, considering all the facts and as you pointed out, no one is indispensable, I feel that my resignation will solve the problems that I now face."

The day of my decision, I took the letter to work and gave it to my boss's secretary to type as an inter-office memo. When she saw what I wanted, she refused to type the letter. I said I'd find someone else to type it. I walked over to the administration building across the parking lot and gave my letter to another secretary. She would not type the letter either, but after I talked to her for a few minutes, she agreed. She gave me an original and several carbon copies. I put each of the carbons in an NBC inter-office memo envelope and hand delivered them to personnel, the head of engineering and the original to my boss, Oscar Wick. (I didn't hand them to people; I left each envelope in their in-boxes.) Then I went back to my editing room to wait for an answer.

I didn't have to wait long. About 20 minutes later, Oscar came into my room and, waving my letter in the air, yelled, "What's this?" I said, "What do you think it is?" He said, "Are you trying to be funny?" After he realized I meant business, his tone became more conciliatory and I told him that the hours were as hard on my family as they were on me. He told me that no one wanted me to leave and asked me what I wanted to stay. I told him it wasn't the money but the long tedious hours that I wanted changed. I told him that after 17 years of loyal service to NBC, the least they could do was to give me nine-to-five and weekends off. Oscar said he would try but that he couldn't promise anything.

I went back to the administration building and spoke with my friend George Habib, then head of the unit managers. I told him of my decision and asked him if there was any possibility I could become a unit manager. George pointed out that NBC had never promoted anyone from engineering directly into the unit manager's position. He could not give me the opportunity that I wanted which would have changed my mind about leaving.

The head of engineering, Jack Kennedy, asked me, "How can you do this to us?" I said, "Who's doing what to whom? I don't think you understand the problem." It seemed that NBC executives were more concerned about *Laugh-In* than my health and my family. I felt that if I continued in the same way I had been going for the past six years, my health and my family would suffer even more than they already had. I was convinced that if I continued to work these same hours and I died, before my body had cooled off, they would have me replaced.

I was told a long time ago that no one is indispensable and I tried to point that out to my boss. Several NBC executives tried to convince me to stay but nothing they said changed my mind. I called the *Laugh-In* office and spoke to George Schlatter about my decision. He was quite upset but said I had to do what was best for me. My wife was in agreement with my decision and I hoped it would resolve our personal problems. I told my boss it was easier to get another job than another family.

My last day was Friday, October 11, 1968. I turned in my keys, my employee identification badge and got my last paycheck. I picked up my briefcase and walked out the door. No thank yous, no party, no nothing. It was just another day, the end of 17 years. After I left, NBC decided to replace me with seven other employees on *Laugh-In*. They discovered (too late, I might add) that there was too much work for the skimpy staff previously assigned to the show. Had they made that decision earlier when I made them aware of the long hours, I most likely would not have resigned.

Laugh-In continued in reruns into the early 1980s; the one-hour shows were cut down into two half-hour episodes, doubling the number of episodes that ran in syndication. However, in my opinion, the re-edited half-hour versions lacked some of the spontaneity of the original hour-long episodes.

I went home very sad that NBC couldn't find a way to give me at least some of what I wanted. I didn't really want to leave but I had no other choice. When I left, I was a union supervisor making $250 a week. I was supporting a family, a home and two cars. Even in 1968, I would not have been able to handle that if not for all the overtime I was making (I often more than doubled my salary every week). I also had a small nest egg in the NBC retirement plan which I withdrew hoping it would carry me through until I found another job. I didn't think I would have too much of a problem since I had four Emmy nominations and two Emmy statues under my belt. Looking back now at the decision I made, I have no regrets. Even though I had no job prospects, I was confident that something would come along soon. As it turned out, within four years, I had quadrupled my salary and had much better hours and I was able to spend more time at home with my family.

When I left NBC, I decided to take some time off and fix up a few things at home. After two weeks, I decided to paint the kitchen. I made one pass on the ceiling with the roller when the phone rang. It was George Schlatter. He told me he was shooting a new pilot called *Cockamamie* and he wanted to know if I would edit it. The program was being shot at NBC but George knew I was now the only editor outside of NBC who could edit with the kinescope work print editing system and cut the videotape as well. I said I would do it. George told me that if the pilot sold, he would set me up in business with himself, Ed Friendly and Carolyn Raskin as the other partners.

George rented a small office in Toluca Lake near NBC and I set to work finishing the show. It was a mess because notes were missing and I spent a long time trying to figure out what went where. Fortunately, I was able to successfully edit the tape and the pilot sold to ABC. I was thrilled. Now I would be in business with three of my friends as partners; they put up all the money to start a post-production company called Burbank Film Editing. We opened up a small office in Hollywood to prepare to edit the series. Although the pilot was called *Cockamamie*, ABC didn't like that name and it was changed to *Turn-On*.

When the finished pilot was shown to Leonard Goldenson, the president of ABC, I sat next to him as he said to George Schlatter, "George, you've got another winner." Well, I thought, we're off and running. The series was shot on 16mm color film with Alan Levi as the director. The film camera was fitted with a video adapter using the same lens as the film camera so the video camera would see exactly what the film camera was photographing. The purpose of this setup was to be able to rewind the videotape after each shot and review it for continuity, lighting and camera moves.

However, we found that the crew spent too much time reviewing each take and it became very costly in terms of wasted time. After a while, the video replay was used only for critical shots. In addition, the film, once edited, would be transferred to videotape and completed at another facility, Vidtronics in Hollywood. The production shooting stage and most of the *Turn-On* offices were in the old Republic Pictures studio facility where the PBS station Channel 28 in Los Angeles is now located. The building was very old and the carpet in the projection room was soaked with water, most likely from a leaking roof. When we walked, it squished. All the water had to be vacuumed up before we could even get started and the musty smell of wet carpet lasted for several weeks.

We had eight editors and assistants for this half-hour weekly series. The contract was for 15 programs. Post-production was a nightmare since animated graphics were added and other special four-way images were built with four synchronous film projectors and a host of other complex mirrors and technical equipment. The mechanics of putting this show together are quite complex and I could write another book just about editing the *Turn-On* series.

By the time the first *Turn-On* episode was ready to air, we had four more shot. However, we had only two completed episodes. This show, because of the complex graphics moving across the screen and other post-production factors, took an enormous amount of time to complete. It was not done with a film work print and no tape was cut *à la Laugh-In*. The show was shot on 16mm film and edited together in segments. These segments were transferred to videotape, assembled electronically and tied together with optical special effects and other complex transitions. Since everyone was working long hours, we were prone to making mistakes.

In one instance, a complex assembly of graphics and other special effects was completed around four in the morning. The editor, Jerry Greene, was preparing to make a backup or protection copy. He would normally grab a blank roll of tape stock, run it through an electronic erasing machine and then load it onto another tape machine in preparation for making a copy from the electronically edited master tape. Since Jerry was tired, he inadvertently picked up the master tape and completely erased it. We were all so numb at that time of morning, Jerry just said, "Let's start over." It took us less time to reconstruct a new edited master since the first assembly was more like a rehearsal. More than 12 hours later we finished, a 30-hour day for all of us.

George had a party at Chasen's restaurant in Beverly Hills to preview the show for the press and others. We had a great time. But when the first episode aired on ABC, the network got so many angry calls about this "nasty show" that most of ABC's stations threatened to pull out of their affiliate contracts if it wasn't yanked off the air immediately. About 15 minutes into the program, ABC went to commercial and *Turn-On* never returned.

The network played something like *Sermonette* to fill out the last 15 minutes of the half-hour time slot. That was the last time *Turn-On* was ever seen. I remember one incident in that first episode in which a nun walked up to a candy machine, put in money and pulled the lever. Out came "The Pill." I'm sure the uproar that caused was one of the reasons the show was pulled. Things like that are tame compared to what we now see on television.

I was told that *Turn-On* made the *Guinness Book of Records* as "the shortest television show ever to air." The day after it aired, I was at home in the shower when wife yelled for me to come to the phone. I asked her if it couldn't wait and she said no, it was important. I got out of the shower dripping wet and picked up the phone. It was Bill Kayden, the show's producer. He said, "Art, the show's been cancelled!" I said, "What? Is this some kind of joke?" He said, "No, the show really has been cancelled by ABC. Tell your crew not to come in on Monday." I was flabbergasted. I remember sitting next to the president of ABC during the screening of the pilot and hearing him tell George Schlatter he had another hit. Wow, what a bummer!

Sadly, I called the crew and told them the bad news. We quickly packed up and moved all the equipment back to my office at Burbank Film Editing. There was so much that I had barely enough room to work until some of it was sent to storage. As it turned out, ABC paid off George's contract for all 15 episodes and it left me with enough funds to continue operation until I picked up other business.

After *Turn-On* was canceled, one of the jobs I acquired was shooting film clips for *Laugh-In*. I had my own 16mm camera equipment and I was able to go out and shoot funny little short sequences which I edited to the soundtrack music (called lick playoffs). These ran five to ten seconds long. I used our kids, our neighbors, trees, rocks, flowers and all sorts of gimmicks to make funny little clips for the show.

I'm sure many of you may remember the person in the yellow raincoat riding the red tricycle and falling over in different ways. The way the raincoat was worn, with the hat pulled over the head, it was impossible to tell who was riding the tricycle. From time to time, I would borrow the yellow raincoat and the red tricycle from the NBC prop department and use my kids as the riders, running into everything imaginable. Once I placed my son in the middle of our neighbor's pool in a little rubber life raft and put the yellow raincoat on him. I told him to paddle furiously and then fall over into the pool.

As mentioned earlier, *Laugh-In* was always in the news. There was a late night talk show where host Tom Snyder asked Dan Rowan and Dick Martin how it was possible to get a thousand or two jokes in every show on a weekly basis. Dick Martin offered that the editor, Art Schneider, had a tremendous task in sorting out all the material and making the jokes work with perfect timing. I thank Dick Martin for giving me so much credit, but it was team work and organization that really got the job done.

After we set up Burbank Film Editing to shoot and edit clips for *Laugh-In*, I also edited many other projects as well. I did a Diana Ross special, a Sammy Davis, Jr., special and so many more that I can't even remember. A ritual we established was to have a weekly Friday afternoon party in our office at Burbank Film Editing. Carolyn Raskin would bring over a bottle of champagne, cold cuts and other goodies. I would pop the cork into the acoustical ceiling tile which would leave a noticeable dent. After several months of these parties, the ceiling looked like it had a hundred bullet holes in it.

Marketing was one of things successful programs did to get additional revenue. As I mentioned earlier, *Laugh-In* was no exception; there were sock-it-to-me bats, comic books and copies of other items often used on the show. Another successful venture was the production of two *Laugh-In* record albums. Jokes were taken from all the episodes and I edited two albums based on this material. The straight line was on the left channel and the punchline was on the right. It was a relatively easy editing job and the stereo effect was quite good.

It seems that even after three decades, friends and acquaintances still remember me for that one series even though I've edited hundreds of other programs since then. It was a fun time and I made many friends and relationships still with me today. I call Schlatter the "Comedy Meister" of television. *Laugh-In* came at the right time in this century and will forever remain in the annals of television history as having left a legacy of comedy and humor in a unique style often copied but never duplicated. As they say, "Imitation is the sincerest form of flattery."

CHAPTER SEVEN

Developments of the 1970s

As the sixties turned to the seventies, a long-standing dream of mine was fulfilled. Ever since I had started editing, I had wanted to see the letters A.C.E. after my name. The letters stand for the American Cinema Editors, an honorary organization dedicated to preserving the skills and traditions of editing. Although my primary skill began as a film editor, I gradually switched to videotape editing when that opportunity presented itself. In 1969, a friend who belonged to A.C.E. asked why I wasn't a member. I told him no one had ever asked me. He said, "Well, I'm asking you."

I filled out my application, but it was more than a year before it was acted upon. Although I had a number of film editing credits, most of my credits were for videotape editing. Since this group knew very little about tape editing at that time, they were at a loss as to how to deal with me. Also, I belonged to a rival union called NABET. Although A.C.E is not connected with the film editors' union, all members at that time were also members of the IATSE union. There was no love between these two unions and they were somewhat suspicious of me for that reason. Eventually, I was asked to come before the board and state my reasons for wanting to become a member.

I went to the board meeting one evening and presented my case. It didn't look good. Then I was asked if there was anything else I could add that would influence the board. "Well," I told them, "I have three Emmy nominations and two Emmy Awards for editing. Will that help?" I went out into the hall while the board deliberated. When I returned, I was told congratulations were in order because I had just been accepted as an active member and had the right to use the letters A.C.E. after my name on any future projects. I participated in many areas and attended meetings as often as my schedule permitted. I was an active member for 18 years until my retirement in 1988 and I still maintain contact with many of those editors today.

One of the founding members of A.C.E. is Jim Blakeley. Jim has been at 20th Century–Fox for many years and at one time was supervising editor for Fox as well as one of the editors on the M*A*S*H television series. I first met Jim when I worked at CFI re-editing the *Planet of the Apes* television series for syndication. Blakeley followed me when I opened up my own business. He was then re-editing old movies for television, removing objectionable violence and language. Jim was an expert at cutting down old feature films without harming the story line.

In 1977 Jim started teaching a class on film editing at UCLA and he asked me to teach one class each semester on videotape editing. I ended up teaching in his class for more than a decade. I would arrive at Jim's house in Beverly Hills around 6 P.M. and he would fix me a drink while his wife Mary made finger sandwiches. Jim at that time was approaching 80 years old and he would swim in his pool every day, one lap for every year of his age. I wonder if he still does that? I would follow Jim to Sunset Boulevard turn left and follow him closely since the campus is sprawling and I could easily get lost. His students often were neophytes in the motion picture and television industries and came to Jim's class to learn about film editing. I showed examples of programs I had edited and explained in detail how some of the special effects were done. I really enjoyed it because with about 50 or so students, there were always enough questions to answer. Often, after class as I was walking to my car, one or more students would follow me, continuing to ask questions. Jim Blakeley was, in a sense, my press agent. He would introduce me to his class in the most glowing terms, and he pushed my two books on editing every chance he got.

In the early '70s, the economy was very sluggish and my partners and I agreed on a mutual dissolution of Burbank Film Editing. I then went to work for a post-production facility called Vidtronics as a vacation relief tape operator and editor for just over a month. When that period was over I was asked to stay on, but I received an offer from Consolidated Film Industries (CFI) in Hollywood in 1971.

Consolidated Film Industries has been in business since the 1930s and is one of the largest motion picture film processing laboratories in the world. I had been dealing with them since 1951 when they processed all of NBC's 35mm kinescope film in the years before videotape. I knew all the top management people and had a good rapport with their technical staff. During the 1970s, many motion picture film laboratories saw the need to get involved in video. The trend was more and more towards producing television programs on videotape and film laboratories saw this opportunity to cash in on it. Sid Solow, the president of CFI and my former professor at USC, was just opening a new video facility and wanted me as their supervising videotape editor. I saw an opportunity to help build up this new video division and decided to accept the offer.

When I started, they had just installed a simplified time code-based editing system made by a company called EECO, the Electronic Engineering Company. It was considerably more efficient than Editec but it was not compatible with another editing system developed by a new company called CMX which was later to become a giant in the editing industry.

The company CMX was a joint venture of CBS and Memorex, hence the name CMX. It was later purchased by the ORROX Company headed by Bill Orr, who led them into developing some very sophisticated editing hardware and software which was way ahead of its time with an exceptionally fast editing system called the CMX-600. A year previous, I had been at a technical meeting where a film of the CMX-600 was shown. I thought, what a great editing system! I wondered if I would ever get a chance to play with it. Little did I realize that a year later, I would not only be editing on it but would be teaching others how to use it. In 1972, CMX chose CFI as a test site for their new equipment. They had developed the fastest editing system in the industry, a "random access editing system." Today, this editing process is known as non-linear editing. In simple terms, shots can be randomly selected and accessed immediately without the winding or rewinding of tape since the material was stored digitally on special spinning data disks similar to those used by banks and other institutions. The CMX-600 used six of these disk units to store about 30 minutes of raw material. Instead of a keyboard, it used a light pen which, when touched to a word on the television monitor, would access a shot or perform a host of other editorial functions almost instantaneously.

For example, if you wanted to find shot 27A-2, you would access the log book and scroll down to that slate number. By merely touching the name 27A-2, the first picture frame of the shot would instantly appear in a still frame on the monitor. From the time I touched the name with the light pen, it took only 1/70th of a second for the shot to appear. That's about twice as fast as an eye blink.

The CMX-600 was designed primarily to edit short commercials, but we soon discovered that by adding the appropriate number of disk packs, it would be possible to edit television programs up to 90 minutes in length. One of the first programs I edited on the CMX-600 was a Julie Andrews special directed by her husband, Blake Edwards. From five hours of raw material, I edited the one-hour special in one eight-hour day. The changes Blake Edwards requested took only another hour. Film editors Peter Johnson, David Newhouse and I were nominated for an A.C.E. "Eddie" award for the documentary "Julie." Peter and David both edited film sequences that were transferred to videotape. Blake Edwards worked with me on this special. After we had a rough cut, Blake invited Julie Andrews to see what we had accomplished in a day. She was absolutely amazed as she watched me select shots and, with lightning speed, edit together sequences in two or three minutes that would have taken several hours using the conventional tools.

Blake thoroughly enjoyed working on this incredibly fast editing system and was so impressed with its ability to edit and make changes that he asked me to go to England and edit his next feature film with him on the CMX-600. You can imagine how flattered I was. However, I knew that the system wasn't yet sophisticated enough to do what he wanted. I hated to tell him it wasn't ready because I really wanted the chance not only to go to England but to work with Blake Edwards. Today, many major feature films are edited on videotape and computer hard drives using even more sophisticated electronic editing equipment and eventually finished on film for worldwide distribution.

On several occasions, Blake and Julie Andrews invited us for lunch, driving us in their Rolls-Royce up to a Chinese restaurant just above Hollywood Boulevard and Vine Street, one of the most famous intersections in the world. Both of them are delightful people, as nice in person as they appear on the screen. When the special was finished, Blake invited 15 couples who had worked on the special to have dinner with them at the Yamoto Inn, a Japanese restaurant in Century City in Los Angeles. My wife was delighted with the invitation and we went into a private dining room reserved for the group. However, we had to remove our shoes before being allowed into the dining room. We sat down randomly at this very low table and ended up seated directly across from Julie Andrews and her husband.

A number of hors d'oeuvres were brought to our table. Julie picked some up and began to eat. I asked her what it was. She said it was sushi

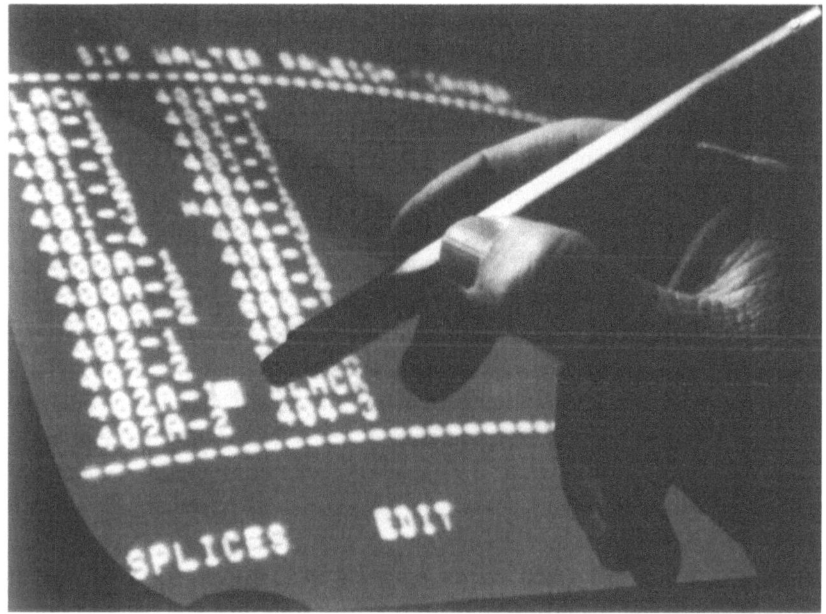

CMX-600 light pen editing system.

and told me to try it. I had heard of sushi but had never eaten any raw fish and wasn't really interested in trying it in front of all those people. Julie egged me on, saying it wasn't fishy-tasting. I looked at my wife and she looked at me with a "what, are you nuts?" expression. I didn't even really like fish but I thought, what the heck, I'll take a little bite.

The sushi was marinated in something like soy sauce. I picked up a small square and tasted it. "You know," I said, "this tastes a little like roast beef." Julie said she knew I would like it. Then I decided to try another piece. The sushi was sitting in a bowl of what looked like shredded coconut. I picked up another piece along with this coconut and bit down on it. What I didn't know was that this "coconut" was really shredded hot horse radish. My mouth was on fire. I grabbed for what I thought was a small glass of water which turned out to be hot sake. It was like pouring gasoline on a fire! A flood of tears ran down my face from the pain. Julie Andrews looked up at me and began to laugh, but I think she really felt sorry for me. My wife kicked me under the table for being such an idiot and embarrassing her. However, the evening turned out all right and we had a great time. That dinner was something I'll never forget, and I'll bet Julie Andrews won't forget it either.

The Julie Andrews documentary we edited on the CMX-600 was well received. That was in August of 1973. The following September, Julie started a new weekly series. Her director at ABC heard how fast we could edit on our CMX-600 and he wanted to try to edit a particularly difficult sequence in which she played several parts. At that time, ABC was using the older Editec editing system and although the editor Nick Giordano was an expert with it, they estimated it would take at least 40 hours of Editec editing to put this 15-minute segment together. I was asked if I would be interested in editing this segment on the CMX-600. I jumped at the chance since I was now well-versed in the use of the system and looked forward to editing this segment on it.

The director carefully went over his notes and selected about two hours of the best takes to be transferred to the CMX-600. The maximum capacity of the system was 27½ minutes per load so that edited segments had to be assembled from several small chunks of material. This was a minor inconvenience since no editing system at that time had the ability to edit at lightning speed. On average, a 27½ minute load of raw or unedited material would generate about 5 to 6 minutes of edited material (roughly a six to one ratio of raw material to the finished product). Selecting and choosing shots to be edited together was a pleasure. The editing system also had the ability to fast forward or rewind any shot at ten times play speed as well as to jog a single frame forwards and backwards.

Another unique feature of this machine was that when a frame was stopped, any associated sound was scanned so that even when the picture was still-framed, you could listen to the sound associated with that frame. This allowed the editor to easily find a hole between musical notes in which to make an edit. The pitch of the note was the same as though it were being played at normal speed. You have to see and hear it to believe it. Even though the CMX-600 cost about $750,000, its ability to edit with incredible speed and accuracy enabled me to accomplish far more in less time than with any conventional editing system. We also edited the NBC special *Dr. Jekyll and Mr. Hyde* which needed 150 digital disk packs to hold all five and a half hours of raw material to generate an edited program of 52 minutes. We had to rent most of the special digital disk packs from Memorex, which depleted their entire stock. The same kind of disk packs we used for editing were also used by banks to digitally store information.

From the time I sat down and made the first edit on the Julie Andrews

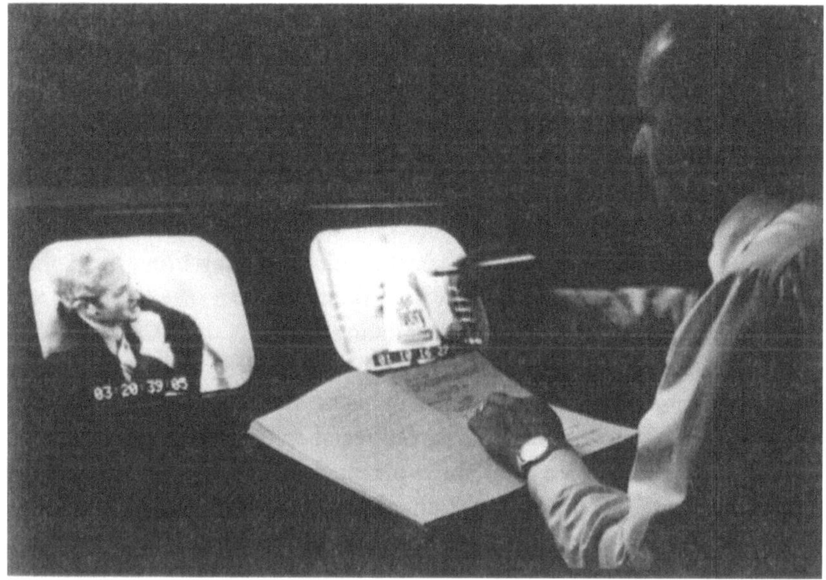

Author at CMX-600 editing console, 1973.

segment, I finished in less than two hours plus another half hour to make changes. The director was beside himself with joy. He was so pleased with the end result that he wanted to do the entire series on our system. After determining the volume of material needed for 26 weeks of shows, we decided that we could not guarantee we would be able to meet their deadlines, primarily because of the enormous amount of preparation needed to get the material ready to edit.

The problems were getting the original production videotape material to and from ABC, transferring it to the CMX-600, and the amount of manpower it would require to get the job done. The editing itself would be a snap; the hard part was everything else around it. So it was decided not to edit her series and possibly mess up the delivery schedule. However, Nick Giordano and I were nominated for videotape editing and were fortunate to win an Emmy award for the first show in her series. This was my third Emmy award and my second Emmy for a Julie Andrews program.

Unfortunately, the high initial cost of the CMX-600 along with its heavy maintenance costs and high hourly rate ($425 an hour) were some of the factors that contributed to its demise. Five CMX-600 editing systems were eventually built, but because of rapidly changing technology, newer and cheaper technology soon replaced them. These newer editing systems provided editors with similar results at a fraction of the cost.

While I was supervising editor at CFI, I was asked to edit a series of five short videos for the Hudson Brothers, Mark, Bill and Brett. This group of guys were real cut-ups and we spent a lot of the time telling jokes. Their five videos were shot on 35mm color film and transferred to tape, but they were not happy with the color. So they brought in their director of photography to consult with them to make sure the color was properly corrected as the videos were being edited.

The basic equipment was not capable of making the kind of color changes they wanted. In order to make even the most subtle change in only a single color, we brought in three special color-correcting amplifiers, each one connected to one of three playback VTRs. As we created the edit master tape, we would make changes primarily to the color portion of the picture but also to the contrast, brightness and saturation of the color as well. The three brothers were a kick to work with and they sent me a nice letter thanking me for my help and my jokes.

In early 1975, I received a telegram stating that I was to be awarded the "Broadcast Preceptor Award" given by San Francisco State University. When I read the telegram, I was somewhat suspicious since I had never been awarded anything of this nature in my life. The telegram also stated that among the other honorees were Barbara Walters, Larry Gelbart and Gene Reynolds (producers of the *M*A*S*H* television series), author Faye Kanin, Bob Keeshan (Captain Kangaroo) and George Nicholaw, vice president of CBS radio in Los Angeles. Each of the above was being honored for their work in various fields. I was selected for "Pioneering the Field of Electography." I hadn't heard the term "Electography" before but it appeared to be an all-encompassing term related to film and television.

Even though the telegram seemed on the up and up, I wasn't really sure it was real. I thought that if I called Mr. Nicholaw, one of the honorees, he would know if it was valid. I called his office and asked his secretary to please verify this information for me. I was put on hold for several minutes. When she returned she said simply, "We strongly urge you to accept since this is a very prestigious award." I was stunned. This was for real.

Due to my long work schedule, I had to work the day of the awards ceremony, but a month later I was invited to participate at San Francisco State on a seminar relating to these awards; I gave a lecture on videotape editing and showed several video clips of material I had edited. While the clips were being played during my talk, people would randomly applaud at some of the material. I was astonished. When the seminar was over, I took many questions about programs I had worked on. All in all, it was a wonderful experience and I treasure my Broadcast Preceptor Award as much as my Emmys.

In 1973, Alan Blye, the producer of *Sonny and Cher* series on CBS, asked me to edit the series at CFI. He was very well-organized and knew exactly what he wanted and wasted no time in editing. He was an accomplished musician and writer along with his many other talents. Because of schedule conflicts, Alan would often send his associate director Jeff Margolis, now a very accomplished television director, to edit with me. Jeff and I put each weekly show together and, except for one or two changes requested by Blye after viewing the episode, we rarely had to redo any of the edits.

During one program, Cher sang "Bridge Over Troubled Waters." It was beautiful, but because the show was long, Blye decided to remove one chorus which would bring the show exactly to time. Since Blye couldn't be there, Jeff Margolis and I had the task of shortening this song. We reviewed it several times, looking for a spot to delete material. It was not easy. Jeff wanted to make the edit at a certain point but I told him the music edit would not work. (The song was prerecorded and Cher had lip synched it.) I suggested we make the sound edit at a music bridge and then re-sync Cher to the track. After several attempts, I was able to make a short audio dissolve which removed the material we wanted. The music edit was perfect but I could not make the picture work at the same edit point. I had to delay the picture change for about 40 seconds because that was the only camera angle I could use to avoid a "jump cut." The biggest problem I faced was finding a camera angle that would work. Luckily, the camera dissolved to a side shot where Cher's lips could not be seen so no one would know if she was really in sync or not. However, when the camera changed to a front shot, Cher was not quite in lip sync. So I remade the dissolve moving the picture edit three frames ahead of where it originally was. It took us nearly four hours to make this one edit but it was worth it since the edit was perfect and even Blye could not tell where we had actually made it.

When Sonny and Cher were breaking up, Sonny would call Blye while we were editing. Then the next day it would be Cher calling. Each time the phone rang in the editing room and Blye would get the call, he'd say something like, "Okay, guys, why don't you take a long lunch break now—like about three hours?" That was all right with us, and the company didn't mind since Alan paid the going editing room rate even while talking on the phone to them. At about $300 an hour, it would be the world's most expensive local telephone call. Sonny and Cher called many times over a period of several weeks, causing a slowdowns and delays every day we edited. Apparently those "fatherly talks" to both of those stars didn't do anything to resolve their marital problems since we know what eventually happened to them. I did other projects with Alan Blye over the years which were highly acclaimed by critics. After Sonny and Cher went their separate ways, Sonny got his own new series and so did Cher, both on different networks.

Another popular program I edited was the *Tony Orlando and Dawn* series. It was easy to edit mostly because it was well-planned. Usually I could edit one episode in an eight-or-ten hour day. Producers Saul Illson and Ernie Chambers were great. I remember one Christmas Eve we had to finish a program to meet a deadline. Since we had to work that evening, Saul Illson's wife brought dinner to the editing room. It turned out she was a gourmet cook. She brought in this bowl of salad that was two feet in diameter along with the other items, and we enjoyed one the greatest meals I have ever tasted. Jeff Margolis, with whom I had worked on *Sonny and Cher*, was also the director of this series. This and other series programs were what is called a format show since the routine of the program is basically the same week after week and there were no surprises in editing. They were so easy to edit that I could almost phone in my edits (not really), but it was a fun show to do because the material was good, the people I worked with were pleasant and we were all professionals.

Dora Hall was a television special put together with love—the love of a husband for his wife. Leo Hallsman, the president and owner of the Solo Cup Company, had a lot of money. One day, he asked his wife, "If you could have anything you wanted, what would you want?" She told him she wanted to be a star. This wish might not seem unusual, unless you consider the fact that she made this decision when she was 78 years old. Leo said fine. He hired the best directors, lighting and makeup people. He brought in vocal coaches and others who were the best in their fields to help give his wife the gift she wanted. I edited the first of many

Dora Hall specials. Another interesting aspect of this project was that so many versions of this program were made that nearly every editor in Hollywood at one time or another did some editing on one of the versions. I think there were at least 11 different versions of the basic Dora Hall special.

Another enjoyable assignment was a series of 75 *Comedy Shop* programs starring Norm Crosby. The show was produced by Joe Siegman, a quiet man who was able to get the funniest comics in Hollywood to appear on the series. Director Perry Rosemond and I had the greatest time editing the series. First, we would just view all the comics on each episode. Each comic would do about ten minutes of material. From that, Perry would pick out the funniest jokes to be used in the show. The procedure he used to determine which jokes would stay in was somewhat unusual.

As we watched these comics, Perry would take notes. If I laughed, Perry would put a check mark opposite that joke. The harder I laughed, the more check marks and underlining that joke got. There were times, however, when I didn't laugh. I'm sorry to say that those comics who didn't make me laugh may now be in some other line of work. I was amazed by how much influence I had in that series.

You can still see many of these comics who got their start on *Comedy Shop* (Jeff Altman and Jay Leno, to name just two). I edited the series at CFI except for ten episodes that I had to finish elsewhere because we were so booked up. Those ten were taken to TAV, a company in Hollywood where my son Robert worked. Although I edited the work print on those ten episodes, my son did the assembly and all the finish work. The producer gave us father and son screen credit on those episodes. That was the first time we ever got screen credit together.

Old friends came calling when Sonny Bono, fresh from his breakup with Cher, launched a show of his own. Alan Blye opted to produce it and asked me to edit. The first episode had Sally Struthers as a guest. She did a number called "In the Mood," a standard made famous by the Andrews Sisters in the 1940s. What was unique about it was that Sally played all three parts, changing dresses and hairstyles to imitate the three sisters. Although it took eight hours to shoot and eight hours to edit, the finished song only ran about three minutes on the screen.

The soundtrack was first recorded with Sally in a studio days before the shooting. On stage, the background picture of the band was then recorded with the musicians playing the song completely through. Next, the background shot of the band was rewound and played back through the studio's control room. At the same time, Sally (dressed as Patty Andrews) was positioned on the set with marks on the floor. Sally then mouthed the words and acted the part of Patty Andrews as the track played. When that composite was recorded, it was again used as a playback for the next take, but this time the tape contained the shot of the band and Sally as Patty. Shooting something like this took a lot of preplanning, and Alan Blye knew exactly what he wanted. The process included some trick optical effects using the Chroma Key process.

Sally then changed costumes, this time dressing up as Maxine. She was carefully positioned on the set so as not to overlap with herself as Patty. The next tape was then recorded, making a composite adding Maxine to the mix. The third and final shot was Sally dressed as Laverne. Now the tape contained Sally as all three Andrews Sisters but with three long shots of Sally side by side on the stage. To enhance the song a bit, before Sally changed her costume each time, a close-up of her in the appropriate dress was recorded. These close-up shots were then edited into the place in the song where Alan Blye wanted them.

Since the soundtrack was recorded in its entirety on the first take on all subsequent takes, Sally listened to the playback of music and lip synched the words. Many takes were made in order to get the best performance from Sally. This was quite a grueling experience for her, and as the day went on, her lip synching of the sound track wasn't always on the mark. However, since I was inserting the close-up shots after the basic editing had been completed, if I saw Sally was a couple of frames out of sync (usually behind the sound track), I would merely adjust the position of the edit to compensate. I was in every case able put her back in perfect lip sync. After we had completed editing the song, Sally was invited in to see it. She was so delighted that she shook my hand and thanked me over and over for a great job.

When videotape came into use in 1956, all editing was done by physically cutting and splicing by hand. This process continued for several more years but in 1963, Ampex brought out the first electronic editor controlled by a small computer. Although it did make good electronic edits, it was not the easiest device to use since manipulating the single frame audio tones that triggered the start and end points of every edit required great skill. The biggest problem was that if the director wanted a change anywhere in the program, there was no way to correlate the edit tones to the new change since every set of edit tones would have to be rearranged or moved upstream or downstream to accommodate the new length of any scene change. This was not only time-consuming but often very frustrating since repositioning those start and stop edit tones was a hit-or-miss proposition.

Four years after the introduction of Editec, EECO developed a method of addressing every frame of a videotape with a unique number (sort of like a consecutive street address) that would allow an operator to log these numbers as editing points. This feature, called time code, was implemented in this new system and it improved repeatability, a major factor in the increased use of electronic editing. Now it was only necessary for the operator to log every set of in and out time code numbers which enabled him or her to modify one or more scenes of a program with much greater accuracy and speed.

Although EECO was a giant leap forward in the field of electronic editing, it still had limitations. There was no method of storing a set of time code numbers so that they could be retrieved and used to make changes or construct another frame-accurate copy of a program. All the time code numbers had to be written down on paper and entered into the editing system one edit at a time.

In 1972, CMX developed the first really practical computer-assisted editing system. All edits were not only printed out on paper by the computer, they were also stored on a punched paper tape containing the same information. By using a paper tape reader, the operator could retrieve all the edits and restore the information so that a program could be easily updated or in other ways modified. The only pitfall to this procedure was that every edit recorded by the computer stayed in its memory so that in the event that the edit list had to be used to fix a program or make another copy from original source material, every edit would be repeated—even those that were later considered as no good. Unless these so-called bad edits were noted by the operator and skipped or deleted from the list, an extra amount of redundant recording would occur (in effect nullifying the benefits of stored edit lists). Later, software programs were developed that could find redundant edits and carefully remove them and even rearrange edits to put them in consecutive program order.

The CMX editing system used a computer manufactured by a company called Digital Equipment Company (DEC). The computer contained only 8K (thousand bytes) of memory. (This is minuscule compared to the standard amount of memory now used in personal computers and those used for editing.) Most current systems contain from 8MB (million bytes) to more than 32MB of memory. The DEC computer weighed in at 100 pounds and cost $10,000. Just compare that to what is available today and you will quickly see why the computer editing of the early 1970s was still a long way from being really efficient.

The term off-line editing is generally construed to mean creating a work print on film or videotape whose purpose is to provide program continuity along with a set of time code numbers that can later be used to assemble a master edited tape for broadcast or distribution for other purposes. Until 1977, there were no truly computer-assisted editing systems available. Of course, a few people devised crude versions of editing systems that were not entirely computer-assisted but that had a few functions making it *appear* they were. In 1973, while working at CFI, we decided to design and build a state-of-the-art computer-assisted videotape editing system since nothing like what we had in mind was commercially available. The software was written by Jim Adams, who previously worked for CMX and was one of the developers of the CMX-600. We used four industrial version one-inch videotape machines. There were three playback VTRs and one record VTR. We decided on this format because these industrial format VTRs could wind videotape from one end of an hour-reel to the other in less than 60 seconds, a feat previously unheard of.

It took a year to build the hardware and write the software but when we began testing the completed system, we were amazed that it worked so well. Since I worked through every stage of development, I wanted to be the first to edit a program on it. It turned out to be the American Film Institute's salute to Orson Welles, which I edited in January of 1974. Because we used these high speed VTRs, searching for material and having three playback VTRs gave me more capacity and speed than anyone had ever seen before. It even had a unique feature called "look ahead" which allowed VTRs that weren't busy making an edit to search for upcoming shots and have them cued and ready to make another edit.

Even better was the fact that if the next source or playback machine was cued far enough in advance of the edit point, the play VTR would go into play, synchronize itself to the record machine and make the next edit without even stopping the record machine. Often several edits could be made if they were long enough to allow the next VTR to cue itself up. This of course depended on where on the reel the next shot was located. Since there were three playback machines available, the number of consecutive edits that could be made without stopping was determined only by where the material happened to be at the time the VTR started to search. In automatic assemblies of television programs, I have made as many as 15 consecutive edits without stopping the record VTR. No one in the industry had yet developed such exotic software. Years later, none of the commercial vendors had duplicated the power of the "look ahead" feature developed by CFI in the middle 1970s. The CMX version, called the CMX-50, came out at the annual National Association of Broadcasters Convention. Even though the CFI editing system was not designed as a commercial venture, its power and editing speed brought many clients to the facility because they could save money and leave with a good product.

When the executives at CMX heard about our in-house editing system, they asked us to give them a demonstration. However, I was against that idea because we had developed proprietary software that was far ahead of anything the industry was using and I was afraid they would try to copy our system and bring out a commercial version. One day a few weeks later, several CMX people including their chief programmer paid us a visit at CFI and I was asked to give them a demonstration. I tried to be as evasive as possible about how certain things worked, but they kept asking the same questions over and over. I knew what they were getting at, so I said I couldn't answer because it was "company confidential." However, I can't help believing that we gave them too much information and their clever engineers used it to duplicate many of the features we had incorporated in our system.

The CMX-50 was designed to edit work tapes and generate time code edit lists that would later be used to conform the raw material into an edited master program tape. The primary difference between the CFI system and the CMX-50 was that the CMX-50 used three Sony VCRs instead of one-inch VTRs. The advantage of these relatively new machines was that the operator merely had to pop in a cassette and the mechanism would automatically thread the tape within the machine. The disadvantage in using VCRs was that they wound tape very slowly. From the beginning of a 60-minute tape to the end would take about six minutes (and another six minutes to rewind the tape to the beginning). Even so, the VCR eventually replaced the open reel VTR style of tape machine because they were much less costly and more reliable than the one-inch VTRs.

At the time, the president of the company, Bill Orr, asked me if I would be part of a 15 minute promotional tape describing the history of editing. I refused at first only because I was somewhat camera-shy based on my experience with Bob Hope and the "Jump Cut" award he gave me in 1965. After he spent several hours coercing me, I reluctantly agreed.

The premise of this promotional spot was the development of editing throughout the last seven decades. I was to star as the "editor" who operated everything from a film splicer to the new editing system CMX was debuting at the broadcast television convention. For each scene, I had to change costumes starting with old fashioned knickers, a horrible-looking wig and a beat-up sweater. I had my own makeup person, wardrobe and lighting. I was starting to have fun. I had very few lines since most of the program was narrated. Those lines I did have were ad libbed.

We shot for several days at CFI in Hollywood as well as at other nearby locations where some of the new equipment had been installed. In some ways it was a definitive dissertation on how editing evolved. On the other hand, some of the production values looked a little corny partly because it was very low-budget. (I think the entire project was budgeted at less than $20,000.) Although some of the crew got paid, I didn't. After all, I wasn't doing it for the money but rather for the fun of it. It was a big hit at the television convention that year and many people still rib me today about my acting debut.

Three years later, Adams formed the Mach One company to build and service his system to the video editing industry. When I returned to CFI in 1980 after a four-year absence, the Mach One software soon replaced the other commercial software used in all the editing rooms at CFI.

In 1984 came the introduction of the first group of non-linear editing systems designed to materially speed up editing and reduce costs. Non-linear editing means that shots and scenes are transferred to 12-inch laserdisc which have access times of one second or less to find material anywhere on a 30-minute disc. The Editdroid and the CMX-600 were two of the first to use laserdisc in an editing system. Compare that to the access time of a 30-minute videotape (about 3 minutes from one end of the tape to the other). The biggest drawback to laserdiscs is their cost and the fact that once recorded, they cannot be reused. About all they were good for after editing was as a Frisbee. Because of the high cost of making the laserdiscs (an average of $80 to $100 for each 30-minute disc), other editing system developers chose a different approach. They opted to use banks of VHS or Betamax VCRs to accomplish the same thing. By putting identical material on all the VCRs, up to two hours on each of 15 VCRs, the editing software would carefully position each of the

VCRs enabling several machines at a time to search out specific shots frame-accurately and play them in continuity without recording a videotape. In this fashion, multiple VCRs would play and switch shots and cue up other shots as needed while the rest of the system was playing material. This process was not as fast as a laserdisc system but is far more cost effective since even 15 or so VCR videotapes could be erased and re-used dozens of times. The Ediflex, Link and Montage non-linear editing systems were just a few of the many editing systems developed in the mid 1980s.

In the early 1990s, the laserdisc and videotape non-linear editing systems were replaced by computers using hard disc drives as the storage medium. Lightworks, Avid, Matrox and D-Vision are just a few of the many high speed non-linear editing systems used to edit not only television programs but feature films as well. These new systems are the most productive of any yet developed and cost even less than the old style videotape editing systems still in use today.

In the early days of computerized editing, there were sometimes computer problems called "bugs" or equipment failures during an editing session with a client. The term used to describe these problems is called "down time." In order for me to look confident in front of the client or to make them think I was in complete control of the situation, I devised a method of hiding from the client the fact that something was amiss or that things were not going according to plan. This was developed because most clients would find any opportunity to get a rebate on their editing session to save money. I had one client who carried a stop watch and noted to the minute how much time should be deducted from the bill due to equipment failure or "down time."

Down time attributed to the client was not deductible from the bill when the client stopped the edit session to take or make phone calls or if a reel of tape was missing and someone had to go get it. In these cases, the philosophy was that if the editor or company had a failure that caused the editing session to stop, then the amount of down time would be deducted from the bill. If the client caused the down time, he or she would have to pay.

Of course, the company hated down time caused by technical problems, and I didn't like it either. Not only did it make our company look bad, it did not reflect well on me as the one in charge. So I came up with a plan to try and eliminate as much non-billable time as possible. This worked only in those instances when either I had a problem entering data into the computer or some other small technical hang-up that could be fixed in a matter of two or three minutes. For obvious problems that could not be covered by a "smoke screen," I would have to alert the client and hope the problem could be fixed as quickly as possible so as not to tie up the client's time much beyond what he or she had booked.

If there was down time due to equipment failure, this posed several problems. First, it would delay the next client waiting to get in. Second, it might delay the client's schedule in another facility where other work was scheduled. Third, even though there was down time, the company had to pay our salaries while we all waited for the equipment to be repaired. This was costly, especially if the problem required several hours to fix. The company could not be profitable if there was too much down time.

Generally, most editing facilities had three or more editing rooms and unless they were all up and running, the company would not make money. It was important to be sure the technical staff and others kept this equipment in top shape through preventative maintenance. The VTRs were the most prone to failure because of high usage. Not only were these machines used for editing, they were also used by the night shift to make copies of programs for duplication and syndication, a term called "dubbing." Often these VTRs would run as much as 20 hours a day, six or seven days a week. It was easy to see how wear and tear could cause a machine failure.

The second type of problem was not so obvious. The software programs used to control the equipment and store all the edits would sometimes malfunction not because of the software changing but because of a "bug" that could only be detected during a certain kind of computer operation. These were the most difficult to fix because they were random in nature. This would generally occur when a change was made to the software to add a feature that somehow interacted with another part of the program. It would sometimes take hours or even days to find bugs and to make corrections so that it did not affect other parts of the program.

In order to protect myself and the company, I would divert the client's attention from any problem I found that I thought could be corrected either by my making a change not to the software program but to my edit list that often could reflect a change to an edit or series of edits that would not cause down time. Because computer editing is a very complex procedure, the chance of error in entering data or modifying the existing edit list is quite good even for the most experienced editor. (Editors are under great pressure not only to do editing but to operate the hardware associated with editing such as the stereo audio board, the video switcher and a host of other highly complex pieces of hardware.)

Setting up this hardware, manipulating the edit list and dealing with the client is a pressure-filled job and, although many editors are well-paid, the pressure is not always worth the monetary reward. Good and highly respected editors generally work longer hours than other editors and spend less time with their families. I was very conscientious when I was editing and often spent long hours away from home. Looking back, I regret not being at home with my family enough when they were growing up. Long hours were the cause of my resigning from NBC and I did not want to fall into the same trap again.

Manipulating the computer edit list which consisted of time code information was a tough job. Each group of eight digits or numbers defined the hours, minutes, seconds and frames of each edit. Every edit line stored in the computer had four different groups of time code numbers. There is the start and stop time of the playback material and the reel number from which it came. Corresponding to that is a second set of start and stop times indicating where that particular edit was located on the master edited tape. In addition, there is video and audio switcher information and even notes associated with some edits to remind the editor to make some change to a particular edit during the automatic assembly.

Whenever I found that I had a problem with the edit list and I didn't want the client to know, I would talk out loud to myself as I was making the corrections. The client had no idea what I was doing and, since these changes generally only took a couple of minutes, they thought I was involved in some complex mathematical computer manipulation and never thought that it might be considered down time. We weren't trying to cheat the client, but to document every one- or two-minute problem wasn't practical. Sometimes, to compensate the client for these changes, the bill would reflect a completion time 15 minutes less than the clock showed when editing was finished.

However, whenever we had a technical failure, I would let the clients know and tried to estimate how long it would take to fix. In order for them not to get anxious and fidgety, I would tell jokes from my vast repertoire to ease their worries. If the repair job appeared lengthy, the company would pay for me to take the clients to lunch or dinner. Fortunately, this only happened a few times in my career, attesting to the ability of our technicians to quickly find the problem and make repairs. Today, because of more highly developed hardware and software, down time due to technical failures or software bugs is becoming less and less of a problem.

I spent about 80 percent of my career editing comedy and musical variety programs. They say that laughter is good medicine. Well, through the years I've had a good dose of it. The rest of the programs I edited were dramatic or other non-comedy programs, but my first love is comedy. I think I have a great sense of humor and a great supply of jokes stolen from some of the best comedians in the world.

CHAPTER EIGHT

More Career Moves

During the summer of 1976, my boss asked me if I wanted to attend a broadcast video symposium given by the 3M company. He told me he couldn't go and that the company would give me paid time off to go to this conference. How could I refuse? He didn't know any of the details and said he would have the 3M representative contact me.

A few days later, I got a call from 3M giving me the particulars of this seminar to be held in a place called Wonewok, Minnesota. I was told just to bring clothes, nothing else, since all other things would be provided. I would be leaving in a few weeks and I would get further instructions. About a week later, my wife Dee received a beautiful silver necklace from 3M along with a letter thanking her for "loaning" her husband to 3M for the week. I could already see this was going to be a classy operation.

I was told to meet on the private side of the Los Angeles (LAX) airport where a plane would be waiting to whisk us to Minneapolis. When Dee and I got there, I said good-bye to her and boarded a 3M private jet, a Grumman Gulfstream. It was a small plane and had only room for nine passengers. The seats were swivel, meaning they could be swung around 180 degrees to face another passenger. The minute we were seated, we were offered sandwiches and other things to eat and drink. The pilot told us to fasten our seat belts before takeoff. We were taxiing towards the runway while I played cards with Tom Mann, a friend from a company called Vidtronics. All of sudden, I was sucked back in my seat and I thought we were going into orbit! I noticed Tom was now directly over my head since he was sitting facing me before takeoff. I said, "Please don't loosen your seat belt or you will fall on me." I swear it felt like we were going straight up. We climbed to 44,000 feet and proceeded to head towards Minneapolis.

The flight was uneventful so I walked into the cockpit and chatted with the pilot and co-pilot. I said, "Can you tell me where we are?" The pilot said he didn't know but if I really wanted to know, he would check with one of the two on-board computers that kept track of our flight path. The only money I lost on the trip was two dollars on a bet. There were two gauges inside the cabin that registered the outside temperature and altitude. I guessed that at 44,000 feet, the outside air temperature would be 35 degrees below zero. It was 85 degrees below.

When we landed, we were whisked away to a motel and dinner. We spent the next day touring the 3M plant before being driven to Wonewok. One of the interesting things we saw was a "quiet room," which I guess was used to test certain kinds of electronic equipment. The room itself had acoustically treated walls. We entered the room standing on a floor grill. When the door was closed, the acoustic material on the walls seemed to suck every bit of sound out of the room. I could only hear my heart beating inside my chest. It was eerie.

When we arrived at Wonewok, we were assigned to two-bedroom cottages. I was bunking with one of the fellows I met on the plane. These cottages were fully furnished, including a bar and refrigerator. There were 24 invited guests and 24 3M employees. My understanding is that the 3M employees were there as winners in sales contests and we were there as clients. CFI at that time did a large amount of business with 3M, buying the bulk of their videotape from them. My part in the seminar was to give a talk on post production and editing since I was the only one at the conference with that background. We spent the first day hearing about the latest in technology and upcoming new television hardware. I gave my talk and showed some video of new equipment we had installed at CFI.

What was unusual is that no women were involved at all except for the camp cook. The meals were great, really fit for a king. For example, we would have wild rice pancakes stuffed with mushrooms for breakfast. During that meal, we would be asked to select something from the dinner menu. Typically it would be prime rib, trout, shrimp or some other expensive food I normally didn't eat at home. The day's activities included trout fishing, skeet shooting, boating, swimming or just lounging around the grounds. There were hundreds of miles of lake shoreline. My friend Jack Calaway and I took out one of the power boats and spent the day watching beavers build a dam. I tried a little of everything that was offered.

Every afternoon, there was cocktail hour. At that time, a huge bowl of shrimp and other items were presented for us to enjoy. Prior to the start of the cocktail hour, all skeet shooting and other use of firearms was halted, for obvious reasons. When dinner was announced, we went into the dining room and sat down at any one of the tables. Within a few minutes, the dinner entree we had ordered that morning was brought directly to us. The tables were not reserved and we couldn't figure out how the waiters knew who we were and what we had ordered. Later we discovered that a 3M representative who knew us was hiding in the kitchen, pointing us out to the waiters. It was a clever idea which made us feel all the more welcome.

At one point, I had forgotten to bring a cap since it was so hot outdoors. I asked one of the 3M fellows where I could get a cap up here, miles from nowhere. He brought me over to a drawer and told me to pick out any hat, courtesy of 3M. Later, I ran out of film and asked the same fellow about getting more film. He went to another drawer and gave me three 36 exposure rolls of 35mm 3M film. He also told me that when I had exposed the rolls, to return the film to him and 3M would process, print and mail the pictures back to me. This was unbelievable. One day I went trout fishing in a pond stocked with fish. Within minutes, I had caught my limit. I could almost reach in and pick them out of the water. As soon as we got back to the dock, our catch was tagged with our names, cleaned, frozen and, a few days later, mailed home ready to be cooked and eaten.

After dinner, several of us would walk around the area but soon discovered we were covered with ticks. We spent the rest of the evening "unticking" ourselves. Without a doubt, it was the best week I ever spent in the company of friends, great food and atmosphere. I take my hat off to the 3M organization for making that seminar one I'll never forget.

In 1976, I was finally able to join the Motion Picture Film and Videotape Editors Guild, Local 776. The Guild's name had been updated to include videotape since the handwriting was on the wall and they didn't want to be left behind. When videotape was added to their name, I thought hell had frozen over because of all the fear and animosity that had been built up over the years which prevented any real cooperation between the two mediums and the various guilds. Soon, I was elected to the Board of Directors of the Guild and was on it for a two-year term representing videotape editors.

Once the Editors Guild decided videotape editing was here to stay, they purchased a CMX-50 editing system to teach their members how to utilize the power of a computer to help make their job much easier. At first, it was hard to convince most members that they should at least be familiar with this new technology. But I must say, the younger members were far more anxious to learn than the older ones because the older members were quite intimidated by the multi-colored keyboard and all the strange terminology. However, as one of the instructors, I was amazed at how quickly some of the them took to this new way of editing.

My friend Fred Berger, who used to edit the series *Dallas*, switched over to videotape editing and has no desire to go back to film editing. One reason is that tape editing is cleaner because there is no actual handling of film or tape. Another editor once told me that he calls tape editing "gentleman's editing" because the rooms are quiet and there is no mess, nor are there any trim bins filled with hundreds of small pieces of film.

In 1976, I was still supervising editor for CFI's videotape division and editing my usual long hours, racking up a lot of overtime. I was editing *The New Mickey Mouse Club,* a five-day-a-week syndicated children's show and the *Dean Martin Roasts* specials one after the other. On very short notice, the head of the tape department resigned and went to another postproduction facility. They didn't know what to do on such short notice so Sid Solow, the president of CFI, asked me if I would consider stepping into the job as the new department manager. I was really taken aback since I really only had experience in management of my own small facility. They were asking me to run a department of 55 people.

The company needed an answer within two days. I thought about it and talked it over with my wife. We decided that it couldn't be any worse than working the long hours I'd been doing for the past five years. Besides, I would be working normal hours and going home at the same time every night. This seemed to me like it would work. I told Sid I would accept the job. That was on a Friday. At the time, I assumed they would lead me through the corporate maze before I could do any serious damage. After all, they were structured and had been in business since the 1930s. I thought I could make it if they gave me some help. It wasn't like I was walking into a new company for the first time. I knew everybody there and they all knew me.

As it turned out, I was scheduled to work that weekend on another *Dean Martin Roast* special. I remember telling the producer that we had to finish by midnight Sunday because after that, I would turn into management. We did finish editing by 11:30 Sunday night, just in time for me to get home and get a few hours sleep because my new job started at eight the next morning.

I was somewhat apprehensive since I had no formal training for this position. I walked over to my desk, put down my briefcase and went to get a cup of coffee. Within the first half hour, all hell broke loose. I was asked to go to a meeting regarding some union problems. I knew something of what was going on but was not briefed before going into the meeting, so I essentially kept my mouth shut. Then I was asked to join a corporate meeting on budgets for the next quarter. I felt like I was in the twilight zone. My head was buzzing and I had no idea of what I was doing. I couldn't wait to get home that night. Did I make a mistake? Well, this was the first day and I kind of had the jitters. Maybe it would be better tomorrow.

Tuesday came and one problem after another hit me that day. It was as bad as Monday. There were different problems but not having any prior knowledge of the situations I was being pulled into, I felt very uneasy. I went to see Sid Solow. I told him of my concerns but he told me not to worry. Things would work themselves out. Wednesday came and more problems surfaced. Someone gave me a Valium in an attempt to calm me down. All this did was make me dizzy. I thought, "What have I gotten myself into?"

By Friday, nothing had improved and I didn't think I could face another week of this. A friend told me what I should do. He said, "He who fights and runs away, lives to fight another day." I wasn't a quitter but I knew if I collapsed, they would have someone taking my place before my body hit the floor. I didn't let this happen at NBC and I wasn't about to let it happen here.

I wrote out my resignation that Friday, only five days into my new job, and gave it to Sid Solow. He was disappointed, but I told him of my lack of prior training for this job and the monumental problems the department faced, and that I wasn't up to the job of manager. I told him had I been minimally trained for this position I probably could have made it. Besides, there were a few people in the film lab who resented the video division. For one reason, our salaries were much higher than those of the lab workers. Solow tried to talk me out of leaving but I'm sure he knew what I was up against and accepted my resignation. I gave CFI three weeks' notice so they could find a replacement.

I called my friend Dick Krown, a producer for Walt Disney on *The New Mickey Mouse Club* series, and told him of my decision. He said, "Why don't you come over to Disney and help get this series off the ground?" I knew a lot of Disney people and thought that it would finally solve my frustrations. I don't like pressure. I waited out the next three weeks knowing I wouldn't have to face any more pressure at CFI. When I ran into a problem, I turned it over to my assistant Dennis Embler whom I suggested the company put in my place since I felt he could handle the job.

I went to work for Disney the first Monday after I left CFI. There were problems on the Disney lot as well, but not to the extent I had at CFI. There was animosity towards the tape crew on the lot since from the time Walt Disney opened the studios, nothing but film had ever been shot there until now. The film people were afraid that the video people would take their jobs. There was deliberate overcharging in some areas to inflate the costs of shooting on video, hoping the studio would reconsider using video crews on the lot.

Producing a five-day-a-week, half-hour show was a massive undertaking. Twelve new kids were used in this series. It was Disney's intent to revive the charisma of the original *Mickey Mouse Club*. I was supervising the editing of the series and coordinating other postproduction areas relating to editing. The logistics of editing five daily programs week after week were more than some of the staff could bear.

There were five different standard openings that I edited before leaving CFI. Several remote crews were shooting segments to be integrated into future shows. Most of the program was live but the timing was critical, especially when segments were switched around. That created severe timing problems and caused a lot of additional editing to keep each episode within the proper time constraints.

Working at Disney studios was pleasant even though the series was a headache to edit. The grounds of the studio were impeccable. Everyone had a pleasant smile and attitude. I seldom went out to lunch since the studio commissary was my favorite. All meals were fresh, homemade and inexpensive. I could stuff myself for about two dollars a meal.

I stayed with Disney for about five months. There were too many problems I couldn't resolve because of various roadblocks. Dick Krown (one of the field producers) and I seemed to be the only sane people on this project. There were personality conflicts and a host of other seemingly insurmountable problems I thought I had left behind me. When I decided to leave, the staff took me out to lunch and gave me a plaque with all their signatures and (of course) a Mickey Mouse wristwatch. I did make a lot of friends during my brief stay but, seeing the pressure beginning to mount again, I decided it was time for me to make a move to quieter pastures.

In 1977, I was asked to consult for the Ampex Corporation. They were unveiling a new kind of electronic editor designed as a self-contained package. Everything was included: switcher, VTR machine control and audio. It even had a learning mode that allowed an editor to create special effects, modify and repeat them. This system was called the EDM-1. I was given training on the system prior to going to the NAB (National Association of Broadcasters) television convention held in Washington, D. C. Although my training with the EDM-1 was limited, I absorbed enough to be able to do the demonstrations needed to sell this kind of equipment at a trade show.

It was a classy piece of equipment and impressed me with its compact design. During the convention, I must have been successful in demonstrating the EDM-1 because Ampex asked me if I would like to go to Montreaux, Switzerland, to demonstrate the system there. What an opportunity! I would be gone for three weeks and I didn't want to leave Dee alone for that long a period. I explained this to Ampex and they agreed to let me take her along.

In June, we were off to Switzerland. We rented a car in Geneva and drove the 45 miles to Montreaux. This was our first time in Europe and not only were we unfamiliar with the customs, but we also didn't speak French. Many people did speak English, but we found it a bit more difficult to converse outside cities with the local residents. Even though many of the shopkeepers spoke English, we found some of them would only speak French, pretending not to understand us. This was quite annoying and I'm sure they lost business because we and others often walked away without buying anything. We bought a French-English dictionary just to be able to converse.

We picked up the basic phrases and were able to "limp" through conversations with the locals. When we first arrived, we stopped at a local restaurant in Montreaux and ordered ham and cheese sandwiches. The waiter said they didn't serve that item. I asked them if they had just ham sandwiches. The waiter said yes. Then I asked him if they had cheese sandwiches. Again the waiter nodded yes. I told him to bring us two of each and we made our own ham and cheese sandwiches.

In order to get a good travel rate, Ampex had to purchase airline tickets and rooms for a three-week stay even though the convention only lasted for eight days. This meant we had almost two weeks of free time to sightsee. Since the convention in Montreaux did not start for a week, we stayed at a local chalet north of the city. It was up in the mountains and was called the Montanard. We had a private one-bedroom cabin with a kitchen and a beautiful view of the mountains. The fields were covered with narcissus flowers so dense they looked like snow. There was no radio or television. The nearest telephone was at the restaurant a quarter mile below us. We were completely isolated.

The first week we spent sightseeing. We went to the nearby village of Gruyere, where the world-famous cheese was made. When we first walked into the cheese factory, the smell of fermenting cheese nearly knocked us over, but after a few minutes, the odor seemed to disappear. The cheese is made under hospital-clean conditions and aged for at least two months before shipping. We viewed the cheese-making process from a glass-enclosed gallery above the factory, watching white-coated people scurry about the room with a certain amount of intensity. Driving in Switzerland was no problem because there are numerous road signs. Even though we didn't speak French, the road signs and graphics were easily understood.

The second week was the convention. When I first went to the convention center to get oriented, we were told that most of the connecting cables had been cut on the Ampex EDM-1 editing system and they suspected sabotage. It took a crew of engineers working day and night to rebuild those cables in time for the show. The system kind of worked during the convention, but there was inadequate air conditioning and low voltage throughout the building which caused much of the equipment (including the EDM-1) to malfunction. Whenever I had a break, I would walk over to the air conditioning vent and stand in front of it with my suit jacket open, hoping to get enough cool air so that I could go back to work. Since we had so many problems with the system, someone dubbed the EDM-1 "The Edit-Maybe" system.

One evening, on our twenty-third wedding anniversary, we were invited to dinner courtesy of my former employer Bill Orr, president of CMX. Since I was working for Ampex at the convention, I felt I had to ask my boss if it was okay to "go to dinner with the competition." CMX manufactured similar types of editing equipment and I thought it would be much wiser for me to ask permission than to possibly create a scene if my boss found out later. The restaurant was located on the other side of Lake Geneva in France (about a 45-minute drive from Montreaux), so we had to go through customs just to go to dinner. We drove around the end of the lake until we came upon the border crossing. We managed to get through customs okay since we told the guards we were only going to dinner and would return later that evening.

The restaurant was in a medieval castle which also had living quarters for the family that owned it. There were four couples and we had a great time. However, after several rounds of drinks, two of the women got into a big argument and it almost came to blows. We had to break up the fight and calm down those involved or we would have been thrown out. The dinner and fight lasted well into the evening until at last we realized we were the only guests left in the room. I looked at my watch and was shocked to see that it was well past 2 A.M. Time does fly when you're having fun!

After the convention was over, we had a few more days to sightsee. Gasoline was nearly three dollars a gallon and, even though we had a fuel-efficient Renault, we spent enough money on fuel to almost buy the car. As it turned out, paying for the three-week car rental drastically depleted our finances. When we landed at LAX, we had only twelve dollars between us, just enough to almost fill up the tank for the ride home.

Some time later, I was again consulting for CMX. Bill Orr asked me to go to London to meet with Stanley Kubrick to try and convince him to use the CMX editing system to edit his next picture, *The Shining*. I flew to London and took a taxi to my hotel near Piccadilly Circus. On the way there, the driver asked me if this was my first trip to London. I told him yes. He asked me if I would like to see a little of the city on the way to my hotel. I said, "Why not!"

When we came upon Buckingham Palace, the driver asked, "How about getting your picture taken with one of the Queen's guards?" At this point in time, I was a little groggy from jet lag so the driver could have taken me anywhere. He said, "Give me your camera and stand next to the guard." I walked over to this guy in his bright red uniform and sheepishly stood next to him. He was well over six feet tall and, with that tall hat, looked about eight feet tall. The driver said "Smile!" and snapped the picture. When I got the picture back several weeks later, I saw this little runt with a pained look on his face standing next to a giant.

The next day, Stanley Kubrick's secretary told me to meet him at one o'clock in a restaurant next door to the studio. I hailed a taxi to take me to the studio on the outskirts of London, some 40 miles from my hotel. The driver was unfamiliar with that section of London but he took me anyway, thinking it would be a big fare and a large tip. When we got to the area where the driver thought the studio was, he pulled over to the side of the road and got out his map. Scratching his head, he looked quite puzzled. After a few moments, a quaint little old lady scurried out of her house and came up to the taxi. "May I help you?" she inquired. The driver told her of his predicament and she pointed the way for us. It turned out that we were less than a quarter mile from the studio.

Luckily, I arrived at the restaurant on time. I walked into this somewhat plain-looking establishment and looked around. I had never met Mr. Kubrick and had not seen any photos of him, so I had no idea what he looked like. There were only four people in the restaurant: Two younger looking men who didn't fill my description of what he might look like, an older woman and a middle aged man with a beard. I figured that was my best bet. I walked over to his table and said, "Mr. Kubrick?" He said, "Yes." "My name is Art Schneider and I was sent here by CMX to see you."

Seating myself at Mr. Kubrick's table, I said, "Before we get started, I'd like you to know that I am not only a videotape editor but also a film editor as well." He heaved a sigh of relief. "Thank God. I was afraid they were going to send an engineer who wouldn't have the foggiest notion of editing." We had a fish and chips lunch and talked for some two hours about editing. He told me what he needed and I took notes and made suggestions.

After lunch, we walked back to the studio but Mr. Kubrick had to get back to work. I asked him where I could get a taxi to take me back to London. He said that it was impossible to get a taxi to come out to the studio and offered to have his limousine take me back to my hotel. I was flabbergasted. I got into this long limo and had a very comfortable ride back to London.

When I returned to California, I gave Bill Orr all my notes along with a cover letter outlining what Kubrick wanted. After several weeks of discussion with the CMX engineers, it was decided that it would not be cost effective for them to build the kind of editing system he wanted. Today, however, it is quite common to transfer motion picture film to videotape, edit it and then release the feature on motion picture film such as he had hoped to do with *The Shining*.

In August, Bill Orr took me to Australia to attend their version of our annual NAB convention. I was to demonstrate a model of the CMX operating on a PAL, a different television standard than is used in the U.S. The basic editing system is quite similar to the type used in the U.S. but it operates at 25 frames per second as opposed to our 30 frames per second. It was a little difficult to get used to editing and trimming frames on an editing system running slower than I was used to.

It was August and winter in Australia, so it was somewhat cold and rainy. We left from San Francisco and flew to Hawaii, then on to the Fiji Islands to refuel. We landed in Fiji on a tiny island with no apparent lighting system. I gripped my seat expecting to land in the water, but then came down smoothly on the runway. The entire 12,000 mile trip took about 19 hours with stopovers. When I asked Bill Orr for expense money, he told me I wouldn't need it. (He was right. He gave me $300 but when I got back to California, I gave back $260 of it. Everything was taken care of for me—hotel, meals, travel, tips, everything. I spent only cab fare to and from the airports.)

We landed in Sydney, Australia, and as we were walking down the exit ramp, I stumbled and said, "That must be because we are now upside down." We spent ten days in Sydney and Melbourne, where the convention was held. I gave several lectures on editing to various postproduction groups as well as the Australian Broadcasting Company.

As it turned out, Sydney is constantly "on strike." At our hotel, the waiters were on strike so we had to eat buffet style the whole time we were there. One day, Bill Orr and I wanted to visit the famed Sydney Opera House on an island. However, in order to get there, one must take a water taxi to the island. This day, all the water taxis were on strike except for one independent taxi which we took over to the opera house. When we got there, we found out that the opera house was *also* on strike, so all we were able to do was to walk around the grounds of the building.

The currency in Australia is in dollars and the maps are indicated in miles, but one thing that was hard to get used to was that everyone drives on the "wrong side" of the street. A friend of Bill Orr's loaned us his Jaguar and we decided to take a sightseeing trip around the city. I opened the door to get in and found myself in the driver's position and Bill found himself in the passenger's side. Driving those streets if you are not used to it can be quite hazardous.

In my freelance editing days, I often did a lot of consulting for large and small companies. Prior to my starting my own company, EVI, I was asked by Bill Orr, if I would be interested in consulting for CMX. (They wanted me to write a new User's Guide for their editing systems. They had seen the training manuals I had written while at CFI and wanted the same "plain English" type of instructive language as opposed to the very technical language used by most manufacturers. I agree with that philosophy since an instruction manual is essentially worthless if the material in it is not easily understood.)

Writing a new version of their editing manual required me to make weekly trips to the factory for several months. I was also asked for my input regarding new editing options from the point of view of film and video editors. Bill Orr and I got along great. We went on lecture tours to Australia and made other trips across the country and Canada to help sell the CMX line. But at that time they were having problems with their software which caused headaches for them and the people that bought these systems.

At that point in time, I was contemplating becoming partners with TV producer Alan Blye in EVI (Electronic Video Industries), a video postproduction facility. Alan was one of those producers who was always in the editing room and became upset at the problems with the CMX system (in several cases it lost edits in the computer's memory that could not be recovered). When this happens, you must remake every lost edit, which is an expensive waste of time. Alan and I signed an agreement to start this new company and he asked me what other kinds of editing systems were available. The only one that I knew of that would do what Alan wanted was the Mach One designed by a former CMX employee, Jim Adams.

When we decided to go with the Mach One instead of a CMX system, I had to tell Bill Orr I could no longer consult for his company because that would be a direct conflict of interest. I called his office and talked to his vice president Al Behr, who told me that he would relay my message to Bill. About two hours later the phone rang and Bill went into a tirade, the likes of which I had never heard before. Among other things, he called me a back stabber, traitor and other names I don't wish to put in print. I tried to tell him the reason for my leaving as his consultant but he would not listen to any of my explanations.

From then on, at trade shows, meetings or any other place where we would run into each other, he just passed me with daggers in his eyes, not saying a word. This went on for more than a year until for some reason he mellowed out and we became friends again, I suspect Al Behr finally was able to get him to listen to the explanation for my leaving his employ. Once we became friends again, I told Bill that I had just bought a new sailboat. He asked me when I would take him out on. My response was, "As soon as I install a plank on the bow!" He kind of laughed, but we remained friends, even though he never did go sailing with me.

After we decided on using the Mach One editing system, EVI was founded by myself, Alan Blye and Bob Einstein, Alan's partner. They put up all the money to start a small off-line editing boutique. We rented space in a film laboratory called Fotokem, located in beautiful downtown Burbank. Since the space was formerly a storage area, we had to install the walls and build our own offices as well as put in an oversized power panel to handle all the electrical requirements of the equipment.

The editing system was the Mach One. However, the company had just gone into business and had only shown a prototype. The designer and owner, Jim Adams, was a genius. Jim could solve any problem related to hardware or software since he was not only a programmer but a hardware designer.

We had a tough time getting going because of a manufacturing problem with the controller boards. Jim and I spent every day for nearly three months correcting the problem and finally got the system working in December. We spent the rest of that month debugging and making improvements to the software. Our first client was Loma Linda University Hospital in Los Angeles. That project worked out well. During our first year of operation, we had nearly 300 clients.

Things were starting to get hectic and I was back working a lot of hours again. We decided to hire another editor Dave Collins, who took a lot of the work load off my back. We hired two maintenance men from Pasadena City College, which has a reputation for turning out skilled graduates in electronic engineering.

As we both found ways to improve the editing system software, I asked my engineer Don Kravits if he knew anything about programming. He said he had taken some courses but that was a few years ago. I asked him if he would like to improve our Mach One editing system and he said he would give it a try. I gave him the technical books and all related material. For more than two weeks, nothing happened. Then one day he asked if he could try something and I said, "Be my guest." He made a very simple alteration in the software, changing the name of the "Mach

One Editing System" to the "EVI Editing System." After that, software improvements were dramatic.

If I were to graph Don's learning curve, it would start out a horizontal line and then in an instant go vertical; it was that dramatic. Kravits made so many improvements that we were head and shoulders above any of our competition in efficiency, which translated into shorter editing hours and lower editing bills for our clients. Among my clients were Stacey Keach, Sr. (Mr. Birdseye). As well as being an actor, he was a commercial producer, mostly making Datsun commercials. Mike Nesmith of Monkees fame was another client. We had other clients such as 20th Century–Fox, and edited most of the series *That's Hollywood*. We did lots of specials as well.

At one time, our company was editing a Beatles special and Ringo Starr was very involved in producing it. When the work print editing was complete, Ringo had to approve it. Somehow the word got around that Ringo would be at EVI but no one knew the exact date. I'm sure that was deliberate to avoid any problems with people gawking at him when he was just trying to do his job without being mobbed. The word was that he was to be there on a Friday, so everyone at the lab wandered around the halls hoping to get a glimpse of Ringo. But he didn't show up until Saturday, when most of the staff was off for the weekend. Ringo managed to see the program without interruption and after making a few changes left the building. I met him briefly as the president of our company but kept out of the way of his entourage.

Probably one of the most memorable clients I ever worked with took me by surprise one day. I was editing when my secretary Linda Moore came over and said there was someone to see me. The guy looked very familiar to her but she couldn't remember his name. I went out to the lobby and immediately recognized the client: It was Allen Funt of *Candid Camera*. Someone had given him my name and he was interested in editing several *Candid Camera* specials. I introduced myself and asked him to come into our lounge and have a cup of coffee. As I poured him a cup, I couldn't resist saying, "Before we start, I'd like to ask you, are we on *Candid Camera*?" He laughed and assured me that we were not. Later, I edited four *Candid Camera* specials for Funt and discovered he edited his specials in much the same way as Bob Hope; he goes for the laugh. If the picture works, fine, but first make it *funny*. I made a number of "jump cuts" in those two specials which is probably why he asked me to edit for him.

I had a good staff at EVI and we often brought in freelance editors as well. They sometimes brought in their own clients, which helped our cash flow for a time. We were quite successful until our neighbor, Compact Video, started to undercut our low editing rates, which made it tough to survive. In addition to competition, the economy was in a slump. Alan Blye asked me to not take a salary except when I was working even though I was president of the company. I couldn't accept that philosophy and when my contract came up for renewal, I elected to leave the company.

After I left EVI, I worked as a freelance editor for a company called Astin-Moore in Hollywood. The company was financed by David Moore and John Astin, the actor. John is very intelligent and would often quote Shakespeare when he came into the office. I edited several more *Candid Camera* specials with Allen Funt at this facility.

One day, I got a letter from *Who's Who in America* in which I was asked to become a subject of the *Who's Who* biography. I wonder who gave them my name and thought that I was worthy enough to be included in this prestigious group. Of course I accepted. The plaque I received states, "The Marquis *Who's Who* Publication Board certifies that Arthur P. Schneider is a subject of biographical record in *"Who's Who in America Fortieth Edition 1978/1979"* inclusion in which is limited to those individuals who have demonstrated outstanding achievement in their own fields of endeavor and who have, thereby, contributed significantly to the betterment of contemporary society." Several years later, I was also included in *Who's Who in Entertainment*. Once in *Who's Who*, you are in for life. I get annual update sheets in case there are more items I want to include in my biography.

In 1980 I began a new venture with my friend, Dick Krown, whom I first met in the mid–1950s when we worked for NBC in Hollywood. Our business, formed on a handshake, was a small company we called Videoedit Systems. Its purpose was to produce educational films showing the damage to the environment caused by pesticides and other factors. Although he and I had made several half-hour films years before, this new partnership was designed to expand our potential and to produce other types of films.

One of our first projects was an environmental film called *A Wonderful Bird Was the Pelican*. This film depicted the destruction of pelican eggs due to DDT and other pesticides the birds were ingesting which made their shells so soft that when that sat on them, the shells were crushed by the weight of the birds. Actor Eddie Albert was in that film.

A second film called *Ah, Man, See What You've Done* was designed to show the damage pesticides can do when washed down into the ocean from streams and storm drains. Another actor of the time, Peter Deuel, narrated. He was so involved with the environment that he offered to narrate the entire film for nothing. It happened to be at the time when Deuel was shooting his television series *Alias Smith and Jones*. He finished shooting late one Friday and showed up at the recording studio at eight the next day. He did take after take until he was satisfied. As it turned out, we needed a few extra lines from him so he showed up the following Saturday to record those lines even though he was very tired.

During the production of the film, we rented a small yacht to take us to Anacapa Island (located off the west coast of Los Angeles) to shoot some footage. Bob Hope's son, Kelly, was working with me at the time and I asked him if he would like to come along to shoot still photographs. We also brought along another friend who worked for Disney. His name was Keith Chaney, a nephew of Lon Chaney, the actor. Keith was a funny character and was always looking for a way to play practical jokes on people. He brought along a high-powered rifle in an attempt to shoot sharks in the ocean if we happened to come across any. On our way out to the island, we were all somewhat bored so Keith pulled out his rifle, walked up to the boat captain and said, "Take me to Cuba!" The captain was not amused and nearly threw Keith overboard. After that incident, Chaney kept the rifle below deck and never brought it out even though we ran across several sharks that day.

Because Krown and I had both worked for Disney, we had developed many positive relationships with that organization. We did several Bank Americard commercials for Bank of America which included several Disney characters (Pluto, Donald Duck and Mickey Mouse) as actors. We shot at several locations all over Burbank and Los Angeles. When mothers saw the camera crew, they ran to get their children to watch us shoot. This happened almost everywhere we went.

Henry Gibson of *Laugh-In* fame was a friend also interested in the environment who narrated several projects for us. We took him on location with us on several occasions to help put together projects we were all interested in. There was a time when Henry called me at home wanting to know if I could get some monster movies for his son's birthday party. As it happened, Dick Krown also worked as a producer for UPA, an organization that, in addition to making cartoon films such as *Mr. Magoo,* also had an extensive feature film rental library. Dick gave me two films for Henry which I picked up and took home with me. I called Henry that evening and told him what I had gotten for him.

He was thrilled and said he would be over to pick the films up the next day. My little son heard this conversation and alerted the entire neighborhood that Henry Gibson was coming to our house. When Henry got off the freeway and onto our street, he was mobbed by dozens of kids along with a few parents. It took almost 30 minutes for Henry to break loose from the crowd. When he finally got to our house, I came out to meet him and apologized profusely for the inconvenience he had to endure. To my surprise, Henry was thrilled that so many people had come to meet him. He told me he spent most of the time signing autographs. To show his appreciation for my getting him the films, he brought me a good bottle of wine.

I was and still am involved in trying to help improve our environment. I got an education while making these films which helped my understanding of the perils we face when we take for granted the God-given things on this earth.

CHAPTER NINE

From Edit One
to the Editdroid

When I left CFI at the end of 1976, I didn't expect to go back. However, some four years later, CFI had new corporate people in place along with plans for expansion. I was asked to come back for a couple of reasons. The department was in need of modernization of the video post-production area. I was willing to return as supervising editor but on one condition: I wanted to bring with me Don Kravits as CFI's in-house programmer since I had great success at EVI with Don in updating our Mach One editing software. I was confident that he would be able to handle any software chore presented to him. They agreed to those terms and I returned in the spring of 1980.

Since CFI was in the film processing business, they wanted a way to edit feature films on video and be able to cut the original camera negative frame-accurately from a number list and release the product to theaters, thereby adding to their overall revenue. That research program intrigued me since my primary training began in film editing at USC. We were given a budget to build a new on-line editing room with state-of-the-art equipment. The staff editors were part of this plan so as to get their input. After all, what's the use in building something no one will use? It was a well-designed room with a beautiful oak console, basic Mach One hardware and software, five Sony one-inch VTRs and other equipment designed to speed up the editing process.

The editing room (or "bay," as some call it) was designed more like a spacious living room setting with comfortable couches, wall-to-wall carpeting, phones and adequate space for the editor and other staff to perform their duties. It was sound-insulated and designed for stereo sound editing. I think most producers and directors, the minute they hit the couch, pick up the phone and start making calls. Trying to get them to approve a complex edit is sometimes done by the producer nodding his or her head while talking on the phone. The editing room often becomes an extension of their office.

We opened our new Edit One at CFI on August 14, 1981, inaugurating it with a series of promotional trailers for 20th Century–Fox. I wanted to be the first to test-drive the new room since I was in on the very concept of the design more than a year before. All the editors loved the system because it took little effort to make simple or complex edits on the CFI system. We were all proud of our accomplishments.

One of the first series I edited on the system was to re-cut the *CHiPs* television series for syndication. The first episode I edited was the pilot, which had wall-to-wall music in it. I had to take out four minutes of program to allow for more commercial time. It was tough but I was able to make smooth transitions, being careful not to up-cut or chop off any music which would make it sound abrupt and off-tempo. I was pleased that it turned out so well. I was editing my seventh episode in the new Edit One when the phone rang. It was the producer of the *CHiPs* series asking who edited the first episode for syndication. I was afraid to answer since I thought it might be a trick question and he would complain about my edits. I asked why he wanted to know. He said he wanted to thank the editor for doing such a smooth job, especially on the music cuts. I heaved a sigh of relief and told him I edited that episode. He thanked me for blending the music and not destroying the storyline.

In order to be most efficient, I would view a 3/4 inch video cassette copy of an episode I planned to shorten for syndication. I would generate a paper list of all possible edits, generally far more than I needed to get the program length to the syndicator's requirements. Then I would type this list into the computer's memory. Since I knew the original length of the program and I knew how many deletions I had listed, I could quickly calculate how many of the tentative deletions I could restore. When the last edit was typed in, the edit list would indicate the total length of the episode. If the overall program length was now short, I would put back any of the edits in my list that approximated the time I needed. If I was still long by a few seconds, I could always start a fade-up a few seconds later to get out those last few seconds. In effect, these additional edits and later fade-ups were a sort of "rubber band" option allowing me to precisely time each episode exactly to the syndicator's time requirements.

Generally, re-editing any series for syndication was a relatively simple matter of pulling out dozens of little shots here and there, a few seconds at a time, without losing track of the story. For example, during a chase, I could cut several seconds out of some shots and in effect speed up the sequence, thereby cutting out some time. Also, when people would exit a room, I would shorten the shot so they left the room quicker. Police cars driving up to a location could easily be shortened and still get the story across. This is typical of how I would remove material without affecting story continuity. Only rarely would I cut out any scripted dialogue since I did not want to confuse the audience by accidentally leaving out a clue or other dialogue pertinent to the story. In those few instances where I was really desperate for time, I would look for superfluous dialogue (which I call "fluff") that could easily be deleted without affecting the storyline.

Once in a while, it would be necessary to make a dissolve to take out a section of material. In that case, I would make a copy of the section I had to dissolve to, make the dissolve then return to the master tape. This procedure was quite rare since nearly all the edits I needed to make for time could be gotten by primarily shortening shots. By making about 50 or 60 separate edits and carefully removing small bits and pieces, some as short as one second, I was able to get every episode to the exact length required for syndication. Because I was, in most instances, pulling up scenes in sequential order, I was able to auto-assemble each episode with incredible speed. I could auto-assemble a one-hour episode in less than 90 minutes, an impressive feat in those days.

A third project I was involved in was designing a compact work print style tape editing system with simplified software that could be easily moved from place to place. I was the only editor on the staff with prior film editing experience so I was able to provide a viewpoint specifically designed for film editors. Of course, as we progressed, film editors from other studios were brought in for their opinions as well. The entire project was successful for many years until better technology came along to replace it.

CFI had a large syndication department, and one of its biggest clients was the *Lawrence Welk* series. The series was edited at ABC and sent to CFI for duplication. However, each week, promotional spots (or trailers, as they are also called) were created from material within each program. These 10-, 20- and 60-second promos were added to the head of each tape, publicizing the show for the following week. In addition, all the commercials were added into blank spots left in the master tape for that purpose. Each program tape was formatted in such a fashion that enough blank space at the head of the tape prior to the start of the program was included for color bars and the three promos.

Associate producer Irv Ross and I would integrate the commercials and build the three spots every week. The entire process would take about four hours. I really had to know what I was doing because I was editing all eight commercials and the three promo spots directly into the ABC edited master tape; this task required me to not only be an editor but a videotape technician as well, since I had to adjust our record VTR to precisely match the ABC master tape so that the commercials and promos wouldn't break up on the air. Once the commercials and promos were integrated, the night crew would make duplicate copies (also called dubs), making as many as 12 at each pass. When you consider that each episode might require up to 100 or more copies, depending on the number of stations taking the program, the copying operation generally took all night. I edited the majority of these syndicated programs and the associate producer and I became friends. Often, he would bring me samples of the sponsor's product—Geritol. He carefully brought the product to me packaged in a plain brown wrapper so my friends wouldn't make jokes about me taking Geritol.

Although I've edited many series, I also enjoyed editing television specials. One in particular I will never forget was *To Will a Miracle*, produced by Dick Clark Productions and starring Cloris Leachman. It is the story of a couple who adopted a blind, developmentally disabled baby, brought him up as their own and gave him the love and devotion that allowed him to live a useful life. When I finished editing, Dick Clark was brought in to view the program. After the screening, he thanked me for a great job. The special got great reviews and has been rerun many times.

Universal was one of the first major studios interested in using videotape as a means of editing their television programs, then converting the data so that the original camera negative could be cut and matched to the edited video image for foreign release. They came to us at CFI in September of 1982 since we had developed a conversion program we felt would fill their needs. We called it Film 5, a software program written for the singular purpose of translating time code information into motion picture film edge numbers and providing a frame-accurate cut list so that the negative cutter, by reading the numbers from the list, could accurately cut a camera negative which would later be printed by the lab.

Don Kravits, the CFI staff programmer, had written the software based on information from me, from other editors and the needs of the negative cutters themselves. Universal decided to try a parallel edit test with an episode of *Magnum, P.I.* One print would be cut by their film editor, while another print of the same episode was being edited by me on video (later to be matched to a duplicate copy of the original camera negative). An episode called *From Moscow to Maui* was selected. I had not seen the series before so Universal sent over a couple of episodes on cassette for me to view so I could get a feeling for the format.

A duplicate negative and a color work print were made for me before the primary material was turned over to Universal. Twenty-eight ten-minute reels were transferred, a running time of about 4.6 hours, providing me with a shooting ratio of almost five to one. Since we were not in a race, our test was just to see if we could do what Universal wanted. The first step was to log the scene and take numbers of all the material. Along with this, we made a punch mark at a convenient frame adjacent to a visible film key number somewhere on the camera slate before action started. Then the film was transferred to videocassette for me to use during editing. After I received the work copy, I would run down to each scene and take and log the exact time code number of the frame with the punch mark and log this information, which would later be used to generate a frame-accurate edit list for the negative cutters.

I cut the episode on videotape as I would any program. I was given a marked script showing all the good and bad takes and where each take started and stopped. It took me about three days and after I finished I called the producer to look at the episode. As he viewed my version, he said nothing. I was a bit apprehensive about what he would say. When the program ended, he turned to me and said, "Not bad. However, you should stay on the star, using more close-ups." I was relieved. He gave me a list of changes they had made on their version so that my cut would closely match the one their editor did.

I did one other thing the film editor could not do. I added opening and closing credits on the work print. On film that's a costly and time consuming task since it has to go to the optical department and is not cost-effective just for use in the work print stage. There was also a shot of Magnum looking through binoculars at someone. I simply used a small circle wipe and, with a joystick, moved it around the screen to follow the action, giving the effect of what Magnum was seeing through his binoculars. Since the optical effects I added were normally available on the video switcher which is part of the editing system, it took only a few minutes to add the credits and special effects. The *Magnum, P.I.* producers were quite pleased with these very simple things I had done on my version.

When I completed editing to the satisfaction of Universal and the negative was finally cut, we determined several things. One, the cost of this test, dollar wise, was about the same. Two, the cost of the editing hours alone (video editing including changes) was two-and-a-half times faster than the same episode edited on film. Part of this is due to the fact that with video editing, there is no hands-on or touching of tape required. Searching for a shot is done by time code. The creative aspect of this project was about the same. However, it should be pointed out that no two editors edit the same. This fact has been documented dozens of times in the past. Third, we did prove that the CFI tape-to-film conversion program was feasible. Taking into account all the variables encountered in this test, we were convinced that this was the way of the future.

Today, editing on tape and releasing on film is a common procedure. More and more feature films and TV series are being cut on video, reducing the cost and allowing faster editing. It also gives greater flexibility to the director and editor which often greatly enhances the final product. Once again I was pioneering in television.

For about five years, I was into sailing. Our first boat was a 22-foot Catalina sailboat with a retractable keel, kept on a trailer in the boat yard at the Marina. It weighed just under one ton so I unofficially called it our "One Ton Sloop." After awhile, we upgraded to a 27-foot Catalina (weighing more than 5,000 pounds) which had to be kept in a slip at the Marina. Our daughter Lori named it "Dream Weaver" after the song. It was great fun but still a little cramped. We then bought a third sailboat, a 30-foot Catalina that was custom-built to our needs and weighed more than 11,000 pounds. I named it "A Work of Art." I quickly found out that a boat is a piece of fiberglas surrounded by water into which you pour money. After about two years, we were not getting enough use out of it so I sold it to a doctor who renamed it (what else?) "Blood Vessel." There is an old saying that goes, "The happiest days in a sailor's life are the day he buys his boat and the day he sells it."

I spent a lot of time volunteering for everything. I was a member of the SMPTE (Society of Motion Picture and Television Engineers) Education Committee. We used to put on seminars from special effects to lighting to editing and everything in between. Many of these projects were in association with my old alma mater, USC. All the seminars that were videotaped, I eventually edited and took out the dull stuff. They were then sold as instructional tapes and were very well received by students all over the country. We even broadcast one seminar by satellite across the U.S. with several colleges participating and the audience's asking questions of the speakers. Each seminar was put together by the education committee, a group of tireless people which included some of the best professionals in their fields. Even though many of the speakers were not experienced to lecture in front of large groups, the response from the audience was excellent. Most of these seminars filled the auditoriums to capacity.

My partner Dick Krown and I would take on all kinds of film and video projects. One interesting project was to make a video cassette version of the Tolstoy classic *War and Peace*. There were several versions made, all of them quite long. The one we had to work with was more than six hours long. In order to make it easier to rent, our client wanted it cut down to no more than four hours which meant it would fit on two two-hour VHS cassettes.

Fortunately, the entire movie was dubbed in English and done extremely well, making it very easy to understand. It took me more than two weeks to trim the slow sequences without disrupting the story. There was a sequence where two people sat looking at each other not saying a word. It ran on for several minutes. I trimmed a couple of minutes and still got the idea of them staring at each other to carry the story point. Much of the war scenes seemed to run on forever and so they too were shortened. Before we assembled the master tape, the client reviewed the entire movie and was quite pleased with the results. I later heard that our version was a best rental movie for many years.

One series I worked on was *The Greatest American Hero*. It was complex to edit and required a large staff of editors on a weekly basis. We were asked to work on one episode called *The Lost Diablo Mine* which had in excess of a thousand edits. The way producers and directors work is that after the first cut is assembled, the editor starts to make changes. Rather than make all the edits over again along with the many changes, the first cut of the work print is used as a playback source to build another version.

The first work tape is copied frame for frame to a new blank tape until a change is required. Then new shots are added or deleted as the case may be. The first cut work print is again copied to the next place where a change is required. Scenes may be swapped, shots added and anything else the director may want to change is done at that time. This process of copying the old work print up to a point, then adding or deleting other material, continues until a second version edited work print has been created. The second version is then reviewed by those interested and notes are taken for more changes.

If extensive changes are required again, the second version of the edited work print is now used as a playback source and copied to a point, and the same kind of changes are made as before. With each revision, another edited version is created along with a new set of time code information of just the changes. This process may go on for as many as ten different versions although generally four to five revisions are made due to budget and time constraints. A heavy action-adventure episode may contain as many as 1500 edits in a single one-hour episode.

The episode I worked on was one of those. However, because of the enormous amount of editing, five editors were working on this project in order to make air date. There were five versions of the episode created and a special software program was required to untangle all the edit information. The way this process worked could in itself fill up a book but because we have more efficient ways of editing now, I only bring this to your attention to show what we were faced with in the days before all the sophisticated editing software became available to us.

The 1500 edit list information was loaded into the computer. The program was started and asked to remove any unwanted edit information, sort the edits in program order and create a new edit list that reflected only those edits approved in the last or final version of the edited work print. Because the software had so many edits to work with, it kind of got choked up and after a while could not continue its sorting and cleaning operation. It was panic time. The programmer who wrote the program was called and he flew down from Northern California that same day. Without his help we could not have completed the operation and no doubt would have missed the air date. As it turned out, not only did we assemble the master broadcast tape from the massive number of edits, but all the editors involved in that episode were nominated for an Emmy

Award for videotape editing. This was the seventh Emmy nomination of my career.

In the spring of 1984, the annual National Association of Broadcasters convention was held in Las Vegas, one of my favorite places to visit. As luck would have it, a company I consulted for, Convergence, was involved in a partnership with George Lucas to develop and market a state-of-the-art random access video editing system. It was called the Editdroid. They called me one day and asked if I would be interested in demonstrating the system at the upcoming convention. Of course, I jumped at the chance. But first, I had to learn how to run the system. The two prototypes were built somewhere in California. I was to have one day of training with several other editors. I was flown to Oakland, California, then driven to a secret hideaway in a place called San Enselmo. They did a good job of hiding their tracks and I had no idea where I was.

Finally, we arrived at a small rundown-looking house on a side street. We went in and stumbled through old cardboard boxes in a back room. What I saw amazed me. Here, among old boxes, junk, tools and mysterious electronic devices stood two elegant-looking big screen editing systems. They were not cluttered with the typical keyboard and complex-looking software as were the systems of the day but rather had a unique look, as though they belonged to the Starship Enterprise. The viewing screen was in the wide screen format and was about three feet across. That must have been the George Lucas touch.

By the time we got settled and began learning the system, we had to leave for the airport to catch our return flight. As it turned out, we had only a little over four hours of training before the unveiling of this new system a few days later in Las Vegas. I was a little worried that I hadn't become proficient enough to do a good sales job for the company at the convention.

When we arrived at the Las Vegas at the convention center several days later, the two systems were all set up. The engineers were working on them to get rid of some technical problems, which is not at all unusual for high-tech equipment of this kind. Two things electronic equipment do not like are low humidity (it makes integrated circuits do funny things and sometimes fail) and ambient room heat. One must realize that the main convention center in Las Vegas is around a half million square feet. Can you imagine what it must be like to air condition such a humongous building and keep the temperature comfortable? Under these conditions, the equipment may become unreliable, which is something you cannot have at a convention where people come to see your equipment work.

The booth where the equipment was set up was carefully covered and shrouded in secrecy and only those of us who were directly involved were allowed in during the setup time. Guards were posted 24 hours a day, partly to be sure our competition didn't peek. When the show opened the next day, it was wall-to-wall people around our booth, in part to see what George Lucas and his engineers had come up with and to see a demonstration of technology that was to change the way editing would be done in the future.

In the year 1984 editing would change forever. For one thing, instead of using tape to record on, laserdics would replace those slow-moving tape machines. Laserdiscs could even at that time access any point on a 30 minute disc in just a few seconds or even faster. In comparison, just to go to the end of a 30 minute videotape, would take about three minutes and of course three minutes back to the other end. You can see why the adaptation of laserdisc to editing was such a big deal to the entire postproduction industry. However, the relative cost of making the laserdiscs along with the fact that they were not reusable limited their use in favor of slower videotape systems. Today, laserdiscs have been replaced by even faster computer hard disc drives that have access times that are nearly instantaneous and that have storage capacities of several hours.

Storage formats were another big change of the 1980s, with most of the change happening late in the decade. With the introduction of the two-inch VTR in 1956, one might imagine the many thousands of two-inch format videotape programs stored in vaults in the past four decades. By now, many have been transferred to other, more modern and better-quality formats, notably the one-inch format. However, in the late 1980s and 1990s, digital has been the format of choice. One important reason for this is, when recording or transferring master tapes in the digital format, duplicate copies made from a digital master do not degrade the picture and sound. Analog format videotapes tend to start degrading the picture after the second or third generation copy, and by the fourth generation begin to look fuzzy and exhibit other technical problems.

Digitally recorded videotapes, on the other hand, can be duplicated many times over without any noticeable loss of quality. By the end of the 1990s, most videotape recording will be in the digital format because the cost of this equipment is coming down and the higher quality of the recorded image will allow archiving of tapes, even those transferred from the old two-inch standard to the digital format. Most series producers have transferred their old analog-recorded programs to the digital format over the past few years since eventually the old two-inch VTRs will disappear. Although more than 5,000 two-inch machines were originally built, today there are only a handful in use due to the difficulty in getting spare parts. Those that are still running are generally only used for playback to get the old two-inch tapes transferred to another format.

Since 1984 was a turning point for high-tech editing, *Entertainment Tonight* interviewed many of us in the Editdroid booth during the convention and did a story with me demonstrating the system. It was a lot of fun but about all you can see is the back of my head and profile.

After taking several months off to catch up on some long overdue projects at home, I went to work for Modern VideoFilm in Hollywood. My daughter Lori was already working there as a quality control operator. The company was just getting into editing and I was asked to help get that going. I was hired as the supervising editor. The company got a large contract from Paramount Studios to re-edit a number of their successful television series for syndication.

They include 60 episodes of *Mannix,* 177 *Laverne and Shirley,* 254 *Happy Days,* 77 *Mork and Mindy,* 117 *Taxi* and 79 *Star Trek.* I had only seen a few of the *Star Trek* programs but after I completed the series, I became a "Trekkie." My assistant editor was the greatest Trekkie I ever saw. He had memorized the series scripts and could actually lip sync the dialogue from memory for nearly every episode. Altogether, these series accounted for more than 800 individual episodes which were re-edited for syndication. In addition, I cut down several first-run features at the time including *Romancing the Stone* and *Yentl.* These features were shortened for the airlines who wanted them kept within a two-hour length.

The re-editing of these series was essentially the same as the *CHiPS* series I did at CFI. This project was different only in that Paramount people would review every episode of every series we did to be sure the continuity of the story was left intact. It was not an easy job because we had a limited amount of material that I would classify as superfluous to each story. It would take anywhere from three to four hours to re-edit an hour episode and about two to three hours to re-edit each half-hour episode. We liked to look at each episode in order to understand the story before starting to make cuts. We had to take into account the total time removed as well as making good edits that did not affect the music or confuse the story line.

The exact beginning and end point was based on the in and out time code of each potential cut and was written down on a log. When we finished the episode, we would add up all the little edits we made and subtract them from the total program time. If we had taken out too much time, we would selectively put back just enough cuts to get us to the required time. We really never had the problem of being too long or too short because of these many optional cuts we could play with.

Once the log was finalized, the edit log data would be entered into the computer and the episode could then be automatically assembled very quickly. The average half-hour episode would be auto assembled in about 45 minutes and a one-hour episode in an hour and a half.

Watching every episode of all those series, was to say the least, boring since I had seen most of them on television years ago. I wanted to scream a few times at the stupidity of the sitcom plots, but couldn't. My daughter Lori worked with me at Modern VideoFilm making copies of feature films for distribution. One of these films, *E.T.*, had massive distribution. She had to see that film in its entirety 55 times. Talk about boring! I only bring this up because I want readers to know that about 95 percent of working television is plain old hard, boring work. What glamour there is restricted to the production end and those few instances in editing where one might get involved with a celebrity. In my case, I made it a point to go on the set every chance I got to meet people. That's one way I was able to come in contact with so many directors, producers and stars. Many of the producers and directors I met during my 17 years at NBC (and others I met after I left to work at other facilities) followed me to each new facility. Once you establish yourself and generate some sort of following, unless you really screw up, these friends and clients will follow you almost anywhere during your career.

CHAPTER TEN

Teledyne Takes Me to Tokyo, and Other TV Tales

In the early 1970s, because of a dispute I don't remember, the Television Academy split into two chapters. The National Academy on the East Coast ended up with the short end of the stick, televising only the daytime awards and sports although they still had the ability to give out awards in the same categories as the West Coast chapter. The East Coast chapter was known as NATAS, the National Academy of Television Arts and Sciences, and the West Coast chapter was called ATAS, the Academy of Television Arts and Sciences.

In 1984, I got an unexpected opportunity to edit an *ABC After School Special* called *Andrea's Story, a Hitchhiking Tragedy*. Martin Tashe the producer, was someone I had known for many years. His programs were all shot on 16mm color film, transferred to videotape, edited and released on tape for broadcast. Since many of Tashe's programs were used in schools for teaching purposes, he developed a way to cut the camera original and use the already mixed track from the TV version to make film release prints for schools and other organizations. Tashe's specials were always well-received by educators since they all carried a message of some sort. I always enjoyed working with him in the editing room since he was well-prepared and the job always went smoothly. Because of that, he saved money and turned out a good product as well.

The daytime Emmy Awards were coming up but I passed on the idea of submitting the program for an Emmy. One day I saw in *Variety*, an industry trade paper, that I had been nominated for an Emmy for *Andrea's Story*. I told my wife, who was just as surprised as I was. The awards were being held in New York, but I wasn't about to go since the cost of the trip and getting the time off was something I wasn't prepared for. The awards were not being televised, so I told my wife to look in the morning paper the day after the awards to see if I had won. I told her only to wake me if I had won and to let me sleep if I didn't. The next day she ran into the bedroom yelling, "You won, you won!" Wow—my fourth Emmy Award! The Emmy was shipped to my home after it had been engraved with my name.

I liked to do freelance editing because I could negotiate a bigger salary and my hours were my own. Alan Landsburg Productions wanted to re-edit the series *That's Incredible* for syndication. It was not a run-of-the-mill editing job since the new shows were sometimes a compilation of several different episodes. In addition, it would often be necessary to run a separate audio track in synchronization with the picture to include sound effects, narration or some other sound source not available on the production soundtrack. This was time-consuming since getting the soundtrack to synchronize with the picture was not always an easy job. I would work from about 5 P.M. to 11 P.M., re-editing one or two episodes each night. Some episodes were more complex than others since there were elements that had to be retrieved from the tape vault and at times they could not be found, delaying the job. Once in a while, if one element was missing, the whole job had to be put aside until someone could locate the missing piece or pieces the next day.

It was fun in a way since working at night was relatively quiet. There was only myself and an assistant editor who would load the tape machines and set up the technical equipment. Sometimes the librarian would work late, getting needed material for the evening's work. Other than that, it was a pleasant editing job and sometimes even boring since the format was basically the same for each episode. My job was to assemble the individual elements in continuity based on a supplied script to blend individual soundtracks together and to make sure each episode came out exactly on time. The syndicator requires a specific running time for each series including opening, closing and commercial spots. Program length was determined by someone who timed each segment and added up the segment times to be sure the episode was not short or long.

A friend called one day and wanted me to interview for a position with a company called Color Systems Technology that had developed a way to colorize black and white movie film. I could not comprehend how this was possible and wanted to find out what this process was all about.

Motion picture film is photographed at 24 frames per second while videotape is recorded at 30 frames per second. There are 1,440 individual film movie frames per minute which are transferred to videotape (the colorization process is designed to work only with a videotape image). When you realize that a feature-length motion picture has a running time of between 70 and 120 minutes, you will realize how many frames must be colorized. It gets even more complex when the film is transferred to videotape. During the conversion process, the videotape is being recorded at 30 frames per second or 1800 frames every minute since the translation process increases the number of frames recorded each second. It was a very complex and secretive process that actually worked. I decided to take the job. There were a lot of bugs that had to be worked out and long hours were spent attempting to simplify the process so that non-technical people could be trained to operate the highly complex equipment.

Imagine having to color each element within a frame a different color, keep track of that color and continue it into the next frame until the image changes. When that image reappears, you must restore the exact color so the audience does not see a color change when cutting back and forth between two scenes. When there is a lot of movement within a given frame, the added color must be tracked with the image since the color did not automatically follow a moving image within a given frame.

I could see that when the system was better perfected, colorizing black and white images would be of great benefit in bringing a new look to thousands of old black and white feature films. This was a new company and I felt the management staff wasn't in tune with what was really needed. I had many meetings with them but eventually discovered they had their own agenda and wouldn't listen to me, partly because what I felt was needed would cost the company more than what they had budgeted for. After about a month, I decided that I was being sidetracked and felt it was time to leave. This was the shortest time I've ever spent with any company.

Soon after leaving Color Systems Technology, I accepted a position with Teledyne Camera Systems, a division of Teledyne, Inc. This division built film and video cameras for the military. These custom–designed and built film and video cameras are used in fighter planes to affirm hits and damage to enemy planes. They also built electronic equipment designed to transfer videotape to motion picture film. The purpose was to provide 16mm color films from videotapes; these films would often be shown in remote villages where only a film projector and a generator were available. (A television system designed to show programs to a large group would require many monitors, a power supply and lots of cables to inter-connect everything. A 16mm film on a simple projector, sometimes using the wall of a building or even a bed sheet as a screen, works better than an expensive television system in remote areas.)

Teledyne Camera was building a very high-resolution or high-definition tape-to-film system for a company in Japan called Imagica. The system they designed was higher in resolution than anything available at that time. The tests we made were of outstanding picture quality, almost as good as direct photographic film quality. I gave a talk on this system at an SMPTE technical meeting on high-definition television and showed one of our film tests. We projected these tests at the Academy of Motion Picture Arts and Sciences theater in Beverly Hills on a 60 foot wide movie screen and there was a lot of favorable comments on the quality of our images.

The Teledyne system generated 1250 lines of video information which yielded incredibly high picture resolution. At the time we made these tests, Sony had developed a similar system using what they defined as a 1125 line system (1125 lines in a single television image was some four times sharper than the home television set which has only 525 lines). On the other hand, the Teledyne system provided a 20 percent improvement in resolution over the Sony standard.

However, there were a few design problems that prevented the full implementation of the Teledyne system. First, the tape-to-film recorder could only record film at one speed, eight frames per second. But any movement in a scene would speed up the action by three times when the film was projected at the normal running speed of 24 frames per second. A special high-resolution videotape machine was supposed to be developed by another company in Japan to run at either the normal 24 frames per second or the eight frames per second needed by the Teledyne system. Nevertheless, Teledyne went ahead building a prototype high-definition tape-to-film transfer system for Imagica in Tokyo, Japan.

In July of 1985, Teledyne Camera sent me to Tokyo to meet the people at Imagica and assure them that the unit would be ready in time for the new addition of their television center, then under construction. I flew from Los Angeles to Tokyo with a stopover in Hawaii. I got off the plane in Tokyo and went into the airport terminal. I could not find anyone who spoke English. After much frustration and fumbling, I was told by someone who spoke a little English that I had to go to another transfer terminal in the middle of the city.

I took a bus there, hailed a taxi and told the driver where I wanted to go. He looked puzzled. I tried several times to communicate with him but to no avail. Finally I wrote down the name of my hotel and gave it to him. He smiled and motioned that he would be right back. In a couple of minutes, he returned beaming. Apparently someone inside had translated my note for him and now he knew where to take me.

An unusual feature of most Tokyo cabs is a built-in color television monitor in the roof of the cab so that the rear seat passengers can watch commercials during their ride through the streets of Tokyo. There is a video cassette player in the trunk which probably holds a good two hours' worth of commercials. In this way, the passengers are trapped into watching commercials. However, it doesn't work for non–Japanese speaking passengers since I had no idea what they were saying. Instead, I took pictures out the window of the cab.

It was a vacation as well as a business trip since I told my hosts it was my first time in Japan. They assigned one of their people to escort me around and show me the sights. The president of Imagica, Fumio Nagasi, was a UCLA, MBA graduate and spoke very good English. The fellow assigned to escort me did as well. My escort (I can't remember his name) loved to walk, so we walked all over Tokyo. It rained most of the time but that didn't stop him (or me). I didn't know if or when I would ever return to Japan so I took advantage of every opportunity to see the sights. I do remember though that we had sushi for lunch and dinner most every day. We often ate at out-of-the-way restaurants and had better food and drinks than was found in tourist establishments.

Across the street from my hotel was a public market. I was curious as to what food prices were compared to what we pay in California. I had to convert at the exchange rate of 242 yen to the dollar. Melons turned out to cost a little over six dollars each and other vegetables were comparably priced. With today's exchange rate, those melons would cost almost three times as much now as they did in 1985. No wonder the cost of living in Tokyo is one of the world's highest!

It so happened that there was a technical exhibition in progress in a community about 40 miles outside Tokyo called Tsukuba, sort of a "think tank" to develop new ideas for electronic products. I was asked if I wanted to see this exhibition and of course I said yes. My escort and I boarded a train. It was nearly empty because everyone was at work. I had a chance to see some of the villages outside the city and was enamored with the lifestyle. In some ways, it had the flavor of rural America in the 1950s.

When we arrived, I was awestruck by the immensity of the area since it was like going into an electronic Disneyland. The exhibits were amazing. I saw a beef steak tomato vine with the largest tomatoes I've ever seen. I would guess some of them weighed more than four pounds and they were grown without dirt, just nutrients in water. They had lettuce and other vegetables rotating on motorized trays with artificial sunlight. There was a robot that could read music and play the organ. That exhibit was so crowded, I had to hold my camera over my head hoping I could get a shot of this incredible robot. It played beautifully and never missed a note.

ShowScan is a unique method of projecting movies on a giant screen using film twice as wide as normal motion picture film and running at an incredible 60 frames a second as compared to 24 frames per second for normal motion picture film. The picture quality is outstanding and because the film was running at 60 frames per second, flicker and other visual distractions normally associated with standard 35mm projected at 24 frames per second were eliminated. The screen itself was at least 40 feet high and about 60 feet wide, covering an entire wall of the building.

Most of the meals I ate consisted of sushi. I was later told that a parasite had been found in local raw seafood that caused many people to become ill. Considering the amount of seafood I ate, I was very lucky I didn't get whatever was going around.

After leaving Tokyo, I headed for Seoul, Korea, sort of a hop, skip and jump from Japan. When I arrived in Seoul, I had no idea who was going to meet me. As I went through customs and entered the main lobby, I saw a man holding up a Teledyne brochure and figured he must be the fellow waiting to pick me up. He spoke English well enough for us to be able to communicate and we drove through Seoul to the Lott Hotel located directly across the street from the American Embassy. Once I settled in and unpacked, I looked out the window at the Embassy and was somewhat aghast at the hundreds of bullet holes in the face of the building. Later, I was told that North Korean infiltrators sometimes sneak across the border and rake the building with machine gun fire, a thought I tried quickly to dismiss from my mind.

I was taken to meet the Teledyne representative (who spoke pretty good English) and I was given a tour of their film processing laboratory as well as a number of other technical areas relating to television. It rained most every day of the five I spent in Seoul, making it a very dreary trip; I couldn't wait to get back home. I came back via Northwest Orient Airlines and we landed in Seattle. As I came up to the customs inspection station, I was asked where I had just come from and told the inspector, "Korea." He asked me why I was there and I said, "Business." He told me to go on. There was no customs declaration, no questions, no inspection of my luggage. I must have looked honest.

After a year and a half, I left Teledyne since the high-definition equipment was finally delivered to Japan and the other line of products they were selling needed to be updated in order to be competitive. Their other product, the Teledyne tape-to-film recorder for 16mm and 35mm, was already an old design. Other companies started using lasers to record film images while Teledyne insisted on continuing with old technology, using old kinescope tubes with electronics that did not meet current needs. I had great difficulty convincing clients to spend money on old technology. I left Teledyne in the summer of 1986 to continue writing my first book on videotape editing.

I was happy to be working at home without the pressures of dealing with clients who sometimes didn't know what day it was. I had to help them resolve their technical problems but we sometimes ended up talking about everything under the sun but editing. When this happened, the meter kept running. Sometimes they got on the phone while my crew and I stood by waiting for them to figure out what they wanted to do next. I've come to the conclusion that some of the people I worked with as clients should have found another line of work. They often wasted my time and a lot of their money because they were poorly organized.

In the fall of 1987, a company called TAV (Trans American Video) called me and asked if I would like to edit promos for the Disney Channel. Since I had been a freelance editor for TAV in the past, I knew most of the people in that organization and felt somewhat comfortable working there. However, I was a little concerned since my son Robert had been working there for almost 15 years. I didn't know how they felt about nepotism but they couldn't have cared less. I felt that was an easy job for me since I would be using the Mach One editing system that I helped design some ten years earlier.

I accepted the job and began work. Within a couple of weeks, I had learned most of what I needed to know to start editing with the Disney people. In a sense, this was my second go-around in connection with the Disney organization having been involved as the supervising editor for *The New Mickey Mouse Club* a decade before. My son used to drop in every now and then while I was editing these promos to give me pointers on setting up specialized equipment I had not used in the past. All in all, I had a great time at TAV.

Trans American Video was located in the center of Hollywood between Sunset and Hollywood boulevards. Even in 1987, the area was beginning to degrade and many big stores closed because business was drifting away to other areas farther from the heart of Hollywood. One of the big problems was that transients and homeless people would use our doorway to urinate and the odor would drift inside the building to our editing room. Some comedian once said, "Hollywood is like a bowl of Granola. What ain't fruits and nuts is flakes." Nothing could be closer to the truth.

My son had two weeks' vacation left at the end of the year and planned to take a trip during that time. He was also scheduled to edit another Bob Hope special during that same period. Robert told me that I would have to edit the special since he wasn't going to change his vacation. I hadn't edited a Hope special in about 20 years.

At first, I was somewhat nervous. I knew everyone and yet I had been away from this organization for so long that I wondered if I could still "cut it" with them. The director was Sid Smith, a veteran of hundreds of television specials. I first started working with him in the mid–1950s on NBC specials such as *Saturday Night Revue*, so it was like working with an old friend. There was an enormous amount of footage to go through, some of it shot by novice military personnel. We had to look at every single frame of this "amateur video" to be sure we didn't miss anything of value even though 99 percent of it would not be used.

My fears about working on another Hope special were soon allayed. Editing this special was no different than it was two decades ago except it was much easier and faster due to the new editing equipment we were using.

The Hope staff still told the same jokes and we reminisced about the old days. In fact, it seems that when they ordered lunch, it was the same kind we used to eat when I was editing at NBC.

One sequence in the special was a dance number with four cameras. Sid Smith would not be able to be at the editing session until later in the day so he told one of the dancers to come to editing to cut the dance number with me. I'll never forgive him for that. This lady didn't have the foggiest idea of what to do and I must have recut the dance number at least a dozen times before she finally gave up and left. When Sid Smith showed up, we recut the number in under a half-hour. That morning was a complete waste of time.

After I completed a rough cut of the special, Bob Hope was called in to view the work print and make comments. When Hope showed up in the editing room, we greeted each other and I told him I came out of retirement just to edit this special. He laughed and made several funny comments about the old days of editing at NBC (Hope has a great memory for people and places). Hope watched the entire program and made suggestions and comments as we went along. Once he left, I went back to editing to make the changes. When Robert returned from vacation, he assembled the master edited tape. As usual, more changes were made during the final assembly, a process generally frowned upon because it slows down the assembly process and increases editing time and cost. This was the eleventh time we received father and son screen credit as editors on the same program.

In 1985 my friends Don, Jerry and I decided to develop a state-of-the-art non-linear video editing system capable of creating an edit list that could be used to transfer the information to film so that the program could eventually be used to cut the original camera film from the video-tape edit log. The name Link was agreed upon since we all thought that the system would be a "link" between videotape and motion picture film, something not yet available at that time.

At first, we looked for venture capital to finance the project but it was impossible to make any kind of deals since the lenders wanted too much of the company in return for their investment. Since I was working at Teledyne Camera Systems and was not able to devote the necessary time to the project, it was decided that I would act as a consultant to Link and also help write the technical manual for the operation of this editing system. Because I was not directly involved with the mechanical design of the hardware or the software program (except for testing and debugging), Jerry and Don both put their own money into the project. Since I had no money of my own invested, I was given two percent of the company as a limited partner in return for my consulting expertise and for writing the user guide.

It took about a year for Don and Jerry to design and build the prototype unit. The heart of the system was a consumer model Apple Macintosh computer. Don wrote the software and Jerry built the hardware. On weekends I would go over to Don's garage where the unit was housed and play with the Link. I was good at breaking things and, in a way, this was good. They were able to fix these problems before any potential investors were called in, avoiding public embarrassment.

After spending a little more than a year tweaking the hardware and software, they decided to try to attract investors to recoup some of their own funds as well as to provide operating capital to build two more units and open up a facility for training and rental of the units. They rented a small one-room office in a Studio City building near several television and movie studios. At about the same time, I left Teledyne, and became more active with Link.

I was brought in by Don and Jerry to help demonstrate the Link to film editors and potential investors. People were generally quite impressed by the flexibility and speed with which one could make edits. There were twelve Betamax consumer-style VCRs connected to the system which would automatically search out material to make edits. The Link worked as well as some of the more expensive commercial units later built by companies with unlimited development funds. Eventually, they got a number of investors to put up enough money to build two more editing systems and allow them to get started in business.

Later, when a small office was opened in Burbank, Jerry became the "chief cook and bottle washer" for Link Systems since I was now employed by Trans American Video. I could not continue actively with Link because it would have been a conflict of interest and because my hours were often unpredictable.

When I retired in 1988, I moved away from Los Angeles and my affiliation with Link essentially stopped although I still had two percent of its stock. Link was barely able to make ends meet, primarily because of competition from other editing systems that were more fully funded. Many of the competitors switched to a more sophisticated method of storing images for editing by using high speed laserdiscs and then switched to an even more economical hard disc drive. Unfortunately, Jerry and Don did not have the funds to update Link and this was a blow to them since they saw opportunities slipping away. Business was slow and it really couldn't support two people. Don left when he got a job with a competing company. Jerry couldn't handle the business by himself, editing and maintaining the three systems, so he also called it quits. He went with a company called Avid as a training instructor and Link was shut down.

My first book on videotape editing, *Electronic Post-Production and Videotape Editing*, was published by Focal Press in 1989. It took about 18 months to get the book ready for publication. Digging up the photographs was a big part of that since some of the equipment I wrote about had been obsolete for several years. A basic text designed for beginners and students, the book was quite well received. It covers basic editing techniques and even how to get along with the client. Someone I later met told me she read my book, especially the chapter on time code. She went in for an interview and was asked a number of questions about time code. Based on the knowledge she gained from my book, she got the job and wrote me a letter thanking me for writing the book in such a manner as to make it so easy for her to understand.

My second book, *Electronic Post-Production Terms and Concepts,* published by Focal Press in 1990, was really the first book I wanted to write. The title is somewhat misleading since it is really more of a dictionary of post-production terms. I argued with the publisher about the title since I felt readers would not understand that "Terms and Concepts" was really a dictionary. Unfortunately, they won out. First sales were not as good as my first book. I knew it would sell much better if potential buyers knew that it was a useful and up-to-date dictionary.

The information and terminology contained in the book will always be valid since most of it will always be part of the television industry's vocabulary. There are more than 650 comprehensive entries of up-to-date information including slang terms and "buzz" words. What's different about this book is that each definition is quite comprehensive; a few of them take up more than a page. In addition, the book is profusely illustrated with sketches, photos and diagrams to help the reader better understand each term and its definition.

I am also a contributing author to two more books, *The American Cinema and Video Laboratories Handbook, Fifth Edition* where I wrote one chapter on videotape and *The Focal Encyclopedia of Electronic Media* where I've written more than 50,000 words.

In 1983, we decided to look for investment property. We contacted local real estate brokers but couldn't find anything we liked.

Every year on vacation trips in the nearby mountains, we would visit real estate brokers looking either for a home already built or possibly a lot on which to build a vacation home. We looked at everything for sale over a period of a year. We were about to give up and start looking elsewhere when the broker showed us the only lot he had left. We bought the lot at the end of 1984. In 1987, lumber prices began a steep rise and we decided to build a vacation home on the lot. Finally, after many delays, we sold our L.A. home in July of 1988 and were settled into our new house by October. What do I do all day in retirement? I'm at least twice as busy now as I was when I was editing. For example, there is home maintenance, a chore that is required of everyone who owns a home, retired or not. Living in the mountains presents different needs since we live at an altitude of 5,200 feet. In the winter, we often spend November through May shoveling snow (we average about 150 inches of snow each season). During summer, we buy firewood to heat our home in the winter and store it in our garage. We mounted a 20-foot long, 10-inch plastic tube to the 20 steps leading down to the front door. When we need wood, we merely slide the logs down the tube and they land on the walkway a few feet from the front door.

Dee has a passion for wild animals and she feeds the birds, squirrels and raccoons that frequent our deck. We've had as many as ten raccoons on the deck at one time. Although we've never seen any deer, we have been visited by several bears and other strange-looking animals. Sometimes the coyotes stand under our bedroom window and howl, keeping us up. The only real pests are the woodpeckers who would have our house for lunch if we let them.

I've been president of our homeowners association, on the board of directors of our community services district, and am still involved with the advisory committee for our county. I am also the secretary-treasurer for our local fire department. My wife and I walk daily and frequently visit our national parks. I also find time to write letters to our local supervisors and other politicians who I feel lack the one thing most of us who are not in politics have—plain old common sense.

Once a year Dee and I go to Las Vegas for the annual television convention where my publisher has a booth and I help sell my books. Other times we go to places like Lake Tahoe or Reno or some other place of interest. Two or three times a year we go to L.A. to visit our family and friends. That's why I keep busy and work twice as hard in retirement as I did when I was editing.

If you are lucky enough to be in the right place at the right time and get a job you really like, spend nearly 40 years working hard, enjoy your work and find a place you can retire to, you may be able to live a long, fruitful and productive life. You can consider yourself very lucky, as we do.